Solutions to Inflation

EDITED BY

David C. Colander

HARCOURT BRACE JOVANOVICH, INC.

New York   San Diego   Chicago   San Francisco   Atlanta

Library of Congress Catalog Card Number: 79-84377

ISBN: 0-15-582450-3

CONTENTS

IV / ECONOMIC INCOMES POLICIES   155

INTRODUCTION

Good sense is of all things in the world the most equally distributed, for everyone thinks himself so abundantly provided with it that even the most difficult to please in all other matters do not commonly desire more of it than they already possess.

DESCARTES

Inflation exists; of that we are sure. We are, however, not so certain about what causes it, and we are probably even less certain of what to do about it. When we are faced with such an enigma, a typical course of action often is to ignore it and hope it will just disappear—we did, and it didn't. In fact, it became progressively worse, accelerating from a rather slow trot, which stirred economists' imaginations more than their fears, to a moderate canter, that awkward speed in between a walk and a gallop that requires one either to know how to ride or to have a well-padded rear end. And now there is talk of inflation bursting into a gallop unless, of course, something is done. But what?

Contrary to the popular conception that we have no answers, many economists have formally proposed plans to curtail inflation. In the classroom and in economists' shop talk, solutions abound—many more than could possibly be included in one book. But economists are not the only ones with an abundance of solutions; politicians and private citizens are also inflated with ideas. If anything, the problem is not a lack of solutions; it is, rather, that none has emerged as the clear-cut favorite.

Some of these solutions have been around for many years, and their pros and cons have been fully explored. Who, for example, has not heard that the solution to inflation lies in holding the money supply down, a prescription that dates back to the writings of John Locke and David Hume in the 1750s? Wage and price controls as a solution have an even longer history. The Code of Hammurabi imposed wage and price controls about 4000 years ago. Other solutions are novel, and their final forms are yet to unfold.

The arguments for and against various solutions are often compelling, and a reasonable person often finds himself agreeing with all, especially the one he read last. Still, a rational choice among the alternatives must be made, and the first step toward making that choice is to have readable expositions of the alternative solutions. This reader is designed to offer just that.

Before leaving you to the mercy of the advocates of various solutions, it is only fair that you be minimally armed with an overview of the range of possible solutions and with the theory that underlies them. The readings in Part I are designed toward this end.

Part II contains solutions with monetarist leanings. Part III considers wage and price controls, and Part IV explores a group of solutions categorized as tax- and market-based incomes policies (TIP and MIP).

I have tried to be objective both in choosing the selections and in making comments. However, the framework within which this volume has been designed reflects two underlying sentiments. I would hope these merely reflect my reasonable approach to the problem of inflation, but because an "unreasonable reader" might consider my framework biased—rather than reasonable—I would like to make these sentiments explicit. (The

1

definition of "unreasonable reader" as used here is the normal one—someone who disagrees.)

The first sentiment is rather subtle: It is that the theories underlying the solutions are not diametrically opposed but are slight variations on a central theme. This implies that there are no major gulfs separating the proponents of various proposals but merely slight differences in emphasis and interpretation of facts.

The less subtle second sentiment is that there are no easy answers to the problem of inflation. The choice is among undesirable alternatives, and we must choose the "least worst." A few further clarifications are in order about both these sentiments.

A FEW NOT SO SUBTLE WORDS ABOUT THE SUBTLETIES OF INFLATION THEORY

The theory of inflation that normally filters down to the lay reader appears to be a rather settled affair: There is cost push, wage push, and demand pull inflation. Cost push is caused by nasty corporations and businesses that push up their prices independently of demand; wage push is caused by nasty unions that push up their wages independently of demand; and demand pull is caused by nasty governments that incur budget deficits beyond levels that are reasonable and prudent.

The apparent result is a pleasant state of affairs for students who can make the neat divisions on their exams, scoring an "A" if they mind their pushes and pulls. The actual state of affairs is, unfortunately for students, much more unsettled and much more confusing. To use an analogy made by Alfred Marshall when he introduced supply-demand analysis, price is determined by both blades of the scissors, and trying to separate them is like trying to answer the chicken and egg conundrum, a pursuit that well serves the purpose of employing unemployed philosophers but that is unlikely to have any other fruitful results. Cost push, demand pull, and wage push are all the same, seen from slightly different perspectives. (Generally the perspective is that the other guy did it.)

There is nothing radical in these statements; most economists agree that the classifications of inflation are much more complex and difficult than ones normally made. We use them in our textbooks and lectures nonetheless, with the rationalization that we must make simplifications to teach students at the introductory level. The result is a dichotomy between professional journal articles, which display a rich and deep understanding of inflation and make little or no distinctions between theories, and the "textbook" theory, which makes neat divisions.

The problem with the textbook theory of inflation is its explanation of push inflation. Cost push is often presented as if it were caused by monopolies raising their prices. This view is insufficient for two reasons. First, when a monopoly raises its price, it is only a change in *relative* price; if other prices did not also rise, the result would be negligible. Monopoly causes high *relative* prices, not a high *price level*.

Second, monopoly causes only a one-time rise in price, not a *continual* rise in price. For monopolization to explain inflation would require an ever-increasing monopolization, a condition that has not characterized the U.S. economy in the past decade. Precisely the same two objections hold for wage push inflation. Unions cause high relative wages, not a continually rising wage level.

What then is meant by cost push or wage push inflation? Generally it means two things: (1) that the economy is only sluggishly responsive to changes in aggregate demand (quantity adjustment rather than price adjustment predominates); and (2) that there tends to be an asymmetrical movement in price and wage changes (prices and wages go up more easily than they go down). These two characteristics of our economy give the price level an internal dynamic that pushes it upward. Then, if the government increases the deficit to offset unemployment, or if it increases the money supply, the upward movement in prices and wages will be *ratified*. Other price and wage increases will follow, bringing the relative prices and wages into the same approximate position. The process then repeats itself.

This description of cost push inflation would receive little flak from many monetary theorists, who would tell almost the identical story. However, instead of beginning with the price push, they would emphasize the monetary pull, saying that inflation is always and everywhere a monetary phenomenon: Unless the money supply or velocity rises, prices and wages will not stay high.

Most cost push and wage push theorists would agree with this monetarist position; it is merely a matter of how many times one should say it. For the push theorists, once said is sufficient; they then emphasize changes in velocity and institutional framework.

For all theorists, inflation is everywhere and always a full circle: Wages rise because prices rise because money or velocity rises because wages rise. . . . Trying to distinguish one as the cause and one as the result becomes a hopeless mess. I am not saying that divisions are not helpful; they are. Slightly different emphases are useful in analyzing difficult problems, as long as one remembers that they are only differences in emphasis, not diametrically opposed visions of reality.

The seeming differences between positions have generally arisen in the heat of debate rather than in the careful writings of the various views. This is normal; in the heat of debate, one is naturally inclined to sympathetically interpret one's own view while choosing the least sympathetic interpretation of the opponent's view. Were individuals not so inclined, far fewer words would be necessary, and the world would likely be a rather boring place.

THERE IS NO "EASY ANSWER"
The second sentiment will not be found in the readings themselves but in the noticeable absence of certain solutions. It has already been said that the sheer number of solutions is overwhelming. Anyone compiling a single volume of readings must make personal choices. I found this extraordinarily difficult, since a case can be made for almost every solution proposed, although the reasoning behind some of these solutions often employs a bit of circuitous logic.

Deciding that rules are better than discretion, I devised a "Cod Liver Oil Test" and applied it to the various solutions. (For those of you young enough never to have been subjected to cod liver oil, it is, in my estimation, one of the vilest substances known to humanity. At the same time, however, it was once widely used because of its beneficial effects.) The test was as follows: Would advocates of the solution support it even if it had no effect on inflation? A positive response caused the solution to fail and, therefore, to be excluded from consideration for the book. However, a solution might fail the test and still prove helpful either as a complement to a real solution or as a remedy for some other malady of our society.

The three broad categories of solutions that passed the test were wage-price controls, economic incomes policies, and the monetarists' solutions. These constitute the last three sections of the book. Solutions that did not pass the test fall into two categories: the "sugar" solutions, which promise only benefits and no costs, and the "sugar for me and cod liver oil for you" solutions.

TWO PROBLEMS WITH MOST SUGAR SOLUTIONS

Most solutions that failed the Cod Liver Oil Test are subject to two common fallacies: the static/dynamic fallacy and the relative price/price level fallacy. The static/dynamic fallacy involves confusing a one-time increase in prices with an increase in inflation. Inflation is a continual rise in the price level, so if a one-time (rather than a continual) decrease in costs is implemented, inflation will not necessarily slow down. If you think of inflation as a speeding car whose gas pedal is tied down, and solutions as a brake, you can see the problem. By stamping on the brake you might slow the car for a moment, but soon it will be speeding forward again as fast as ever. Only a continual application of the brake will work. In other words, if a proposal is to slow inflation, it must have some mechanism that applies a *continual* brake and eases off the gas.

There may be a long-run effect from a once-and-for-all decrease in price rises if, when the inflation temporarily slows, expectations of future inflation also are slowed. The connection with expectations is tenuous, though, and at this point it is based more on wishful thinking than on actual theory or empirical evidence.

The second problem with sugar solutions is the relative price/price level confusion. Inflation is a rise in the price level, so the contribution of any one price to the total price level is minimal. Therefore, solutions that decrease some relative prices will only have a minimal effect on inflation, unless that decrease in relative price is somehow translated into a general decrease in all prices (which of course must then be translated into a decrease in inflation). Combined, these two fallacies lead one to disparage most of the sugar solutions.

PROBLEMS WITH SPECIFIC SUGAR SOLUTIONS

Probably the most often cited sugar solution is the "efficiency" solution. That is, if only the economy were made more efficient, costs would decrease and inflation would subside.

The first problem with the efficiency cure for our ills is the static/dynamic fallacy. Most efficiency measures are one-shot deals, while inflation is a continual process. A second problem is that whenever there is an increase in efficiency, the individuals involved generally commandeer the resulting gains, translating them into wage or profit increases rather than into decreased prices or wages. The result is little gain on the inflation front.

Similar arguments can be made for curbing regulation and repealing inflationary special interest laws. Each of these may or may not be worth doing; economists generally favor them, but whether or not they are done makes very little difference to inflation. Once again, they involve a once-and-for-all decrease in costs, while inflation involves a continual rise in prices. After they have had their effect, unless the decrease in costs is somehow translated into decreased anticipations of inflation for the future, these efforts will merely be a hiccup on the inflation rate, and a small hiccup at that because the total effect is so small relative to the total.

A second group of sugar solutions is the tax-cutting or subsidy solutions. Both are seductive but both failed the Cod Liver Oil Test. One version of the tax-cutting solutions suggests that since taxes enter into prices, if taxes are cut, then prices can be cut. A second version suggests that if business taxes are cut, investment will increase, costs will fall, and inflation will stop. While these consequences may be correct, they are not the whole story. If taxes are cut without decreasing expenditures, either taxes must be increased elsewhere, causing offsetting rises in prices, or the government must borrow, placing the Federal Reserve Bank in the position either of cutting off credit and increasing the interest rate (again raising costs) or of increasing the money supply. Only if the total real output increases sufficiently to raise total tax revenue (an unlikely result in today's economy) would the tax-cutting solutions help inflation. And even if they do, the static/dynamic fallacy still holds.

SUGAR FOR ME, COD LIVER OIL FOR YOU SOLUTIONS

This category of solutions includes a broad range of proposals. The "voluntary sacrifice" solutions, of which limiting government wage increases or freezing executive pay are examples, can be so categorized. Any of these, if implemented, would be the beginning of a solution, *but it would only work if others followed*. If they did not, then voluntary sacrifice would soon end, and the group would try to recoup its fair share. A ten years' search has failed to discover an individual who feels his or her price or wage increase is inflationary; it is always the other person's.

A story about Robert Strauss, the former "Inflation Czar," neatly makes the point. According to a reliable source, in July 1978 Strauss was called in by President Carter and asked how he was doing on the inflation front. He answered that he had two-thirds of the problem solved. Elaborating, he said that he had held discussions with leaders of labor, government, and business and had asked each of them what the cause and solution to inflation were. From government, he learned that the problem was with business and labor raising their prices and wages; from labor, he heard that it was the government's and businesses' fault, and that they must be controlled; and according to business, naturally, the problem was labor and government. His conclusion—that two-thirds of the problem was solved—demonstrates his brilliance as a politician and the problems with voluntary sacrifice solutions.

Another group of solutions falling under the sugar/cod liver oil heading are the "competitive" solutions. Generally, business means by this that we should break up unions, while unions favor breaking up big business. Everyone is in favor of competition for the other guy; no one favors competition for all. But even if it were possible to institute more competition broadly throughout the economy, no one has estimated how much more competitive the economy must be made for this to have any effect on inflation. Over the past decades there has been little or no decrease in competition, yet inflation has substantially increased; thus the relationship between competition and inflation seems tenuous.

Finally, there are the "cut the deficit" solutions. In the minds of reporters and the public, the government deficit is probably the most important cause of inflation. One of the reasons we need economists is continually to remind people that they are wrong in this belief, at least as it is often expressed. Bluntly put, *there is no simple causal relationship* between government deficits and inflation. Now this does not mean that economists believe that government deficits are good, or that government spending should, or should not, be cut. Opinions differ drastically on these issues. It merely means that deficits do not cause inflation.

To see why, think of a firm deciding whether or not to invest in a new project. If it decides to undertake the project, it sells bonds, which means that it borrows money from the investing public. In other words, it incurs a deficit. But because we call this "investment" and enter it on the capital account, not on the current account, of the firm's budget, the firm's decision is not called inflationary. One must always remember that *deficits are merely accounting measures* and are dependent on the particular accounting system used.

To avoid confusion, some have suggested that the United States should institute a separate capital and current account, while others talk in terms of a "full employment deficit," or what the deficit would have been had the economy been at full employment.

However, these suggestions merely sidestep the issue and cause still more confusion.

The important question in deciding on government expenditure is whether the project is worthwhile. If it is not worthwhile, it should not be undertaken, regardless of its effect on inflation. While it is true that private investment increases capacity and lowers prices in the future, the same argument can be made about government investment. Products would be far more costly were it not for the transportation system built by government. Similarly, without an adequate legal system or police protection, businesses would find it difficult to carry on even their most normal business transactions. Government investment is every bit as necessary as business investment. It should be pointed out, however, that some government activities probably involve waste; no one disputes that efficiency in government is desirable, *but efficiency is a desirable goal even if inflation were not a problem*. To argue that we should cut the government sector in order to stop inflation is not a strong enough indictment of inefficiency. If the government is inefficient, these cuts should be made even if there were no inflation.

The above reasoning does not mean that the government deficit argument is wholly without merit. Far from it. A much stronger case for government deficits causing inflation makes the argument through the money supply and total demand. But then the argument must be made in terms of *total borrowing*, forcing increases in either velocity or the money supply. The reasoning goes something like this: When people or businesses borrow, they are spending more than they take in; in other words, they are increasing total demand. When people or businesses save, they are decreasing total demand. If savings and borrowings are equal, total demand remains the same; if borrowings exceed savings, the total demand rises and the excess must be financed, which places the Federal Reserve Bank in the position of having either to increase the money supply or, if it wants to hold total demand constant, to choke off investment with credit restrictions and increased interest rates. Whether it should or should not increase the money supply depends on total supply or capacity. If there is unused capacity, increasing total demand will lead to growth; if there is not, it will lead to inflation.

There is still much debate about the limits imposed by capacity constraints, the mechanics of the process, and the amount of control that the Federal Reserve Bank actually has over the money supply. These are unanswered questions. For our purposes it is sufficient to point out that if there is a connection between the deficit and inflation, it is via the money supply, velocity, and total demand, not through any direct mechanism.

THE 100 PERCENT SOLUTIONS
If the sugar and the sugar/cod liver oil solutions do not work, what, if anything, does? Theoretically the answer is straightforward. Somehow, aggregate demand must be made equal to aggregate supply, or in less technical terms, it must be made clear to everyone that there is only 100 percent of the pie to go around. The solutions presented in this reader are designed to achieve this end; theoretically they will work, since by definition they must. Unfortunately, definitional solutions only work in theory; the really tough issues concern the practical application of the theory. To make the leap from theory to practice, a proposal must not only be fair and administratively feasible, it must also be perceived as such by most, if not all, individuals. That task I leave to the advocates of the various solutions.

I /INFLATION:
THEORY AND POLICY OPTIONS

"What is a Caucus-race?" said Alice.

"Why," said the Dodo, "the best way to explain it is to do it." (And, as you might like to try the thing yourself some winter day, I will tell you how the Dodo managed it.)

First it marked out a race-course, in a sort of circle, ("The exact shape doesn't matter," it said), and then all the party were placed along the course, here and there. There was no "One, two, three, and away" but they began running when they liked, and left off when they liked, so that it was not easy to know when the race was over. However, when they were running half an hour or so, the Dodo suddenly called out "The race is over!" and they all crowded round it, panting and asking "But who has won?"

This question the Dodo could not answer without a great deal of thought, and it sat for a long time with one finger pressed upon its forehead (the position in which you usually see Shakespeare, in the pictures of him), while the rest waited in silence. At last the Dodo said "Everyone has won. . . ."

LEWIS CARROLL

Inflation is very much in the news these days. Television stations have run "inflation specials"; stores have instituted "inflation tips for the thrifty shopper"; newspapers report the latest news on inflation in their lead columns. Because of inflation's celebrity, economists have found their views much in demand: Reporters generally attempt to give a balanced view on issues, so someone who has something to say on inflation that is novel or different (or, for that matter, even if it is not so novel) can usually find an eager audience. Some cynics have even suggested that economists have created the inflation so that they would be needed to explain why it exists and what we can do about it.

Despite their popularity, economists frequently lament the economic reporting. They complain that issues that have political importance or that "sound good" often receive more attention than is "economically warranted," and that the difficult choices handed us by inflation are not made clear.

These perceived shortcomings are understandable: Reporters are in an extremely difficult position. They must collect the writings of various specialists of all fields, condense their views, and then find opposing views that can be reduced to a pro/con position suitable for an article. Unfortunately, economists and other specialists seldom speak in black-and-white terms. Instead, they punctuate their writings and conversations with qualifying statements on top of qualifications. And as most students know, reducing the equivocating views of economists to a short summary is a hazardous occupation.

Probably the most severe fault that economists find with the press is the way in which it characterizes the costs of inflation. Reporters use inflation as the scapegoat on which all manner of evil is blamed: sometimes "robbing from the poor," other times "stealing from the rich." Both statements, in particular instances, may be true, but they make poor generalizations. In fact, probably the most appropriate, although logically suspect, generalization about inflation is that generalizations about inflation are themselves

7

inappropriate. The fact is that who gains or loses in an inflation depends primarily on who last raised prices or wages. Since the timing of price and wage rises is continually changing, any generalization thus becomes suspect.

Another often heard characterization about inflation is that it "makes everyone poorer." At best, this statement is misleading; usually it is simply wrong. Whenever prices or wages rise, those who raise their prices gain (if they can sell as much as they did before the price increase) and those who pay the increased prices lose. If the two are averaged together—as they must be, since the price someone pays is the price someone else receives—the gains just offset the losses. On average, inflation makes people neither richer nor poorer. (This is not to argue that there is no cost to inflation; there *is*, but it has to do with its effects on the social fabric of society and is therefore a much more complicated argument than is generally made in the press's discussions of inflation.)

The result of this characterization of the costs of inflation is a misinterpretation of numerous individual price fluctuations. Many of the relative price changes that the press jumps on as "inflationary" are both necessary and useful, serving the function of allocating the goods that are available. Often, if relative prices do not rise, shortages would develop that would have more serious consequences than a rise in price. This need for relative price changes is especially apparent with agricultural goods, for vagaries in harvests necessitate substantial changes in prices within short periods of time. There is nothing necessarily inflationary about these price rises, nor is there anything deflationary about decreases in these prices. They only become inflationary if other prices adjust up to these higher prices and then do not adjust down when they fall.

I originally selected examples of what economists might call "bad reporting" to include in this book but then decided to leave those articles for individuals to find on their own. Instead I chose an excerpt from one of the best pieces of recent economic reporting on inflation, a special *Newsweek* report. It provides both a readable summary of the various approaches to inflation and a list of the policy options.

As with almost every social problem, private individuals have definite and often outspoken views on what should and should not be done to cure inflation. The *U.S. News & World Report* article gives readers a chance to sample some of these beliefs and to compare them with their own. These "lay solutions" warrant attention for two reasons:

1. They come from individuals unencumbered by the weight of economic theory, which can be a heavy burden that stifles creative thinking.

2. The solutions demonstrate the mood and thinking of the general population and give one an idea of the issues that must be addressed if one is to "sell" a solution.

Politicians face a quite different constraint than do reporters and students. They are not selling newspapers; they are selling themselves, and mistakes can be very costly. If the press condenses their positions into the wrong phrases, their careers can be ruined. For example, a statement made at a press conference saying, "If motherhood actually did have the consequences you state I would not support it, although I do not believe that it has those consequences," could very well be reduced to headlines stating, "Representative X opposes motherhood." Because of real or imagined fears that precisely such a thing will happen, politicians generally are very careful with their pronouncements on inflation and inflationary policy, relying on sugar-coated solutions wrapped in stock phrases. This interplay between politicians and the press results in a reporting bias toward sugar-coated solutions.

The third selection, which consists of two speeches on inflation by President Jimmy Carter, demonstrates the careful approach politicians follow. Notice, especially, how a statement that wage and price controls will not be instituted can be quickly changed into one that states their virtues and paves the way for their introduction.

Robert Solow's self-described "large dog of an article" provides the framework within which economists discuss inflation. It offers no solution; in fact it takes the position that there is no solution. Thus, in a sense, it is a critique of all the "solutions" put forward in this collection. Primarily it is simply an extremely well-written primer explaining economists' jargon and their intellectual framework. It provides a statement of what inflation is; how it is measured; how inflations are classified; what the costs of inflation are; and what causes inflation. It is well worth a careful reading.

In the final, more difficult article excerpted from a longer article of the same name, George Perry briefly reviews the recent history of anti-inflation policy and then presents a synopsis of the "mainline economic model." He argues that the Keynesian revolution did not get everything wrong, although he suggests that it stopped short of an adequate model. He then discusses the problems with some of the popular solutions to inflation and concludes with a consideration of potential solutions.

The Inflation Surge

LARRY MARTZ, RICH THOMAS, PAMELA LYNN ABRAHAM

The reporting coverage of *Newsweek* has been some of the best in the United States. In the following article three reporters—Larry Martz, Rich Thomas, and Pamela Lynn Abraham—combine their skills to present a readable and insightful overview of the inflation process.

Here it comes again.

But then, it never really went away. Inflation has been punishing America for more than a decade, and the damage of the past few years can be called "creeping" only by merciful contrast with the galloping double digits of 1974. Now, no euphemisms are possible. Led by food prices, the consumer price index is surging upward once more, and wholesale prices have been rising at an ominous annual rate of 12.8 per cent for the past three months. Jimmy Carter has declared inflation Enemy No. 1 and has cobbled up a program to cope with it—mostly jawboning and a reduction of his proposed tax cut. But business is bracing for the worst, possibly including another taste of wage and price controls, and there are signs of panic buying among some consumers.

Why is the country entering the inflationary whirlwind again? How bad will it be this time? Can inflation be stopped short of double digits or a punitive recession?

For all the experience the U.S. has had with the problem, nobody can say with certainty what is triggering the renewed inflationary spurt. There are all sorts of immediate causes: rain in the West that drowned much of the lettuce crop, a turn in the beef cycle, the dollar's long decline—itself a symptom of deep-seated difficulties—making imports more expensive.

In a strategic sense, the government has played a major role, running budget deficits that average more than $50 billion for three consecutive years of expansion and printing the money to finance them. The economy is moving fast, possibly into a new bout of excess demand, while costs are rising and productivity is slumping. It could be, too, that people are simply so used to inflation that they help create it with their own expectations—demanding wage boosts and going along with price hikes in the glum conviction that worse is to come.

UNDERMINING THE BASIC STRENGTHS

It's a token of the damage that inflation has already done that Wall Street sees a recession as the bullish alternative. The nation has paid its dues. Nearly everyone has a personal sense of outrage at rising prices; in the familiar litany, the old and those on fixed incomes suffer most. Even at a 4 per cent rate, inflation cuts the buying power of a dollar in half in just eighteen years (chart, page 14), and at a 5 per cent rate, a 65-year-old pensioner can expect his check to erode by 41 per cent in ten years.

But inflation also undermines the nation's basic strength. It starts with industry, says Treasury Secretary Michael Blumenthal, and a vicious circle results: "You can't figure your real return, so you postpone investments. Your costs rise, your real profits shrink, your stock values go down, it costs more to borrow. It goes on and on." In turn, efficiency drops because of the lagging investment, and prices have to rise to cover costs. In the end, the nation falls behind its trade competitors and loses international influence, as Britain did when 200 years of monetary discipline collapsed after World War I.

"A WORLD IN WHICH NOBODY KEEPS HIS WORD"

Beyond that, inflation takes a toll in national morality: like Chinese water torture, it wears away the social contract. "People have learned the government is out to cheat them by creating excess money," says William Fellner of the American Enterprise Institute, a member of Richard Nixon's Council of Economic Advisers. Alan Greenspan, chief adviser to Gerald Ford, describes it as future shock: "The ability to plan the future erodes. What is being disturbed is the basis on which people live their day-to-day existence." Henry C. Wallich, a governor of the Federal Reserve System, calls it "a form of fraud, perpetrated by everybody on everybody. It is a world in which nobody keeps his word. Even if you could adjust perfectly for it, it would be a very unpleasant world."

Inevitably, inflation fosters tax cheating and a kind of underground economy. . . . And perhaps predictably, conservative economists tend to see the remedy in almost Calvinist terms. "No one wants the recession, but it's unavoidable," says Fellner. "The government must demonstrate that it is out to establish stability and stop cheating people." That might mean a 7 per cent unemployment rate for up to three years, he says, but "there is no other way."

"THE GREAT AMERICAN DREAM IS A BALLOON"

That conclusion is debatable, but hardly anybody doubts that the nation is in trouble. In a Gallup poll released [the week of May 22, 1978], 54 per cent of a national sampling named inflation as the nation's worst problem—up dramatically from 33 per cent last February, and three times as many as singled out unemployment. Across the country, a near-record rise in home-mortgage rates has failed to slow a rush to buy houses and invest in real estate. The boom in diamonds and other jewelry continues, and the University of Michigan's latest consumer survey found a third of its sampling buying cars and other durable goods in anticipation of higher prices.

At times, the griping about prices has an edge of hysteria. "The great American dream is like a balloon," warns Bob Denton, a 44-year-old salesman in Vacaville, Calif. "Don't inflate it too much or it will blow up. I envision things like after the war in Germany, when people had to go to the store with a bagful of money to buy a loaf of bread."

There is no such explosion in prospect; most economists see even a return to double digits as a long shot in the next few months. But those odds are disquieting enough that there was a wave of relief last week at Carter's announcement that he would scale back his proposed tax cut, reducing the prospective Federal budget deficit for fiscal 1979 to about $53 billion. G. William Miller, who has taken on the Burnsian mantle of chief inflation fighter as Federal Reserve chairman, called the announcement "a major step" and hinted that the Fed would keep money relatively loose. Treasury Secretary Blumenthal said the deficit might be cut further, and some business leaders took the episode as evidence that Carter would back his rhetoric with action. DuPont chairman Irving Shapiro, heading a meeting of the Business Council at Hot Springs, Va., said happily: "The message I got is that this isn't just a shadow dance, this is real."

RECESSION OR WAGE AND PRICE CONTROLS?

In response, some businessmen—including automen Henry Ford II and Thomas A. Murphy of GM—are promising at least token cooperation with the President's call for voluntary restraint in raising prices and executive salaries. Murphy last week put a ceiling of 5 per cent on pay raises for GM's 50 top executives, and said he would "prudently evaluate" raises for 135,000 others. But as Carter's people see it, the biggest problem is going to be with the big unions. And when old George Meany brusquely turned down Carter's personal appeal for cooperation—"It's not my job to make it work. It's his job"—the prospect looked bleak.

Whatever happens, Blumenthal pledged last week that the Administration would not try wage and price controls. But the real alternative, admitted director Barry Bosworth of the Council on Wage and Price Stability (COWPS), is a recession—and a good many economists now see that as nearly a sure thing. "The Fed is not going to accommodate what is happening in prices," predicts Arthur Okun, chief adviser to Lyndon Johnson. "The Fed is going to give us a recession." Most experts do not welcome that prospect, but the Administration seems resigned. "We weren't born yesterday," says a senior hand. "If there's got to be a recession to keep a handle on this economy, then it better be early next year than later."

The need for any recession is a long way from being universally accepted. Apart from Carter's exercise in moral suasion, remedies for inflation are being offered in bewildering profusion: the government is variously advised to raise taxes, cut taxes, cut spending, and put more people to work, control prices, crack down on unions, encourage business investment, or give up and index all prices and wages to anticipate inflation. These proposals have two things in common: they usually reflect the interests of their sponsors, and they mirror a basic debate over what causes inflation and what kind of inflation is now besetting the nation.

DOLLARS OUT OF THIN AIR

Classically, inflation is too many dollars chasing too few goods: the definition of the demand-pull excess that results from an overheated economy with bottlenecks in the labor force or production. But even without excess demand, inflation can come from the cost-push of the familiar wage-price spiral: rising costs force prices up; to keep up, workers demand pay increases; that raises costs again. Recent history suggests that this process can be speeded and reinforced as businessmen, workers and consumers learn to expect inflation and try to stay ahead of it, and this is precisely what Carter hopes to stop. "We must stop adding on that extra per cent or so when we negotiate a pay raise or increase a price," exhorts chief jawboner Robert Strauss, "that little extra that . . . actually becomes the basis of more inflation." But more basically, government itself can be the engine of inflation—in two ways.

The government's role in inflation starts with the budget process. As FDR and the New Deal demonstrated, a budget deficit can help stimulate a lagging economy and soak up unemployment by putting new dollars in circulation. In Keynesian theory, accepted these days even by most conservative economists, such a deficit isn't inflationary as long as there is slack in the economy in the form of unused production capacity and unemployed workers, since the added demand won't create shortages. But the extra dollars must come from somewhere. In practice, most of them are created out of thin air: the Federal Reserve System makes new money by buying its own debt back from the big banks, thus replacing the notes with checks that the banks can count as reserves and lend out several times over.

As some see it, the money-creating process is itself the heart of inflation. The influential monetarist school of economists, led by Milton Friedman, holds that the rest of the inflationary process is irrelevant, since none of it can happen without the money supply growing faster than the output of goods and services. Thus the economy can be kept healthy simply by restraining the money supply to no more than the long-term rate of healthy growth—about 4 per cent a year. In practice, this is not as simple as it sounds, since a money squeeze can be devastating and the Fed's control is imprecise. And in any case, most economists believe the inflationary process is far more complex than the monetarist model allows.

MOVING AND SHAKING

A large part of this complexity stems from government's other role, as a mover and shaker of the economy. Determined to maintain high employment and avoid disruptions, Washington will flinch when a recession deepens or a credit crunch threatens major bankruptcies. In practice, this means that while prices and wages may be made to rise more slowly, they will never actually fall—and secure in that knowledge, workers and companies alike can deepen their debt with impunity. Government finds it increasingly difficult to control its own expenditures, since more and more of them consist of income transfers to citizens who can't be cut off: the old, the poor and the sick. Such outlays, only 22.5 per cent of the Federal budget in 1960, came to fully 40 per cent last year.

Government at all levels also pushes up prices in thousands of specific programs and actions, all of them intended as beneficial and most of them taken for granted: sales and property taxes, utility regulation, farm-price supports, minimum-wage laws, social-security payroll taxes, the regulation of trucks and railroads and pollution and safety rules.

That list barely scratches the surface, and it's pure conjecture what impact such government action may have on the consumer price index. But Barry Bosworth recently estimated that direct regulatory actions of the Federal gov-

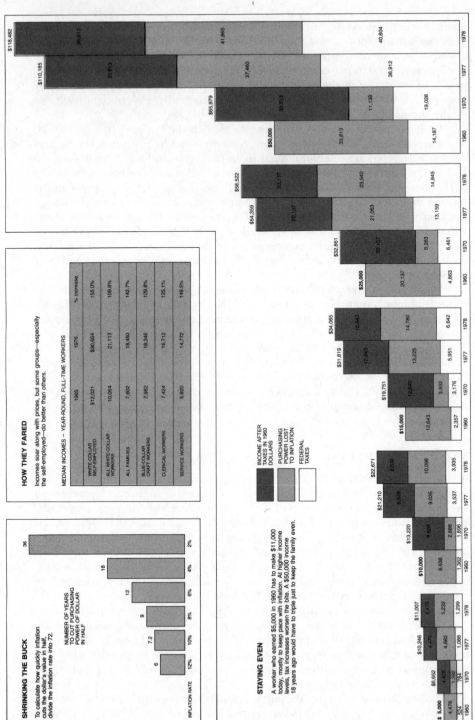

Source: The Conference Board

ernment may fatten the index by 0.75 per cent a year. Administration officials concede that their proposed wellhead tax on crude oil might add as much as 0.4 per cent, while outside economists say it might be twice that. Murphy of GM told his stockholders last week that government regulations will add $800 to the cost of each GM car by the early 1980s, and food retailers maintain they could save $330 million a year if the government would let their trucks carry loads in both directions rather than run empty a third of the time.

MORE ATTENTION TO INFLATIONARY RULES

In a largely overlooked part of his anti-inflation program, Carter ordered that more attention be paid to the inflationary effect of such government actions. As one result, government agencies must now prepare an inflationary-impact analysis of each new rule, to be submitted to a review board headed by chief economic adviser Charles Schultze. Schultze has already persuaded the National Highway Traffic Safety Administration to accept the automobile industry's way of meeting one proposed standard instead of following government specifications. But, says Assistant Treasury Secretary Daniel Brill, "We don't crow about those changes, because it brings the environmentalists, the safety promoters and everybody else down on our heads." A major change, begun in the Ford Administration, has drastically cut airline fares by reducing regulation of the industry, and with that precedent in mind, Carter has told the Interstate Commerce Commission to study a similar easing of trucking regulations.

In the larger picture, the government's regulatory impact contributes to cost-push inflation—a process that is rolling all too fast with no help at all. Cost-push has been the dominant factor in U.S. inflation ever since 1973, when the OPEC oil-price increase and a disastrous world harvest combined with the ending of Nixonian price and wage controls to send the index into orbit, and it shows no signs of ebbing. Food prices, initially expected to slow their rise later this year, are now likely to keep their momentum, largely on the strength of a dismaying increase in prices for beef. Labor productivity, the basis of industrial efficiency, showed a decline in the first quarter and remains a major dilemma. . . . But the biggest challenge to Carter's call for restraint, Bosworth concedes, is posed by the big unions, which must be persuaded to accept smaller-than-average wage increases, at least in percentage terms. "We're going to have to bite the bullet. There's no alternative," Bosworth says.

Labor's response to that notion was summed up by the AFL-CIO after Meany's chat with Carter: "Wage increases are an attempt to catch up and to stay even. They do not start the inflation cycle." In truth, a COWPS study has acknowledged that in the 1970s, wages "have just barely kept pace with prices." But the gains of big unions in concentrated industries have far outstripped those of smaller unions and the unorganized. A worker whose last raise was only 3 per cent shouldn't have to settle for less than that, Bosworth says, but one with a gain of 10 per cent already in the wallet should be willing to lower his sights by several points.

THE NEXT BIG CRUNCH

The real test, as a top business leader says privately, is "how strongly government will back the first business that decides to take a strike rather than bust the guideline." Ever since 1959, when the Eisenhower Administration turned on the steel industry, government has tended to push for settlements whatever the cost. The next crunch: July 20, when the contract runs out for 570,000 postal workers. They and the 238,000 railroad workers, who come up next, have vowed to match the 37 per cent, three-year increase won by the nation's coal miners in their strike this spring.

Until recently, it was taken for granted that there is no major threat of inflation from the demand side, with unemployment still at 6 per cent and manufacturers using only 83.5 per cent of their rated capacity. Normally, in a relationship first noted by Arthur Okun and dubbed Okun's law, it takes economic growth at a 4 per cent rate to absorb the growth in the labor force and prevent a rise in unemployment; after that, it takes 3 points of growth to cut the jobless rate by 1 point.

FULL CAPACITY?

But Okun's law has been repealed—or at least suspended. In recent months, employment has been growing and layoffs falling even while the real gross national product actually declined. One implication is that a good deal of industry's rated capacity may in reality be old and inefficient, that there is little real slack left in the skilled labor pool, and that the American economy may thus be running near its real capacity ceiling. If all this is true, says Fed governor Wallich, "We're now very close to full employment. Six per cent is it, or perhaps 5.7 per cent." And in that case, the economy's real growth would have to be cut back from rates of 4 to 5 per cent; to avoid inflation, growth would have to match the long-term trend of 3.5 per cent.

Such a judgment may well be premature, and economists at the White House are particularly reluctant to accept it because of its implication that no more can be done outside of special programs to help the unemployed. In fact, despite four years of record peacetime expansion, the jobless rate for black youth is hardly lower now, at 35.6 per cent, than it was when Carter took office. "We've had erratic movements in employment and productivity before," says Carter adviser Lyle Gramley. "It behooves us not to jump overboard." Okun himself is reluctant to accept the implication, concluding only: "It's the biggest puzzle I've seen in years."

Some think the answer may be found in inflationary psychology—the sheer expectation of rising prices that tends to feed the spiral. In the early stages of inflation, says Georgia State University economist Donald Ratajczak, consumers resist a price rise by looking for bargains elsewhere. But "after a time, there is a natural tendency to say, 'I hate this, but I don't see any sense in changing stores.'" After that, consumers may even begin buying hard goods ahead of schedule to beat price rises they see as inevitable. "My friends and I all bought Betamaxes because they'll be that much higher next year," says Los Angeles economist Stanley Sheinbaum. "The fact that we did has a further pressure on prices."

One danger in such anticipatory buying is that businessmen tend to mistake it for a real signal of rising demand. In reality, says consumer pollster Jay Schmiedeskamp of The Gallup Organization, buying in advance seldom lasts long before consumers feel overextended. But businessmen who think it will continue build up their inventories just in time for a decline. "We're selling the 1979 cars now," worries Ratajczak. "I think it will stimulate a recession."

Businessmen tend to resist rising costs longer and harder than consumers, but they, too, are vulnerable to the pressure. "So many businesses are desperate for supply," says Bram Goldsmith, chairman of Los Angeles's City National Bank. "They find people willing to buy a product, and they're not paying attention to price. It's a spiraling problem." In an inflation, businessmen try to cut their costs, improve cash flow, cut waste and and trim their payrolls, says an executive of a Midwest auto supplier, but above all, "you raise prices when you can get away with it. That's the first watchword." Such price boosts are hastened when Administration talk of jawboning leads to fear of controls; economist Allen Sinai of Data Resources, Inc., believes anticipatory increases already account for a full percentage point of the inflation rate. And fear of controls is rampant, no matter how many times Carter's men renounce them. Lawyers at one major New York-based conglomerate are dusting off contract language left over from the Nixon era to protect themselves if controls are imposed.

BUYING ADDITIONAL TIME

Given all those crosscurrents, the strength of the economy and the staying power of its surprising burst of speed are even less clear than usual. If the economy is running anywhere near capacity, there could be a dangerously inflationary injection of demand even from Carter's scaled-back tax cut, and his advisers admit to some nervousness at that prospect. Some economists at the Fed think the limit may be close, but Miller himself believes the superheated growth of the second quarter, which could run at a 10 per cent annual rate even after inflation, is merely a catch-up after the lull of the first quarter. In that perspective, he says, "Nothing about the average rate of growth in the first half is at all unusual."

Miller's endorsement of the trimmed tax cut was widely taken to be an accord with the White House—an unspoken promise to provide enough new money to keep the expansion going without a major upward push on interest rates. But in an interview with NEWSWEEK, Miller said he saw the scaleback as buying only about three months' additional time before capacity ceilings are hit. The only way to raise them, he said, is through an increase in investment and productivity; given that and a judicious mix of policy, the four-year-old expansion could continue "for some considerable time."

But that's an iffy proposition, and meanwhile prices keep rising. Economists outside the government now tend to predict a rise of 8 per cent in the consumer price index for a full year, almost a point higher than Schultze's latest maximum. And given the danger of a new demand-pull, the betting now is that the Fed will yank on its monetary string before long. "The Fed will surely prevent a complete runaway in prices, even at the expense of a recession," says Fellner. "The only question is when. I'd guess by early next year."

"NO PRESIDENT LIKES A RECESSION"

That timing would certainly make political sense. As even a top Administration hand concedes, a mild recession in early 1979 implies a recovery in election-year

1980. And for all Miller's semblance of independence from the White House, says a conservative economist in San Francisco, "I have to suspect that he's doing exactly what he was put there to do." Whatever the logic, a veteran of the political wars has his doubts about that scenario. "If you're a sensible political operator, that's the way you would behave," says Alan Greenspan. "But no President likes a recession at any time, under any conditions, because he never believes he will recover from it. That idea is too farsighted for our system. I wish the people who predict that had to sit through meetings when such an idea is actually proposed to a President of the United States."

In fact, neither politicians nor economists like to admit that most recessions are deliberately triggered, and considerable ink has been spent in recent years to demonstrate that they can happen without human intervention. By this theory, the price spiral creates such uncertainties and imbalances in the system that investment dries up, creating widening ripples of layoffs, shrunken demand and dwindling sales. If the process is allowed to go that far, the theorists argue, the resulting slump is far more severe than one deliberately triggered, and far harder to reverse. For the record, Miller himself continues to hope that the Fed can walk the line between doing too much and doing too little. He wants no recession, he says, but it will be "inevitable sooner or later if we do not bring down inflation."

On that, at least, everyone seems agreed. Perhaps a better question is, will a recession actually cut inflation?

Time was when the trade-off was reliable. As recently as the 1950s, the relationship between unemployment and the price index was codified by the Australian economist A. W. Phillips as the "Phillips curve," in which prices would hold steady at a "full employment" rate (originally, about 4 per cent on the jobless index in the U.S.), but rise predictably as unemployment fell below that level. And after three mild recessions during the Eisenhower years, inflation duly subsided to a rock-bottom rate of 1.5 per cent, providing a solid base for the expansion of the 1960s.

But then Lyndon Johnson launched the inflation of 1966 by insisting that Vietnam guns and domestic butter could both be had without a tax increase. After seven years of gyrating monetary policies, mini-recessions, and experiments in wage and price controls, inflation averaged 12.2 per cent for 1974—and after the worst recession since the 1930s, with unemployment soaring to 9 per cent of the labor force, inflation subsided only to 4.8 per cent in 1976. The Phillips curve seemed to have shifted off the chart—and now, after four years of expansion, unemployment stands at 6 per cent with inflation back up to 9 per cent in the first quarter.

GROPING FOR REMEDIES

Given that history, even those who are firmly convinced that a recession is coming are not optimistic about its outcome. "You get so little deflation from recessions now that it's like burning down your house to bake a loaf of bread," says Okun. So the academicians and government planners are groping for new inflation remedies—and polishing up old ones—to try out as less punitive instruments of policy. Among them:

- **LIVING WITH IT.** Brazil, after all, has lived for decades with inflation gyrating between 15 per cent and 92 per cent, and has managed to expand real output and improve living standards. One key to this success has been indexing—the automatic adjustment of wages, prices, taxes and interest rates to the rate of inflation—and Milton Friedman, for one, has proposed similar tactics for the U.S. to minimize inequities as long as inflation lasts. But critics reply that Brazil's solution is enforced by a dictatorship, and in any case Brazil is still importing technology and capital to sustain its boom and doesn't have to run its currency as the world's chief store of value.

- **CUTTING FEDERAL SPENDING.** This is the odds-on favorite remedy among businessmen, usually dismissed by government officials as an irresponsible suggestion that would wreak social havoc and create recession. But Democratic Rep. Jim Mattox, a freshman member of the House Budget Committee, maintains that "if Congress were really serious about inflation, it would be relatively simple to cut the budget"—and he suggests $7 billion in job-training, public-works, revenue-sharing and defense appropriations. Would it work? Vermont Royster, emeritus guru of The Wall Street Journal, recently wrote that deep budget cuts had been tried three times since World War II—by West Germany in 1948, France in 1958 and the U.S. in 1953. Each time, said Royster, inflation subsided.

- **STIMULATING CAPITAL INVESTMENT.** Among other conservatives, Miller argues that the failure of recent policy has been its reliance on spurring demand in the economy rather than providing new and efficient means of production. Some economists claim there's no evidence that increased investment will work, Miller says, but "the only time we've tried it in the postwar era was 1961 to 1965, and it worked beautifully. Capital spending in that expansion doubled—doubled—and we had zero inflation. Real income rose by about 3 per cent [annually], and every American was better off."

- **IMPOSING CONTROLS.** All but unanimously, people who have had anything to do with administering controls regard them with something like horror. "They don't really work," says C. Jackson Grayson, chairman of Nixon's Price Commission. But even some businessmen tend to speak kindly of controls in frustrated moments, and polls show the public consistently in favor. "It's like aspirin: you get instant relief, and then the pain returns," says Grayson. He expects to see them tried again.

- **TAX INCENTIVES.** The idea of using the tax system to punish or reward companies that follow price and wage guidelines dates back to 1970, but it is the newest proposal around—and stirring up considerable interest. . . . Whatever its merits, Blumenthal observes, "it is not something for this year or next. It'll take a lot of study, and then consideration and passage by Congress. We can't afford to ignore any possible approaches, but it's just not here yet."

That leaves the problem of inflation pretty much where Jimmy Carter found it when he arrived in Washington, with little sign of any cure on the horizon beyond his voluntary program. Few give that much chance of working; indeed, says former Presidential adviser Paul McCracken at the University of Michigan, "it may be counterproductive." The frustrating thing, says Bosworth, is that "the amount of restraint needed isn't great. You're talking about 1 to 2 per cent or so for the big unions, and that's hardly an immense act of faith." But people have to be pulled to the brink of national disaster—as they were in Britain two years ago, or in the hyperinflation of Weimar Germany—before they willingly conclude that beating inflation is worth what it costs. And, concludes Bosworth, "we're still a long way from that."

THE FED KNOWS BETTER

Fortunately, hyperinflation is also a long way off. Nobody knows precisely what mechanism tips ordinary inflation into the nightmare lived out as recently as 1946 in Hungary, where prices doubled on average every two to three days. But it apparently doesn't happen before the inflation rate climbs well into three digits, as it has recently in Argentina. In any case, says Greenspan, hyperinflation has never been possible without massive printing of money by the government, and the Fed knows better than that.

Perhaps the worst portent for today's inflation is the spreading cynicism that anything effective will be done. Even those who think they know the remedy don't believe it will be given a chance to work.

"LIKE BEING A LITTLE DRUNK"

Peter I. Berman, monetarist economist at the Conference Board, says a steady squeeze on money growth for the next five years could cut the inflation rate to 1.5 per cent—"but it is unlikely that the medicine will be administered." As policy is applied, says economist Jerry Jordan of the Pittsburgh National Bank, "it's like being a little drunk. The next day you start drinking again to cure the hangover. And so you never stop drinking even though you know the final hangover will be the worst of all." Assessing the prospects, The Wall Street Journal raised White House hackles with a dry editorial, titled "Ask for That Raise Now." Bosworth, it said, "keeps peeling away the layers of his battle strategy. One of these days he will get to the core. Anyone who needs a raise or a price increase had better try to get it before then."

For the coming months, the most optimistic scenario foresees consumer prices peaking at about a 10 per cent rate within the next month or so, with food prices subsiding enough to lower the rate in the second half. Conceivably, that might be evidence enough to help persuade big labor to restrain its demands in next year's heavy schedule of bargaining; meanwhile, the Fed may be able to walk its monetary tightrope and keep the expansion going, even at a reduced rate. And for the longer term, Paul McCracken remarked at the Business Council meeting that there is a limited number of wrong answers; since the nation has now tried most of them, it will be forced to the right one sooner or later.

And pigs might fly: Mcracken was speaking in bitter jest. The smart bet now is that the inflationary trend is still up, and that no government wants to pay the price of turning it down; and so—with occasional ups and downs in the rate, a recession or two and quite possibly more experiments with controls—inflation is now a fixture of economic life.

When the White House Asks for Ideas on Fighting Inflation

U.S. NEWS & WORLD REPORT

U.S. News & World Report is one of the top business and news weeklies in the country, and it generally keeps a close pulse on business feelings. In the following article, one of the magazine's reporters examines stacks of letters received by Robert Strauss when he was President Carter's chief inflation fighter.

If there is one subject on which Americans hold strong and clear-cut views, it's how to halt inflation.

Robert Strauss, President Carter's chief inflation fighter, discovered just that when he asked the public for suggestions on how to combat soaring living costs. Dozens of letters are pouring into Strauss's office weekly, bearing the ideas of citizens convinced that they know not only what's causing price hikes but what to do about it.

Strauss's correspondents range from businessmen to housewives, from farmers to famed economist John Kenneth Galbraith—the latter sending along some of his articles and wishing Strauss luck in his "far-from-easy task."

Suggestions range from meat-ax cuts in federal spending to reimposition of price and wage controls. Blame for the continued rise in prices is spread among bureaucrats, unions, businessmen, hospitals and others. Even the President and Strauss come in for their share of accusations.

U.S. News & World Report examined stacks of letters in Strauss's office. A sampling of what was found—

SOLUTIONS FROM EVERYWHERE

A writer from Atlanta thinks uncontrolled credit is the main cause of inflation and urges that consumers be required to put down more cash for installment purchases. He adds: "This is another way our government may put a big tooth in the bite of the jawbone policy to control prices and wages without controls."

Many of the letters, particularly from the elderly and those living on fixed incomes, demand that the government slap on a price-wage-rent freeze. A couple from Mountain Home, Ark., appeals for controls and urges: "By all means, include rent controls. The scandalous rise in property values in the large cities has now reached the point where landlords are hiking rents outrageously to get an investment return commensurate with the hugely inflated values of their property.

"We have a daughter caught in this economic squeeze. Soon millions of renters who are wage earners will be forced to leave the cities and their jobs because they can no longer pay the exorbitant rents. Every month more people on fixed incomes are going under financially. The only end in sight is the economic ruin of the nation—unless you act!"

A widow in Louisville, Ky., agrees, saying: "I am one of the million widows on a limited income from Social Security who does not qualify for government programs, and two thirds of income goes for rent."

An 80-year-old man in Ukiah, Calif., joins the plea for government controls, arguing: "You are simply whistling in the dark if you think the people will voluntarily [give up] the lush living they have today."

A Fort Lauderdale, Fla., man asks for one hour with Strauss to explain his plan for controlling inflation: "1. Put a limit on all prices, effective immediately. 2. No strikes. 3. Establish an economic court."

Many taxpayers think salaries in the government are too high and suggest that top officials take a cut. A man in Cedar Rapids, Iowa, writes: "If you are going to be a leader, you must set the example. I am talking about the President doing something like reducing his salary by 5 percent or maybe just 1 percent or 2 percent and making this move with his entire White House staff."

That suggestion is echoed in this letter from a Richmond, Va., resident: "Don't you think President Carter should set the example by cutting the salaries of his cabinet as well as his own?"

A writer in East Stroudsburg, Pa., suggests that all her fellow public officials refrain from seeking pay increases. She explains: "If a movement were made by those of us who opted for public service, who have asked for voter support knowing the salary that went with the offices we sought, to live within that salary instead of continually striving for pay raises, our combined public example across the land would certainly have impact. Someone has got to stand up and do something about inflation. If public service was ever needed, this is it. And the time is now."

To get off the inflation treadmill, a Teaneck, N.J., writer ticks off these suggestions: "Freeze all utility rates. Eliminate cost-of-living adjustment clauses. Eliminate all override and cost-plus contracts. Require governments to invest billions into small-business ventures. Eliminate farm subsidies. Restrict the amount of oil imports to a specific dollar amount for the next two years. Move toward a balanced budget."

From an 80-year-old woman in Camden, Me., comes a suggestion to relieve inflationary pressures by issuing $100 bonds dedicated to reducing the national debt.

A Gadsden, Ala., man sums up his ideas briskly in saying: "Get tough. Cut out the spending on waste. We can't afford any more harebrained social programs."

WHO'S TO BLAME?

When it comes to fixing the blame for inflation, practically nobody escapes people's wrath.

An investment counselor in Spokane, Wash., is typical of those who point the finger at Washington, saying: "The people are beginning to realize that the government is the source of inflation, and that budget deficits are the problem.

The federal government is out of control and someone must catch hold of the reins.

"The administration should press for an immediate across-the-board cut in all federal spending of between 5 and 10 percent. When the chips are down, any good business can institute an austerity program. Surely such bloated bureaucracies as HEW, HUD, DOE and DOD can do the same. The current phase of jawboning on inflation is a complete and utter waste of time and energy."

Similarly, a businessman in Burnt Hills, N.Y., accuses the bureaucracies of running the country. He adds: "The government shoves huge Social Security taxes down our throats and gives the civil servants their pensions outside of the [Social Security system] and, essentially . . . lets the civil servants decide what their pay should be—because they make the alleged impartial surveys—and then wants the taxpayers to tighten their belts and sacrifice.

"We taxpayers have more grievances against our present government than the colonists did against King George. Cut the budget, cut the payroll and tolerate no deficit spending, and we will not have a problem with inflation."

The Postal Service is cited repeatedly as a major engine of inflation. A Waco, Tex., man suggests that private enterprise be "given a chance to deliver the mail."

Others join in expressing outrage at the recent increase in postal rates. A San Diego executive complains: "Aren't you aware that the post office just ordered an increase of over 30 percent, forcing most mail-order firms to raise their prices? Aren't you aware that the Postal Service has raised their prices over 300 percent in the last five years and their services continue to deteriorate? Evidently, your pompousness has caused you to hide your head in the sand like an ostrich."

A Gainesville, Fla., resident chimes in: "Why should my labor, which requires special skills and certain judgment, be sucked dry by postal clerks who earn more money than I do? Yet their jobs require no skills, no judgment and no creativity. Mr. Carter has a God-granted opportunity to show he means business. If they strike, the Army can deliver the mail. They did it before."

The No. 1 inflation fighter himself doesn't escape the writers' attention. Irritated by Strauss's response to a previous letter, a New Jersey housewife fires back: "Since you are the one who got the appointment, how come you ask me for ideas?" She terms his $66,000 salary a "ripoff," although a man in Athens, Ga., writes that Strauss is "vastly underpaid."

A lawyer in Caledonia, Minn., defends farmers against charges of causing inflation and turns on unions. He writes: "Now that the law of supply and demand has finally preponderated in favor of the farmer, everyone, and especially labor, is crying their hearts out over the situation. George Meany has been muscling everyone from the President through Congress for years to keep wages high without regard to anyone."

But a woman in Pueblo, Colo., asserts: "You ask that unions take only cost-of-living wage increases to fight inflation. International Brotherhood of Electrical Workers Local No. 12 voted to take no raise and no cost-of-living increase. What do union wives do when we shop with less money and higher prices? We stand alone and unappreciated in our heroics."

A retired resident of Muskegon, Mich., focuses his anger on grocery stores, telling Strauss: "If you will have your department watch what's going on at the supermarkets, you will find prices on many items advancing far above the inflation rate and with no reason such as shortages or seasonal effects. They are just getting it. Why can't price and wage increases be held to the inflation rate? You have no problem holding my Social Security check to the inflation rate."

Big business is the villain, acording to a man in West Allis, Wis., who says: "The administration won't resort to controls because BIG BUSINESS is in control of the economy. Every industry in the country is gouging the public."

A foundry executive in Veedersburg, Ind., agrees with Strauss that some environmental regulations spur inflation. He reports: "We calculate the regulations to be 6½ percent of sales just on our melting operation alone. This does not include administrative time in dealing with the regulators. Add this to the cost of OSHA [Occupational Safety and Health Administration], and we're certain you will see double digits."

A man from Tampa, Fla., turns on hospitals: "The culprit is the voluntary nonprofit hospitals, which comprise the greater block of hospitals in the U.S. Human frailty in hospital management has thrived during a period of weak hospital-medical administration and ill-informed local politicians who manage and govern hospital and health-care operations."

Then there is the regular writer from Minneapolis, whose brief notes arrive almost daily. One of his latest reads: "You have met the enemy. He is *Carter*. Carter causes inflation. *Watch Carter*."

AND A FEW SURPRISES

Some of the letters sound unexpected themes.

For instance, a proposed change in federal noise standards on motorcycles, which would increase their cost, inspired a flood of mail. A Topeka, Kan., cyclist seethes: "Most new motorcycles already meet 1978 standards, but we must draw the line here. I am appalled at being classed as a Hell's Angel just because I ride a motorcycle. That's like calling you a Nixon. How do you like that?"

An Alabama man notes, on a newspaper clipping dealing with the rising costs of shoes, that he would like to get a pair of Strauss's discards.

Every letter gets an answer. Strauss regularly reviews a cross section of the mail, usually reading the letters while traveling on airplanes. He says: "I get some mean mail, but so many letters represent good will of people and give you a lift. The best is so much better than the worst."

The President Talks about Inflation

JIMMY CARTER

Jimmy Carter was elected president of the United States in 1976. His economic policies have been called both liberal and conservative, but most commentators have found it impossible to classify either him or his policies. In the following passages he demonstrates the fine line politicians tread when they discuss inflation. The first selection, an excerpt from his speech "Inflation: To Sacrifice for the Common Good," was delivered to the American Society of Newspaper Editors in Washington, D.C., on April 11, 1978. The second is excerpted from a speech given to the nation on October 24, 1978, in which he announced his new guidelines policy.

Inflation: To Sacrifice for the Common Good

Inflation has now become imbedded in the very tissue of our economy. It has resisted the most severe recession in a generation. It persists because all of us—business, labor, farmers, consumers—are caught on a treadmill which none can stop alone.

Each group tries to raise its income to keep up with present and anticipated rising costs and eventually we all lose the inflationary battle together. There are no easy answers. We will not solve inflation by increasing unemployment. We will not impose wage and price controls. We will work with measures that avoid both these extremes.

Our first and most direct efforts are within Government itself. Where Government contributes to inflation, that contribution must be lessened. Where Government expenditures are too high, that spending must be reduced. Where Government imposes an inflationary burden on business, labor and the consumer, those burdens must be lightened.

Wherever Government can set an example of restraint and efficiency, it must do so. The budget that I propose for our next fiscal year is both tight and capable of meeting the nation's most pressing needs.

The prospective deficit in the budget is as large as we can afford without compromising our hopes for a balanced economic growth and a declining inflation rate. But, as always, pressures are developing on all sides to increase spending and to enlarge the deficit.

Potential outlay increases in the 1979 budget, which are now being considered seriously by Congressional committees, would add between $9 billion and $13 billion to spending levels next year. The price of some of these politically attractive programs would escalate rapidly in future years.

I'm especially concerned about tuition tax credit, highway and urban transit programs, postal service financing, farm legislation and defense spending.

Jimmy Carter, "Inflation: To Sacrifice for the Common Good," *Vital Speeches of the Day*, May 1, 1978, pp. 418–421. Reprinted by permission.

By every means at my disposal I will resist these pressures and protect the integrity of the budget. Indeed, as opportunities arise, we must work to reduce the budget deficit, to insure that beyond 1979 the deficit declines steadily and moves us toward a balanced budget.

I will work closely with the Congress, and if necessary I will exercise my veto authority to keep the 1979 budget deficit at or below the limit that I have proposed.

The Federal Government must also act directly to moderate inflation.

Two months ago I proposed that each industry and each sector of our economic—of our economy—that wage and price increases this year be voluntarily held substantially below the average wage increases for the last two years.

I'm determined to take the lead in breaking the wage-and-price spiral by holding Federal pay increases down. Last year Federal white-collar salaries rose by more than 7 percent. I intend to propose a limit of about 5½ percent this year, thereby setting the example for labor and industry to moderate price and wage increases.

This year I will also freeze the pay of all executive appointees in the Federal Government and members of my own senior staffs. I believe that those who are most privileged in our nation, including other executives in government and also in the private sector, should set a similar example of restraint.

States and local governments employ every seventh worker in our nation. And I've sent letters this week to every governor and to the mayors of our major cities asking that they follow the Federal example and hold down their pay increases.

I've also asked that if those governments plan to reduce taxes that they first consider lowering sales taxes, which add directly to the consumer's burden.

The Federal Government will take several other steps to reduce inflation: All executive branch agencies will avoid or reduce the purchase of goods and services whose prices are rapidly rising unless by so doing we would seriously jeopardize our national security or create serious unemployment.

I'm also asking that all new or renegotiated Federal contracts which contain price escalation clauses should reflect the principal of deceleration. We must cut the inflationary costs which private industry bears as a result of government regulations.

Last month I directed executive regulatory agencies under my control to minimize the adverse economic consequences of their own actions.

I'm determined to eliminate unnecessary regulations and to insure that future regulations do not impose unnecessary cost to the American economy.

Our efforts to reorganize the Federal bureaucracy and to streamline the Civil Service—it's vitally important, it will help us put the Government's house in order.

I support Sunset legislation to insure that we review these regulatory measures and programs every few years and eliminate or change those that have become outdated.

I also urge Congressional budget committees to report regularly to the Congress on the inflationary effect of pending legislation, much as the Council of Economic Advisers and the Council on Wage and Price Stability do to me now.

The combined actions of my Administration and the Civil Aeronautics Board have already led to substantial cuts in some airline passenger fees.

Despite the opposition of private interests, the airlines regulatory reform legislation must be enacted this year.

We are also re-examining excessive Federal regulation of the trucking industry, an effort which may result in increased efficiency for reducing freight transportation costs and retail prices.

In addition, I'm asking the independent regulatory agencies to try to reduce inflation when they review rate changes and to explore regulatory changes that can make the regulated industries more efficient.

Last fall major new legislation was passed which will improve economic conditions for farm families, and we've announced additional administrative action to raise farm income this year.

Unfortunately the Senate has just passed a bill that would raise food prices by 3 percent and the overall cost of living by four-tenths of 1 percent, would shatter confidence in the crucial export market for America's farm products, create havoc with administrative machinery of the Department of Agriculture and cripple American farm famiies through increased costs.

It's bad for farmers; it's bad for the consumer; it's bad for our nation.

I will veto any farm legislation beyond what I have already recommended that would lead to higher food costs or budget expenditures.

Housing construction rates have been running about 2 million a year. And this has caused costs to go up rapidly, partly because of sharp increases in prices of raw materials such as lumber. Since lumber accounts for about one-fourth the cost of a new house, we can obtain some relief by increasing production and using our existing lumber output more efficiently.

Therefore, I've instructed the Department of Agriculture and Interior, the Council on Environmental Quality and also my economic advisers to report to me within 30 days on the best way to sustain expanded timber harvests from Federal, state and private land and other means of increasing lumber yield in ways that would be environmentally acceptable, economically efficient and consistent with sound budget policy.

Daily hospital costs have jumped from $15 in 1950 to over $200 today. And physicians' fees have gone up 75 per cent faster than other consumer prices. It's very important that Congress act now on the proposed hospital cost containment bill as the most effective means that we can take toward reasonable hospital prices.

Failure of Congress to act on the hospital cost containment legislation will cost the taxpayers of our country more than $18 billion in needless Government spending over the next five years.

Together with the airline deregulation bill, this is one of the two most important measures the Congress can pass to prevent inflation.

These measures so far have been delayed by the opposition of powerful lobbying groups. I will continue to give this legislation my full support, and I call on the leaders of Congress to do the same.

Such Government actions as I have discussed briefly can be an important step toward controlling inflation, but it is a myth that the Government itself can stop inflation.

Success or failure in this overall effort will be largely determined by the actions of the private sector of our economy.

I expect industry and labor to keep price, wage and salary increases significantly below the average rate for the last two years. Those who set medical fees, legal and other professional fees, college tuition rates, insurance premiums and other service charges must also join in.

This will not be easy, but the example of Federal action must be met. Inflation cannot be solved by placing the burden of fighting it wholly on a few.

The Council of Wage and Price Stability recently began a series of meetings with representatives of business and of labor in major industries such as steel, automobiles, aluminum, paper, railroads, food processing, communications, lumber and the Postal Service.

In consultation with these private parties, and others, the Council will identify the rate at which prices, wages and other costs have been rising in recent years, the outlook for the year ahead and the steps that can be taken to reduce inflation.

Let me be blunt about this point: I am asking American workers to follow the example of Federal workers and accept a lower rate of wage increase. In return they have a right to expect a comparable restraint in price increases for the goods and services they buy.

Our national interests simply cannot withstand unreasonable increases in wages and prices. It's my responsibility to speak out firmly and clearly when the welfare of our people is at stake.

Members of my Administration have already discussed this deceleration program with a number of leaders of labor, business and industry. Many have already promised their cooperation. Later I expect to meet with business and labor leaders to discuss contributions that they can make to help slow the rate of inflation.

One of the most important contributions that they can make is to show that restraint applies to everyone—not just the men and women in the assembly line, but also the managers in the executive suites.

Just as I will freeze the pay of the top executives in the Federal Government, the American people will expect similar restraints from the leaders of American business and labor.

I'm determined to devote the power of my office toward the objectives of reduced inflation. Our approach must be flexible enough to account for the variations in our complex economy. But it must be comprehensive enough to cover most of the activities of our economy.

In the long run, we should develop a special program to deal with individual sectors of the economy where Government actions have the greatest potential for reducing inflation. These include housing, medical care, food, transportation, energy and the primary metals industry.

The members of my Cabinet will work individually and also with the Council on Wage and Price Stability to develop and to announce early action to reduce inflation within their own areas of responsibility. . . .

Reducing the inflation rate will not be easy and it will not come overnight. We must admit to ourselves that we will never cope successfully with this challenge until we face some unpleasant facts about ourselves, about the solutions and about our problems.

The problems of this generation are, in a way, more difficult than those of a generation before. We face no sharply focused crisis, or threat, which might make us forget our differences and rally to the defense of the common good. We all want something to be done about our problems when the solutions affect us.

We want to conserve energy, but not to change our wasteful habits. We favor sacrifice, so long as someone else goes first. We want to abolish tax loopholes, unless it's our loophole. We denounce special interests, except for our own.

No act of Congress, no program of our Government, no order of mine as President, can bring out the quality that we need to change from the preoccupation with self that can cripple our national will to a willingness to acknowledge and to sacrifice for the common good.

As a nation prepared for the challenge of war, nearly 40 years ago, Walter Lippmann addressed these words to the American people, and I quote from him:

"You took the good things for granted," he said. "Now you must earn them again. It is written for every right that you cherish, you have a duty which you must fulfill. For every hope that you will attain, you have a task that you must perform. For every good that you wish to happen, you will have to sacrifice your comfort and ease. There is nothing for nothing any longer."

A Frank Talk about Inflation

I want to have a frank talk with you tonight about our most serious domestic problem. That problem is inflation. Inflation can threaten all the economic gains we have made, and it can stand in the way of what we want to achieve in the future.

This has been a longtime threat.

For the last ten years, the annual inflation rate in the United States has averaged 6½ percent, and during the three years before my inauguration it had increased to an average of 8 percent.

Inflation has, therefore, been a serious problem for me ever since I became President. We have tried to control it, but we have not been successful. It is time for all of us to make a greater and a more coordinated effort.

If inflation gets worse, several things will happen. Your purchasing power will continue to decline, and most of the burden will fall on those who can least afford it. Our national productivity will suffer. The value of our dollar will continue to fall in world trade.

We have made good progress in putting our people back to work over the past 21 months. We have created more than 6 million new jobs for American workers. We have reduced the unemployment rate by about 25 percent, and we will continue our efforts to reduce unemployment further, especially among our young people and minorities.

But I must tell you tonight that inflation threatens this progress. If we do not get inflation under control, we will not be able to reduce unemployment further, and we may even slide backward.

Inflation is obviously a serious problem. What is the solution?

I do not have all the answers. Nobody does. . . .

I have spent many hours in these last few months, reviewing with my own advisors and with a number of outside experts every proposal, every suggestion, every possibility for eliminating inflation.

If there is one thing I have learned beyond any doubt, it is that there is no single solution for inflation.

What we have, instead, is a number of partial remedies. Some of them will help, some may not. But we have no choice but to use the best approaches we have—and to maintain a constant search for additional steps which may be effective.

I want to discuss with you tonight some of the approaches we have been able to develop. They involve action by government, business, labor, and every other sector of our economy. . . .

I will concentrate my efforts within the government. We know that government is not the only cause of inflation. But it is one of the causes and government does set an example. Therefore, it must take the lead in fiscal restraint.

- We are going to hold down government spending, reduce the budget deficit, and eliminate government waste.
- We will slash federal hiring and cut the federal workforce.
- We will eliminate needless regulations.
- We will bring more competition back to our economy.
- And we will oppose any further reduction in federal income taxes until we have convincing prospects that inflation will be controlled. . . .

The federal government deficit is too high. Our people are simply sick and tired of wasteful federal spending and the inflation it brings with it.

We have already had some success. We have brought the deficit down by one-third since I ran for President—from more than $86 billion in fiscal year 1976, to about $40 billion in fiscal year 1979—a reduction of more than $25 billion in just three years.

Reducing the deficit will require difficult and unpleasant decisions.

We must face a time of national austerity. Hard choices are necessary if we want to avoid consequences that are even worse. . . .

To keep the governmment to a manageable size, I am tonight ordering a reduction in federal hiring. This order will mean a reduction of more than 20,000 in the number of permanent federal employees already budgeted for this fiscal year, and I will cut the total size of the federal workforce.

I have already placed a 5.5 percent cap on the pay increase for federal employees, and federal executive officers are receiving no pay increases at all.

It is not enough just to control government deficits, spending, and hiring. We must also control the costs of government regulations. . . .

Where regulations are essential, they must be efficient. Where they fight inflation they should be encouraged. Where they are unnecessary, they should be removed.

Early this year, I directed federal agencies to eliminate unnecessary regulations and to analyze the costs and benefits of new ones. Today, for instance, the Occupational Safety and Health Administration eliminated nearly 1,000 unnecessary regulations.

Now we can build on this progress.

- I have directed a Council of my regulatory departments and agencies to coordinate their regulations to prevent overlapping and duplication.
- Most important, the Council will develop a unified calendar of planned major regulations. The calendar will give us, for the first time, a comprehensive list of regulations the federal government is proposing, with their costs and objectives. . . .

Of all our weapons against inflation, competition is the most powerful. Without real competition, prices and wages go up—even when demand is going down.

We must therefore work to allow more competition whenever possible so that powerful groups—government, business, labor—must think twice before abusing their economic power. . . .

Another reason for inflation is the slowdown in productivity growth. More efficient production is essential if we are to control inflation, make American goods more competitive in world markets, add new jobs, and increase the real incomes of our people.

We have made a start toward improving productivity. The tax bill just passed by the Congress includes many of the investment incentives that I recommended last January. Federal support for research and development will continue to increase, especially for basic research. We will coordinate and strengthen federal programs that support productivity improvements throughout our economy.

Our government efforts will attack the inflation that hurts most—inflation in the essentials: food, housing, and medical care.

We will continue to use our agricultural policies to sustain farm production, to maintain stable prices, and to keep inflation down.

Rising interest rates have always accompanied inflation. They add further to the costs of business expansion and to what consumers must pay when they buy houses and other consumer items.

The burden of controlling inflation cannot be left to monetary policy alone, which must deal with the problem through tight restrictions on money and credit that push interest rates up.

I will work for a balanced, concerted, and sustained program under which tight budget restraint, private wage and price moderation, and responsible monetary policy support each other.

If successful, we should expect lower inflation and lower interest rates for consumers and businesses alike.

As for medical care, where costs have gone up much faster than the general inflation rate, the most important step we can take is to pass our bill to control hospital costs.

This year, the Senate passed it. Next year I will try again, and I believe the whole Congress will act to hold down hospital costs—if your own members of congress hear from you. . . .

In the last ten years, in our attempts to protect ourselves from inflation, we have developed attitudes and habits that actually keep inflation going once it has begun. Most companies raise their prices because they expect costs to rise. Unions call for large wage settlements because they expect inflation to continue. Because we expect it to happen, it does happen, and once it's started, wages and prices chase each other up and up.

It is like a crowd standing at a football stadium. No one is willing to be the first to sit down.

Except for our lowest paid workers, I am asking all employees in this country to limit their total wage increases to a maximum of seven percent per year. From tonight on, every contract signed and every pay raise granted should meet this standard.

My price limitation will be equally strict. Our basic target for economy-wide price increases is 5¾ percent. To reach this goal, I am tonight setting a standard for each firm in the nation to hold its price increases at least one-half of a percentage point below what they averaged during 1976 and 1977. . . .

We will also make better use of the $80 billion worth of purchases the government makes from private industry each year. We must be prudent buyers. If costs rise too fast, we can delay those purchases as your family would—or switch to another supplier. We may not buy a fleet of cars this year, for example, if cars cost too much, or we may channel our purchases to suppliers who have observed our wage and price standards rather than those who have not.

We will require firms that supply goods and services to the government to certify their compliance with the wage and price standards. We will make every effort, within legal limits, to deny government contracts to companies that fail to meet our wage and price standards.

These steps can work, but that will take time, and you are the ones who can give them that time. If there is one thing I am asking of every American tonight, it is to give this plan a chance to work—a chance to work for us.

You can help give it that chance by using your influence.

Business and labor must know that you will not tolerate irresponsible price and wage increases. Your elected officials must know how you feel as they make difficult choices.

Too often the only voices they hear are those of special interests, supporting their own narrow cause. If you want government officials to cut inflation, you have to make sure that they hear your voice.

I have heard you with unmistakable clarity.

Nearly 40 years ago, when the world watched to see whether his nation would survive, Winston Churchill defied those who thought Britain would fall to the Nazi threat. Churchill replied by asking his countrymen, "What kind of people do they think we are?"

There are those today who say that a free economy cannot cope with inflation, and that we have lost our ability to act as a nation rather than as a collection of special interests. And I reply, "What kind of people do they think we are?"

I believe that our people, our economic system, and our government are equal to this task. I hope that you will prove me right.

The Intelligent Citizen's Guide to Inflation

ROBERT M. SOLOW

Robert M. Solow is regarded as one of the top theoretical economists in the United States. A professor of economics at the Massachusetts Institute of Technology, he served as a senior staff economist on the Council of Economic Advisers under President John F. Kennedy when wage-price guideposts were in use.

Although his specialty has been growth and capital theory, his writing is so readable and his mind so keen that regardless of the topic his articles are highly respected and widely read. In this overview article, "The Intelligent Citizen's Guide to Inflation," excerpted from a longer article of the same name, he provides a solid foundation to the economic analysis of inflation.

Two broadly opposite frames of mind seem to dominate the current discussion of inflation. One says that we are beset by some utterly mysterious plague of unknown origin. If it is not stopped soon, it will cause unimaginable, or at least unspecified, disasters. The only hope is that some Pasteur or Jenner or Ehrlich will discover The Cure. The other view is that it is all quite simple. There is some one thing we have failed to do: control the money supply or balance the budget or legislate price controls or abolish the unions. As soon as we do it, the problem will then go away.

This essay is written in the belief that both these currents of opinion are wrong. I do not, however, have an alternative solution to offer. Indeed, I rather doubt that there is a Solution, in the sense of some policy that your average mixed capitalist economy can reasonably be expected to pursue which will drastically reduce the tendency to inflation, without substituting some equally damaging and intractable problem instead.

What I can hope to do is to explain the vocabulary and intellectual framework evolved by economists for discussing and analyzing inflation. By itself, this will contribute to clarity of thought—much, perhaps most, of current popular discussion is hopelessly confused. I hope to be able to go further than that, however. There are some positive statements one can reasonably make about the behavior of modern mixed economies. We know less than we would like to know, but much more than nothing. Where I verge on speculation, or where there are real differences of opinion within the economics profession, I will try to be honest about it.

WHAT IS INFLATION?

Inflation is *a substantial, sustained increase in the general level of prices*. The intrinsic vagueness of "substantial" is harmless. One would not want to use a heavyweight word to describe a trivial rise in the price level; granted, but it will

Robert M. Solow, "The Intelligent Citizen's Guide to Inflation." Reprinted with the permission of the author from *The Public Interest*, No. 38 (Winter 1975), pp. 30–49, 52–57, 65–66. © 1975 by National Affairs, Inc.

never be perfectly clear where to draw the line, but neither can it be important since only a word is at stake. "Sustained" is a little trickier. One would not want to label as inflationary a momentary (six-month? one-year?) upward twitch of the price level, especially if it is soon reversed. There is no point in being forced to describe mere short-term fluctuations in prices as alternating bouts of inflation and deflation. "Sustained" also carries some connotation of "self-perpetuating" and that raises broader questions. It is obviously important to know whether each step in an inflationary process tends to generate further inflation unless some "outside" force intervenes, or whether the inflationary process is eventually self-limiting. The answer need not be the same for all inflations, and it certainly depends on what you mean by "outside." So it is probably best not to incorporate this aspect as a part of the definition.

It is the notion of the "general price level" that will lead us somewhere. Economists make a sharp and important distinction between the system of relative prices and the general price level. Relative prices describe the terms on which different goods and services exchange for *one another;* the general price level describes the terms on which some representative bundle of goods and services exchanges for *money.* Imagine an economy in which the only goods produced are meat and vegetables, and first suppose that all exchange is barter; some people trade meat for vegetables with other people who want to trade vegetables for meat. If one pound of meat exchanges for three pounds of vegetables, then the relative price is established. But since there is no money, there is no such thing as the general price level. Notice that inflation is inconceivable in a barter economy. It would be logically contradictory for "all prices" to rise at the same time. Suppose that, because of a change in tastes or a natural catastrophe, one pound of meat should come to exchange for six pounds of vegetables. One could say that the price of meat (in terms of vegetables!) had doubled. But that is exactly the same thing as saying that the price of vegetables (in terms of meat!) had halved. A carnivorous farmer would find himself worse off; but a vegetarian rancher would be sitting pretty.

So inflation has intrinsically to do with money. Now let us introduce some greenbacks to serve as money in our meat-and-vegetables economy. Suppose meat goes for $1.50 a pound and vegetables for 50 cents a pound—i.e., one pound of meat for three of vegetables, as before. Now suppose that at a later time meat goes to $3.00 a pound and vegetables to $1.00. The relative price is unchanged. From most points of view the meat-and-vegetables economy goes along as if nothing has happened, and from most points of view nothing has. (Not quite nothing: A tradesman or a miser who happened to be sitting on a load of greenbacks at the time will have taken quite a beating.)

We can go a step further. Suppose the average daily diet consists of one pound of meat and one pound of vegetables (though very few individuals may actually consume exactly the average diet). We could agree to measure the general price level by the money cost of the average consumption bundle. In that case, we would say that the price level was 200 in the initial situation, and 400 after the price increases. (It is the custom to choose some year as "base year" and set its price level arbitrarily at 100. If the initial year is the base year, then the later price level would be 200.) In any case, we would certainly want to say that the general price level had doubled, and if it had doubled in exactly 12 months, we would say that the rate of inflation had been 100 per cent a year.

Since the prices of all goods and services had exactly doubled, it is no trick to say that the general price level had doubled. But we now have a routine that will take care of less obvious situations. Suppose meat goes from $1.50 to $2.40 a pound and vegetables from 50 cents to 60 cents. The price of meat has risen by 60 per cent, that of vegetables by 20 per cent. But the cost of the average consumption bundle rises from $2.00 to $3.00 (or the price index from 100 to 150). So we could say that the price level had gone up by 50 per cent. Notice also that this time relative prices have also changed: A pound of meat exchanges for four pounds of vegetables at the new prices. The vegetarian rancher gains at the expense of the carnivorous farmer, but *that is because of the change in relative prices*. In the case of "pure inflation," when *all* prices change *in the same proportion*, nobody loses (except owners of money) and nobody gains (except owers of money).[1]

Perhaps the simplest way to define inflation is as a loss in the purchasing power of money. That has the merit of emphasizing the fact that inflation is essentially a monetary phenomenon. But there is a possible semantic trap here. Some economists believe that the whole inflationary mechanism is primarily or exclusively monetary, in particular that the main or only cause of inflation is too rapid a growth in the supply of money. They may be right or they may be wrong. (I happen to think that doctrine is too simple by half.) But the mere fact that you can have inflation only in a monetary economy is neither here nor there, just as the fact that you can't have a drowning without water doesn't prove that the way to understand drowning is to study water. I will come back to this analytical question later.

MEASURING INFLATION

In the real world there are thousands of goods and services, whose relative prices are changing all the time in complicated ways. The measurement of the general price level thus becomes a major statistical enterprise. But it is done, and generally according to the principles just described. In fact, the American reader is confronted with at least three separate indexes of the general price level: the Consumer Price Index (CPI), the Wholesale Price Index (WPI), and the GNP Deflator. Since there are some conceptual differences among them, and since they may occasionally say different things, it is worthwhile to understand exactly what each of them means.

The CPI (what is sometimes called the cost-of-living index) is produced and published monthly; it is closest in principle to the kind of price index described earlier. At intervals of a decade or more, the Bureau of Labor Statistics (BLS) conducts an expensive survey of the spending habits of families of different size, income, and other characteristics. From this survey it calculates the typical budget of a middle-income, urban wage-earner or clerical worker with a family of four. Then each month it actually prices out that budget in a number of cities around the country. If the cost of that bundle goes up or down by one per cent, the CPI goes up or down by one per cent.

---

[1] The smart kids in the class will now ask: If meat gets more expensive relative to vegetables, won't consumers buy less meat and more vegetables, and won't that change the make-up of the average consumption bundle, and what will that do to the price index? They can go on to the course in Index-Number Theory, but they will find it dull.

That is certainly a reasonable and meaningful price index, but it does have some drawbacks. (Of course, any method of reducing all those thousands of price changes to a single number will have drawbacks.) It relates only to consumers; the prices of industrial machinery and raw materials could go sky-high, and the CPI would register that fact only later, when cost increases filtered down to retail prices. Moreover, the CPI relates only to some consumers—those middle-income, urban, wage-earning families of four. Old people, or poor people, or oil millionaires, who buy different bundles, may have different experiences. Finally, economists have a technical reservation. The CPI covers, as its concept dictates it should, everything consumers spend money on, including sales taxes, monthly mortgage payments, used cars, and so on. It reflects changes in state and local taxes, interest rates, used-car prices, etc. For some purposes, economists would prefer a price index confined to currently produced goods and services. Certainly it matters whether a rise in the CPI reflects mainly higher sales taxes and interest rates or higher prices for food and clothing.

The WPI, also available monthly, is based on prices collected at the wholesale level. Its coverage is wide but rather peculiar, for several reasons. For one thing, it omits all services, medical care, house rents, etc. For another, it counts some prices over and over again, and thus gives them more weight than they deserve. For example, a change in the price of raw cotton will appear first as a crude material, then again as it is reflected in the price of cloth, then again as it is reflected in the price of clothing. This pyramiding overemphasizes crude material prices and can cause the WPI to behave quite erratically, especially when the prices of materials are changing. Its main utility is that, just because of its coverage of the early stages of fabrication, it often catches price developments early. The WPI, like the other indexes, is broken down into sub-indexes (in the case of the WPI, farm products, processed foods, industrial materials, various categories of finished manufactures, etc.), and these may be very informative.[2]

THE GNP DEFLATOR

The GNP Deflator is by and large the economists' favorite. Unlike the CPI, it covers only currently produced goods and services, and unlike the WPI, it avoids all double-counting. But it is constructed in a more complicated way. The Department of Commerce calculates every quarter the country's Gross National Product. This is essentially the value at current market prices of the current flow of newly produced final goods and services. (The force of "final" is that one omits goods and services which are immediately used up in the production of something else, because their value will be included in the value of the final product.) At the same time, Commerce also calculates the GNP "in constant prices." That is, it takes the current flow of final goods and services, but instead of valuing them at this quarter's prices, it values them at the prices of some fixed year, currently 1958. For instance, in 1973 the GNP in current prices was

---

[2]For more on the WPI, and for a very informative and interesting article complementary to this one, I recommend "Inflation 1973: The Year of Infamy" by William Nordhaus and John Shoven in the May/June 1974 issue of *Challenge* magazine.

$1,295 billion, but the GNP in 1958 prices was $839 billion, because 1958 prices were lower than 1973 prices.

How much had prices risen between 1958 and 1973? The natural computation is $1,295/$839=1.54, for an increase of 54 per cent. If the 1973 flow of output valued in 1973 prices is 54 per cent higher than the *same* flow of output valued in 1958 prices, then the obvious inference is that the general level of prices must have risen by 54 per cent since 1958. So the general formula for the GNP Deflator in year X is: GNP in year X in current prices/GNP in year X in base-year prices. (Exercise: Convince yourself that the GNP Deflator for the base year itself is automatically 1.00 or 100, because in the base year GNP in current prices and GNP in base-year prices are the same quantity.)

Economists like this price index for the analysis of inflation not because it is obscure, but for the reasons I mentioned before: It eliminates double-counting, and it focuses on the pricing of currently produced goods, not existing assets. For that very reason, of course, it may not reflect exactly the experience of consumers. Another disadvantage is that the GNP Deflator is available only at quarterly intervals.[3]

All price indexes suffer from a common difficulty. Commodities change in character and quality. How can the BLS price the same consumer-bundle in 1955 and 1975 when many of the things consumers buy in 1975 did not exist, and so had no prices, in 1955? How can the Commerce statisticians value 1975 GNP in 1958 prices, when there were no 1958 prices for some of the items entering the 1975 GNP? If the price of an ordinary shirt rises 10 per cent in the course of a year, but simultaneously the wrinkle-resisting properties of the shirt are improved, how is one to decide how much of the 10 per cent represents the greater value of an improved product and how much represents pure price increase? The agencies do the best they can, but it is hardly a job that can ever be done perfectly. It used to be thought that there was systematic underallowance for quality improvements to such an extent that an annual rise of one or two per cent in the measured price level could be ignored as not being a true price increase; but no one knows for sure. Perhaps the best conclusion is that one ought not to attach great significance to small changes in price indexes.

This discussion of price indexes has given us another concept of absolutely fundamental importance for rational discussion. GNP in constant prices is in an important sense a "physical" concept. It is an attempt to measure the size of the flow of actual production in a way that is independent of inflationary and deflationary aberrations. When GNP in constant prices changes, it is because the production of goods and services has changed, not because prices have changed. In terms of my earlier example, the difference between the 1968 GNP of $707 billion in 1958 prices and the 1973 GNP of $839 billion in 1958 prices permits us to say that "aggregate output" rose by 18.7 per cent between those years. In the jargon, GNP in constant prices is called "real GNP" or "real aggregate output." We will be coming back to it.

---

[3]There is another minor problem. The basis for putting a price on the output of governments—education, police services, "plumbers'" services, etc.—is pretty tenuous, though these are all part of the GNP. It is possible to produce a price index for privately produced GNP, nearly all of which is actually sold on a market.

THE LAST 100 YEARS

The two charts on the following pages show what has happened to the general price level since 1867. The price index used is the GNP Deflator.[4] Figure 1 shows the price index itself on what is called a logarithmic scale, to draw attention to the proportional changes that really matter. The base year is 1929=100. The fact that the price level in 1973 (291.5) is almost four times that in 1867 (78.0) is not to be taken as utterly precise, in view of the vast difference between the commodities making up the GNP in 1867 and those actually produced in 1973. But for orders of magnitude, the figures will do. Steep portions of the curve represent periods of more severe inflation; when the curve points downward, the price level was actually falling.

FIGURE 1
The Price Index, 1867–1973 (1929 Base)

[4] I owe the figures to Professor Benjamin Klein of the University of California at Los Angeles, who pieced them together from estimates made by Robert Gallman for 1874–1909 and Simon Kuznets for 1910–1946, and the official Commerce Department figures for 1947–1973. The earlier figures are based on very sketchy data.

Figure 2 converts the price index into percentage rates of inflation and deflation; prices are rising when this curve is above the zero line, and falling when it is below.

The broad outlines of the history of the price level are easily read from the charts. From the end of the Civil War to the end of the 19th century, the predominant trend was deflationary. The GNP Deflator fell by more than 40 per cent between 1867 and 1896. Although the curve turned upward about then, by the eve of the First World War the price index had gone back up only to the level of 1873.

Really big inflationary bursts are associated with major wars, and their aftermath. Between 1914 and 1920, prices almost doubled. Between 1940 and 1948, prices almost doubled. The Korean War added only about 10 per cent to

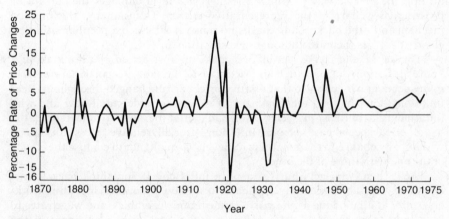

FIGURE 2
Percentage Rates of Inflation and Deflation, 1870–1973

the price level. In the case of the Vietnamese War it is hard to know where to start; between 1966 and 1972, the index rose about 30 per cent.

But that is only half of it, and in some ways the less interesting half. There were at least two years of deflation after the First World War; by 1922 the index was back to the 1917–1918 level. The depression of the 1930's, like those of the 1870's and 1890's, pushed the price level down. The index, pegged at 100 in 1929, fell to 73.3 in 1933, rose to 80.3 in 1936, and stayed there until the eve of the Second World War in 1940. But the last minus-sign on Figure 2 appears briefly in 1949 when the first of the mild postwar recessions lowered the price index by a point. (On a quarterly basis one could find a somewhat bigger decline.) From 1950 on we have had a quarter-century without a dip in the general price level. The best one can find is the period beginning with the recession of 1958, running through the milder recession of 1960, and continuing during the slow return to approximate full employment at the end of 1965. During that interval, the Deflator rose at an average annual rate of about 1.5 percent. It is simply not possible to know with any confidence what would have happened if the escalation of the war either had not occurred or had not been allowed to overheat the economy in the last years of the Johnson Administration.

WHY IS PURE INFLATION A BAD THING?

There seems to be universal agreement that rising prices are a cause for alarm and perhaps fear. Candidates for office accuse incumbents of having fostered inflation or failed to prevent it, and promise to eliminate it themselves. Incumbents announce that they are working on the problem. And surveys of public opinion show that very many ordinary people regard inflation of the price level as one of the most serious problems they face, or at least as an important background worry. Yet it is fair to say that public discussion offers no insight at all into the precise way in which a rising price level damages the current or prospective welfare of the representative citizen. Occasionally, the implied mechanism in the background makes no sense at all. Such a peculiar situation clearly deserves the most thorough investigation.

For the sake of clarity, let us first make an abstraction and think about a "pure" inflation, during which all prices rise at the same proportional rate—so many per cent per year—so that relative prices are unchanged throughout. Real inflations don't happen that way; but if we are to understand how and why inflation is a burden on society, we had better be able to understand the hypothetical special case of a pure inflation. After all, relative prices can change without any change in the general price level; we ought not to confuse the effects of the one with those of the other.

Well, then, who gets hurt in a pure inflation? If you think back to our meat-and-vegetables economy, it is hard to see how producers, including workers, suffer at all. So long as the prices of meat and vegetables, and wage rates in both industries, go up at the same percentage rate, every participant in the economy continues to have the same purchasing power over all goods and services as before. The inflation appears to have no "real" effects. The general point is that a person's economic welfare depends on the prices of the things he or she buys and sells, including labor and the services of property; if the prices of all those things go up or down in the same proportion, then economic welfare stays the same.

Now there is an optical illusion that clearly plays some role in popular discussions of inflation. Many people see no connection between the prices of the things they buy and the prices of the things they sell. The ordinary person works hard and feels that each year's wage increase is deserved. When it turns out that prices have also increased, so that all or part of the wage increase is illusory, the ordinary person regards that price rise—inflation—as a form of theft, a hand in his or her pocket. But of course, wages could not have increased had prices not increased. I cannot estimate how widespread this illusion may be, but there can hardly be any doubt that such an illusion does exist.[5]

---

[5] No one could make that mistake in the simple meat-and-vegetables economy. But the real world is more complicated. For instance, the timing of price and wage increases is irregular, with some temporary advantage from getting in early, and some loss from getting in late. Moreover, the normal experience is that standards of living rise as productivity improves. Then only part of a wage increase is eroded away by price increases, but even the loss of that part is felt as robbery.

If you want to know how the country as a whole is doing, then the course of the price level will not tell you. In narrowly economic terms, the proper measure of success is the flow of goods and services produced and made available to the society for consumption and other uses. The closest thing we have to look at is the real GNP, which we have already met. GNP in constant prices is the most comprehensive available measure of the performance of the economy in doing what it is supposed to do—the generation of want-satisfying commodities. It is far from perfect for reasons that involve the treatment of depreciation, environmental effects of economic activity, the organization of work, the "quality of life," governmental activity, and other things, but none of them has to do with inflation. So if inflation is a net burden to society, that ought to show up in a reduction of real GNP, or at least a slowing-down of its normal upward trend. But that is not what happens; in fact the opposite is more nearly true. Periods of prosperity are somewhat more likely to coincide with periods of inflation and periods of recession are somewhat more likely to coincide with intervals of stable or more slowly rising prices.[6]

Is the social cost of inflation a mirage? There is one earlier hint that needs to be followed up. In a monetary economy—the only kind that can have inflation—holders of cash see their real wealth eroded by a rising price level, even in a pure inflation. So do creditors who hold claims for payment fixed in money terms. Offsetting at least some of these losses are the gains of debtors, who can pay back in dollars of smaller purchasing power what they had borrowed and spent in dollars of higher real value. Perhaps the true social costs of inflation are to be found among the holders of money, or among cash creditors more generally.

ANTICIPATED INFLATION

Another distinction—this time between anticipated and unanticipated inflation—is required for this analysis. So let us take the strongest case first: a pure inflation which is confidently and accurately expected by everyone in the economy. Suppose you lend me a dollar today and I agree to pay back $1.05 a year from today. Then we have agreed on an interest rate of five per cent annually. (You laugh, somewhat bitterly. But it's just an example.) If we both correctly expect the general price level to be quite steady during the next year, then that is all there is to it. You as lender and I as borrower are both willing to make the transaction at an interest rate of five per cent a year. Now imagine instead that we both confidently expect the general level of prices (which means each individual price and wage, since we are talking about pure inflation) to be four per cent higher a year from now. I would be delighted to take your dollar today and pay you $1.05 in a year. Why not? If meat is a dollar a pound today and will be $1.04 a pound in a year, then in effect you would be lending me a pound of meat today, and I would be obliged to pay you only 1.05/1.04 or about

---

[6]There is an exception to all this, but it need not concern us. Imagine a country which must import a large fraction of its basic necessities, like food and oil, and pay for them with exports of other commodities. Such a country may experience steady or rising real production, but if world food and oil prices are rising faster than the prices of its exports, its own standard of living could deteriorate. The United States is not in that position because it is so nearly self-sufficient; but of course it is hardly a hypothetical possibility for Japan and some European countries.

1.01 pounds of meat next year. In *real* terms, you would be getting interest at one per cent a year, not five per cent. Of course for the same reasons that I would be pleased at the transaction, you would not be. In fact, if we were both prepared to make the deal at five per cent with stable prices, we ought both to be prepared to make the deal at nine per cent when we both confidently expect the price level to rise at four per cent a year; in the real purchasing power terms that matter, you will then be collecting interest at five per cent per year. In the professional jargon, the *real* rate of interest (five per cent) is the *nominal* or *money* rate of interest (nine per cent) less the expected rate of inflation (four per cent). Thus the very high interest rates of early 1974 have to be read against the substantial inflation of the same period. Real rates are not as high as nominal rates; in fact, they are lower by about the expected future rate of inflation — about which we can only guess. Of course, anyone who borrows long and is locked in at high interest rates is left holding the bag if the inflation should unexpectedly slow down or stop.

What follows? *If* the inflation is fully anticipated by everyone, *if* everyone has complete access to the capital markets, and *if* all interest rates are free to adjust to expectations about the price level, and do so quickly and smoothly, then borrowers and lenders will be able to protect themselves against inflation. Once again, the inflation would seem to have no real effects.

Well, not quite. Those qualifications are pretty strong. Obviously, we will have to consider the case of unanticipated inflation; but even before we get to that there are some important things to say. First of all, some assets bear no interest at all: the important ones are currency and balances in ordinary checking accounts. They constitute the money supply. It would be mechanically difficult for the Treasury to pay interest on currency. Commercial banks are restrained by law from paying interest on checking accounts. (They do the next best thing by providing financial services free of charge, or at a fee that diminishes with the size of balance; but that is hardly the same thing and cannot in any case serve the same purpose as a nominal interest rate in adjusting to expectations about rising prices.) So, even if the inflation is correctly anticipated, holders of currency and checking accounts will suffer (as they would symmetrically gain if deflation should ever come back into style). These losses to holders of money are not, so to speak, net losses to society, because there are corresponding gains to others. In the case of checking accounts, the gainer is the bank and its stockholders, who earn the higher nominal interest rates on their own assets and pay no interest — except for those free financial services — on deposit liabilities. In the case of currency, the U.S. Government, in the person of the Federal Reserve, is the issuer of the paper, but it is rather special paper, and a special kind of liability, and in any case not very important.

THE "DEADWEIGHT LOSS"

Since anticipated inflation redistributes to others part of the wealth of holders of money, it is natural that businesses and people should try to reduce their holdings of money when they expect prices to be rising. One can hardly do without any cash in the modern world, but nevertheless it is usually possible to substitute effort for liquidity. Corporations can buy relatively liquid short-term securities and try correspondingly harder to synchronize inflows and outflows of cash. Individuals can rely more on savings banks as a repository of funds, making correspondingly more frequent trips downtown to deposit and withdraw cash, and to transfer funds to a checking account just before large payments have to be made. Indeed they can, and the figures suggest that they do. It is true that this minimization of cash holdings costs time, trouble, and shoe leather. Clever comptrollers are thinking about cash management when they could be worrying about higher things. Moreover, and this is the point, these expenditures of time and effort are a real net burden to society, not merely a transfer to others. They are sometimes described as a "deadweight loss" to emphasize this. They are a true cost of inflation in the same sense that the maintenance of expensive police forces is a cost of crime. Some economists seem to regard these losses as the main social cost of pure inflation. But in that case, something very peculiar is afoot, because one finds it hard to believe that they amount to much. For *this* governments tremble and people cry on the pollster's shoulder? Even if you add in the computational difficulties of planning with changing prices, the discomfort that comes from not knowing whether your anticipations about future price levels are approximately right or dangerously wrong, it is hard to get excited.[7]

There is one other important "real" effect of anticipated pure inflation; it works through the tax system. Think of any progressive tax, a tax that takes a higher fraction of a higher income than of a lower income. Now let all prices, and thus all before-tax incomes, rise in the same proportion. Nobody's purchasing power has changed. But the general rise in nominal incomes will drive everyone into a higher tax bracket. If the general rise in prices amounted to X per cent, incomes after tax will rise by less than X per cent, because of the higher effective tax rate, and the government's revenues will rise by more than X per cent, for the same reason. So taxpayers suffer a loss in purchasing power after taxes, and their loss is the Treasury's gain. Our tax system is not as progressive in action as it is on paper, but nevertheless this effect is quite real. The sharpest case is that of someone whose income is low enough not to be taxable at all; pure inflation can push such a person into the taxable range and thus impose a loss of real income.

In summary, a perfectly anticipated pure inflation imposes a small deadweight loss on society, mostly through a waste of effort directed toward economizing on the holding of money; in addition, it redistributes wealth, from holders of cash and checking accounts to banks, and from everyone to the Treasury. Not good, one is tempted to say, but no worse than a bad cold. Real GNP, for all its faults, is the best measure we have of the current production of valued goods and services; that's the number to watch.

---

[7]In very rapid inflations—what are usually called "hyperinflations"—the losses from holding money are so great that one observes a genuine flight from the currency, whence come the stories from Germany in the 1920's of children meeting their fathers at the factory gate to bicycle madly into town and spend the day's pay before it has had a chance to depreciate further. In such cases there may be a return to barter. This kind of disorganization of the economy and society can be very costly, but it is not what we have to talk about. Even at relatively small rates of inflation, a little ingenuity can sometimes invent substitutes for the non-interest-bearing checking account—e.g., the NOW account.

UNANTICIPATED INFLATION

Now real-life inflations are not perfectly anticipated. Neither do they come as a complete surprise. But different people have different opinions about the future of the price level; not all of them can be right, and most of them can be wrong. The consequences of this fact are important, but still special. Interest rates cannot adjust to cushion both debtors and creditors from the effects of pure inflation. Some people will be caught with their pants down: those creditors who have locked themselves into long-term loans at interest rates that do not fully reflect the particular rate of inflation that happens, and borrowers who have agreed to pay high nominal interest rates in the expectation of faster inflation than actually materializes. Of course, for each of these unlucky lenders and borrowers, there is a lucky borrower or lender. Needless to say, when the losers include the broad class of pensioners whose expectations of a viable old age are dashed, it is not a trivial matter.

These gains and losses are not restricted to loans. *Anyone* who has concluded a long-term contract of any kind, stipulated in money terms, stands to gain or lose, depending on which side of the contract we are talking about and whether the rate of inflation turns out in fact to be higher or lower than had been expected when the terms of the contract were agreed. (If rapid inflation continues, we can expect to see more long-term contracts with renegotiation clauses, or with rates of payment explicitly tied to some index of prices. These are a form of insurance against windfall gains and losses from unexpectedly fast or slow inflation.)

Finally, it should be realized that many people, especially non-rich people, are more or less excluded from the benefits of higher nominal interest rates in an inflationary period. Small savers lack either the knowledge or the minimal stake needed to gain access to the sorts of assets whose yields will provide protection against inflation. The small saver is limited in practice to savings accounts and Series E government bonds. The rate on Series E bonds is not set by a market but is managed by the Treasury, and usually kept low enough to constitute a swindle on the non-rich. (One wonders what would happen if Secretaries of the Treasury were required by law to keep all their private wealth in Series E bonds.) The maximum deposit rate payable by savings banks is also limited by law, and by the peculiar role of those institutions as essentially nothing but mortgage lenders. Heaven does not protect the working girl.

The net result of all this is that imperfectly anticipated inflation—the only kind we have—generates massive redistribution of wealth between some borrowers and some lenders, some buyers and some sellers. From a very lofty point of view, these are still transfers, not a net burden on society as a whole. But that doesn't make them good. Moreover, in the public mind these transfers come to look like a net loss: The gainers attribute their gains to their own perspicacity, energy, and virtue; the losers attribute their losses to inflation.

"IMPURE" INFLATION

Pure inflation is an abstraction, though a necessary and useful one. If you can't understand the workings of pure inflation, you will never be able to understand what is actually happening. What is actually happening, of course, is a mixture: The general price level is rising, and at the same time relative prices are changing, sometimes drastically. The price indexes I described earlier are supposed to measure the pure inflationary component of the complicated set of price changes we experience. When I tell you that in the 12 months between June 1973 and June 1974 the CPI rose by 11.1 per cent, the WPI by 14.5 per cent, and the GNP Deflator by 9.7 per cent, I am saying something like: It is approximately as if there were a pure inflation of about 10 per cent, accompanied by a "pure" change in relative prices around a stationary level. In fact, I can add such information as this: The price of food went up by 14.7 per cent during the year, while rents went up by 4.7 per cent, so there was clearly a rise in the price of food relative to rental housing.

That is conceptually clear (though not quite as clear as I am pretending). The trouble is that what you observe and feel in the course of the year is the Total Experience, and it is by no means easy to sort out in one's mind the causes and consequences of a rising general level of prices and the causes and consequences of simultaneous changes in relative prices. This difficulty is complicated further by the fact that price movements are not synchronized. Even if, when all is said and done, the price of A and the price of B are both going to rise by X per cent, A may take off first and B only later. You would think that these timing differences would all come out in the wash, but they may actually have important independent consequences of their own.

The important thing to say about an inflation in which some prices and some incomes rise faster than others is that the *redistribution* of income can become both quite drastic and quite haphazard. It may be that real GNP is high and rising, so that the country as a whole is not being deprived of goods and services and the satisfactions they bring. But definable groups in the population may find their own standards of living deteriorating, either because the prices of the things they buy are rising faster than the average, or because the prices of the things they sell—including their labor—are rising slower than the average of all prices. And often enough it will appear to them that the inflation is the cause of their troubles, when in fact the real thief is the accompanying change in relative prices. Some economically and socially pointless or harmful redistributions can happen just because certain prices and incomes are less flexible than others and adapt sluggishly to a generally inflationary climate.

There are fewer valid universal generalizations about these redistributions than one might think. The rhetorical commonplaces are not always true. It is often said that inflation is especially hard on the poor. One careful study by Robinson G. Hollister and John G. Palmer found that this was not the case in the inflationary episodes of the 1950's, and until 1967, if by "the poor" you mean those below the official poverty line (that is, pretty damn poor). Their figures show that a cost-of-living index weighted the way the poor spend their incomes rose no faster than, perhaps slightly less fast than, the official middle-income CPI. The sources of income that matter for the poor—mainly wages and salaries, Social Security benefits, and various forms of social assistance—just about kept pace with other forms of income in purchasing-power terms. And the poor have little wealth exposed to the risk of erosion. Hollister and Palmer conclude: ". . . because the relative position of the poor seems to improve during inflationary periods and overall real income gains per capita occur during such periods, the poor as a whole must be gaining both absolutely and relatively in economic well-being during periods in which inflationary processes operate."

But not all inflations are alike. Between 1947 and 1967, food prices rose a little more slowly than the CPI as a whole. In 1973, I hardly need tell you, food prices went up about three times as fast as the rest of the CPI. Poor people spend a larger fraction of their incomes on food than richer people do. Moreover, as it happens, food costs at home went up faster than restaurant prices in 1973, and hamburger faster than steak. It would not be surprising to find that the inflation of 1973 did contribute to a redistribution of income away from poor people.[8]

I have seen one press report—but not the details—that says that a poor person's cost-of-living index rose by 11.6 per cent in 1973, while the CPI was going up by 8.8 per cent. Moreover, it was one of the mysteries of 1973 that wage increases were smaller than almost anyone had expected. On both counts, then, the Hollister-Palmer result seems to have been overturned in 1973; in that year, inflation was at the expense of the poor. Others, though of course not every single person, must have gained.

WAGES VS. PROFITS

It is harder to be clear about another important question: how inflation affects the distribution of income between wages and profits. Pure inflation, by definition, has no effect at all; the question is whether the changes in relative prices typical of inflationary periods are biased one way or the other. The reason why it is hard to give a simple answer is that the effects of inflation are mixed up with other systematic effects, especially those having to do with upswings and (mild) recessions in economic activity. It is a fair generalization that, while everyone gains in an upswing, profits gain relatively more. That is primarily because profits are the main beneficiary of the special gains in productivity and savings in overhead that come from using industrial plant near its rated capacity. Correspondingly, in recessions, everyone loses, but profits fall more sharply than aggregate wages. Now, by and large the general price level is likely to rise more rapidly in upswings than in recessions (though, as we shall see later, one of the contemporary puzzles is an apparent weakening of this relation). So it may appear that faster inflation is associated with a redistribution of income away from wages and toward profits, when in fact what is happening has less to do with the inflation and much more to do with the real fluctuations in economic activity. The situation is made even more complicated by the fact that there may be other, longer-run forces operating on the distribution of income between wages and profits.

If one tries to allow for these other effects, it appears that minor differences in timing can make a perceptible short-run difference. There are episodes of inflation in which wages keep up or even ahead, as in the "creeping inflation" of the middle 1950's, and there are episodes in which wages lag behind, as apparently in 1973. But these timing effects are not permanent. The most important generalization one can make is this: The rate of inflation by itself has little or no long-run effect on the distribution of income between wages and profits. If, over

---

[8]Poor people spend a larger fraction of their income on housing than rich people do, and a smaller fraction on transportation, especially automobile transportation. So the run-up in oil prices has more complicated effects: The rise in fuel oil prices hits the poor worse than the rich, but the rise in gasoline prices affects the rich more than the poor. Of course, all this is apart from the fact that any reduction in purchasing power is harder to take when you're poor.

the next decade, say, we imagine the average annual increase in the price level to be three per cent in one case, or six per cent in another, the distribution of income between work and property is likely to be about the same in either case. The division of those years between prosperity and recession is likely to be more important both for the level of real income and its distribution.

I have a more speculative suggestion to make—and you will see that the adjective is apt. Whenever prices are changing rapidly and drastically, there are opportunities for large speculative gains and losses. This is so even in the absence of inflation; if some prices go up and other prices go down, you can get rich quick by being on the right side. Inflation itself creates further opportunities for speculation, and makes the whole spectacle more opaque and confusing. The importance of speculative profits is magnified by the way our tax system favors capital gains. In an inflationary period, therefore, most of us watch the big rewards going to those who are clever enough to see what is happening a little faster than other people, or are simply privy to inside information, and who are sufficiently rich and well-placed to take advantage of their knowledge. At such a time the more traditional virtues of simple competence, diligence, and honesty do not pay off. Most of us do not like that. (Or do I simply mean that I don't like that?) Is this perhaps the redistribution of income that bugs us most about irregular, imperfectly anticipated inflation? . . .

WHAT ARE THE CAUSES?

There is a vast and subtle literature on the causes of inflation and the mechanism of the inflationary process. I cannot hope to survey it fairly, especially since it contains contradictory strands. My sketch of the state of play may be idiosyncratic.

One of the central issues in the theory of the subject—with roots going back hundreds of years in economics—concerns the nature of the connection between monetary goings-on and the real economy of production, consumption, and relative prices. The very concept of inflation presupposes a monetary economy, as we noted earlier. Moreover, our discussion of the simplified meat-and-vegetables economy seemed to lead to a proposition like this: You could imagine two identical islands, one of them (A) with unchanging prices and the other (B) experiencing perfectly anticipated pure inflation at X per cent per year, but with exactly the same *real* events taking place on both of them. The main preconditions for this conclusion are (1) that the money supply should be increasing X per cent a year faster on island B than on A, so that the amount of purchasing power represented by the money supply could be the same in both places, and (2) that it be possible to pay interest on whatever is used for money, say bank deposits, so that the nominal interest rate could be X per cent per annum higher on island B, to keep the real rates of interest equal.

Now that is pretty abstract; but the further development of such reasoning leads one school of economists to conclude that the real and monetary spheres are in principle separate, and that the true and only cause of inflation is excessively fast expansion of the money supply. It follows that the only way to reduce or stop inflation is to slow down the growth of the money supply. Moreover, if the real and monetary spheres really are separate, then doing so will not have real effects, and will thus be quite harmless. (Of course, one can argue that if inflation has no real effects, or negligible ones, there is hardly any point in stopping it.)

I hasten to say that this is a caricature. This school of thought recognizes perfectly well—and the recognition goes back to David Hume—that real-life inflations are not pure and perfectly anticipated. Any attempt to slow or stop an inflation by tightening money will certainly have redistributional effects and may well cause recession, diminished production, unemployment, and excess capacity. All the "new Quantity theorists" claim is that these real consequences will not last forever. Eventually, as the new state of affairs comes to be embedded in expectations and business decisions, the real effects will disappear. Island B will get to be like Island A. The intervening period of bad times has to be regarded as an investment whose payoff is the reduction of inflation, whatever that is worth.

A practical man would want to know how long that period of bad times is likely to last. The new Quantity theorists are not really able to say, and it is hard to blame them. It is a difficult question, and the experiment has never been tried. The sterner protagonists of this view have occasionally hazarded the guess that the period of purification might conceivably last a long time, to be measured more nearly in decades than in quarters. A political figure like Herbert Stein will not say that, but he did say in July [1974] that inflation is "a serious and dominant problem which will require the maintenance of a policy of restraint for the remainder of this year and beyond that."

This question of timing is an analytical question as well as a practical one. The opposing school of thought holds—to caricature once again—that there is a permanent connection between the monetary sphere and the real economy. But what does "permanent" mean? Presumably it does not mean literally forever; nothing is forever. If it means "a long time"—as, for instance, decades—then the distinction between the two schools seems to be more a matter of emphasis or taste than of principle, and more a matter of applied economics than of pure theory. But those questions of application are terribly important, as we will see.

THE "TRADE-OFF" VIEW

I shall give a grossly oversimplified sketch of one version of the alternative doctrine. It is based on the famous "Phillips curve," named after A. W. Phillips, who started the whole thing with a purely statistical study of British figures. Let us take it for granted that for extended periods of time in many countries there is a reliable inverse relationship between the unemployment rate (to be thought of as a measure of the degree of prosperity) and the contemporaneous percentage rate at which the level of wages rises. That is to say, in a year in which the economy is strong and the labor market is tight, workers—individually or through their organizations—will be inclined to hold out for relatively large wage increases, and employers will be inclined to offer them; in a depressed year, when the unemployment rate is high, workers will be less pushful and employers will feel more hard-pressed and hard-boiled. Naturally, there are other forces affecting the behavior of wage rates, but this is the one we are concentrating on. Observe carefully: The Phillips curve is a relation between the rate of increase of wage rates (a *monetary* magnitude) and the unemployment rate or level of production (a *real* phenomenon). I have given a plausible but casual rationalization of such a relation; I must warn you that this apparently simple proposition has been the object of whole volumes of the most subtle theoretical and empirical research, which is only beginning to converge. There are still wide differences of opinion within the profession.

So much for wages. If there were no improvements in productivity, labor costs per unit of *output* would move along in step with wage rates (i.e., labor costs per *hour*). Since productivity is generally rising, though not uniformly, labor costs per unit of output rise more slowly than wage rates. In fact—subtleties aside—unit labor costs rise when wages rise more rapidly than productivity in percentage terms, decline when the opposite holds true, and remain constant when wage rates and productivity both rise at the same percentage rate.

But we are interested in prices, not only wages. The simplest acceptable preliminary explanation of the behavior of the price level in the private non-farm economy is that it is cost-determined. Market conditions are clearly part of the story too—think of oil!—but for simplicity let us just keep that in the background. Suppose that the general price index simply comes out as a mark-up on unit cost of production. That is practically the same thing as a mark-up on unit labor cost, since labor costs amount to more than three quarters of all costs in the economy as a whole. If the price level is roughly proportional to unit labor costs, then the price level will rise when unit labor costs rise, fall when they fall, and stay the same when unit labor costs are stable. So the price level will rise, fall, or remain unchanged according to whether wage rates are rising faster than, slower than, or at the same pace as productivity.

But the wage level—apart from the other market forces we are now ignoring—rises faster when the unemployment rate is low, and slower when it is high. And so the price level—again ignoring other market forces—rises when unemployment is low and the economy prospers, and falls when unemployment is high and the economy is depressed. This is the famous "trade-off between inflation and unemployment" that has found its way into everyday talk. A stable price level can be achieved only at that unemployment rate that allows wages to rise about as fast as productivity is increasing.

According to this line of argument, the real and the monetary are intimately connected. The rate of inflation is governed by the real condition of the economy, in particular by its "tightness" or prosperousness. Moreover, the options for policy are clear but limited. Society can have a slower rate of inflation or no inflation at all, if and only if it is prepared to generate and maintain enough unemployment and excess capacity to hold prices and wages in check. Years ago Paul Samuelson and I conjectured that the corresponding unemployment rate might be in the neighborhood of 5.5 per cent of the labor force; and events suggest that it would now be higher. If the policy choice is really limited by the "trade-off" then there is no avoiding the question: How much is it worth to reduce the rate of inflation, and how much does it cost to live with higher unemployment and lower production? If you think back to our discussion of the social costs of inflation, at least of moderate inflation, it is hard to avoid coming away with the impression that they are minor compared with the costs of unemployment and depressed production—especially since the redistributive costs could in principle be cancelled out by actions designed to protect or compensate the potential losers.

The reply of the trade-off school to the monetary school is: Yes, tight money and balanced budgets can stop inflation, but only by depressing the economy for a long time, perhaps a very long time. The "old-time religion" preached by Herbert Stein and his successor Alan Greenspan is (as Karl Kraus said of psychoanalysis) the disease of which it purports to be the cure.[9]

AN UNSETTLED QUESTION

The doctoral dispute I have been describing obviously goes deeper at the level of analytical principle than at the level of practical economic policy. At the analytical level there are wheels within wheels that I haven't even mentioned. So far as policy is concerned, it seems to be mainly a matter of timing. Whatever their sterner members mutter, the monetary school acts as if you could squeeze the inflation out of the system in real time; the period of restraint and unemployment would not be so long as to be impractical or worse. Their opponents estimate the period to be longer, and they are less willing to swallow the intervening unemployment anyway. So there is a difference, but a vital difference, mainly in tone. That is why the newspapers report that "liberal" economists have nothing especially new and different to offer in the present circumstances. (Perhaps I should mention, for those who have not seen a scorecard, that members of the "monetary" school tend to be politically conservative and members of the "real" school are more likely to be politically liberal, though there are exceptions.)

The actual behavior of the American economy from the end of the Korean War price controls to the middle 1960's seemed generally to confirm the trade-off view. That is to say, there seemed to be a reasonably reliable relation between the tautness of the economy and the behavior of wages and the price level, after the various other market forces had been taken into account. Beginning about 1966 there was a perfectly classical inflation associated with the deliberate malfinancing of the Vietnam War. (Can it be that wars get the economic policy they deserve?) But thereafter something seemed to go haywire. There has been, more or less ever since, a tendency for wages and prices to rise faster than those old, previously reliable relationships would have predicted. In retrospect, for instance, it appears that the belated tax increase of 1968–69 did, somewhat slowly, have the right sort of effect on real GNP; but the softening of the economy failed to slow down the inflation as effectively as it might once have done.

The profession responded to these happenings in several ways. George Perry made a strong and interesting case that the trade-off had worsened, mainly for reasons connected with the age and sex composition of the labor force, and the

---

[9]I should mention two quite different policy options, though I don't want to discuss them in detail. One is the imposition of price and wage controls of varying degrees of strengency. There are arguments and counter-arguments as to whether such controls can be effective, and, if they are stringent enough to be effective, whether they are likely to have destructive side-effects on the working of the system. The second option is an organized attempt to "improve the trade-off"—i.e., to make a lower rate of wage and price increase correspond to any given unemployment rate, either by union-busting or trust-busting, or by a program of manpower policies designed to improve skills and open up labor markets. Some people say that recent experience shows that manpower policy doesn't work; others point to the small size and piecemeal character of the programs and argue (as Bernard Shaw said of Christianity) that manpower policy has not failed, it hasn't been tried.

differential experience of women and the young in the labor market. Otto Eckstein concluded that a trade-off was pretty sound so long as the unemployment rate was higher than some critical value in the neighborhood of 4 or 4.5 per cent, but that near the critical rate the labor market tended to explode and behave more or less the way the monetary school thinks it always behaves. The monetary school argued that it all went to show that there could be only a short-run connection between real things and monetary things. Workers and employers are *really* interested in *real* things; as soon as they see what is happening and learn to *expect* the inflation, they will behave so as to disconnect all real events—like the unemployment rate—from any relationship with purely nominal magnitudes like the rate of inflation. Thus any attempt to use the short-run trade-off must come to naught eventually.

The dust has not yet settled on all this. Statistical analysis of the one run of observations history gives us is a poor substitute for controlled experiment, but it is all economists have. It may be a long time (that word again!) before this question is settled. . . .

WHAT IS TO BE DONE ABOUT IT?

The tail of conclusions on this large dog of an article is going to be short. This analysis of contemporary inflation does not lend itself to a sweeping Solution. In fact, it suggests that there has been altogether too much leaping to Solutions without any clear understanding of the nature of the Problem. On close inspection, the social costs of ordinary inflation turn out to be mostly a matter of socially useless or harmful redistributions of purchasing power. Since there are straightforward ways of repairing that kind of damage if we seriously want to do so, it appears that most of the sweeping solutions that have been proposed—such as a prolonged dose of unemployment and underproduction, or universal and rigid price controls—are likely to be at least as costly to economic efficiency as the problem they are intended to solve.

We might better be concerned to find effective ways to protect or compensate the innocent losers from inflation. There is no need to contemplate anything so drastic as universal indexing, as some have proposed, but a little well-aimed indexing would certainly be a step ahead. The most important such step has already been taken—the automatic correction of Social Security benefits for changes in the cost of living. Second, it could only be a good idea to provide a limited issue of a special saving instrument for small savers, a Treasury bond that pays a stipulated *real* rate of interest. The third such reform that comes to mind is a bit touchier, but only a bit: the indexing of the personal income tax, so that inflation does not automatically increase the effective tax rate, especially on those near the bottom of the income scale. The only reason for hesitation is that in classic demand-pull inflations the rise in the effective tax rate is an automatic stabilizer, tending to damp the inflation itself. But surely it would be better to have sensible discretionary fiscal policy.

Such devices would make moderate inflation easier to live with, if it should turn out to be inevitable. They may also contribute to the effectiveness or at least diminish the riskiness of anti-inflationary policies. To the extent that they divorce the real from the monetary, they make it less dangerous to tinker with the price level.

It has been suggested to me that the implications of this whole argument are defeatist: Democratic governments will always or often allow the economy to drift into an inflationary situation, if only because that will frequently be easier than confronting difficult choices; having done so, they will be unable to confess error and set about rationally trying to protect those who might unjustly be hurt by the initial mistake and its consequences. I am not completely convinced by this story as a piece of political science, nor do I know what follows from it anyway. Perhaps I should be interpreted as wishing that it might be regarded as an even graver confession of error to inflict recession and unemployment on the economy and thus hurt nearly everyone merely to cover up an inability to correct the distributional consequences of an essentially unavoidable "mistake." I especially deplore the habit of excusing this policy by attributing to inflation all sorts of costs that have, in fact and logic, very little to do with inflation itself.

I have suggested that slow inflation may be endemic to modern mixed capitalist economies that are determined not to tolerate severe slumps and are known to have both the determination and the ability to avoid them. Inflation is their characteristic way of adapting to change. The unusually rapid rise in prices during the past year and a half may simply reflect the fact that the world has been called upon to absorb some unusually large changes. In that case, it will burn itself out. The current situation is certainly not pleasant—it is a prize example of an unanticipated impure inflation. But panic-stricken policy responses will simply add injury to insult.

Slowing the Wage-Price Spiral: The Macroeconomic View

GEORGE L. PERRY

George L. Perry has been an important leader in the modern development of macro-economics. An author of numerous articles on unemployment and inflation, he is known in Washington as a veritable fountain of information on empirical forecasts of inflation and unemployment. He is currently a co-editor of the *Brookings Papers on Economic Activity* and a Senior Fellow at Brookings Institution, occupations that keep him on top of the theoretical and policy changes that continue to occur in the field of macro-economics. In this article, excerpted from his 1978 paper "Slowing the Wage-Price Spiral: The Macroeconomic View," he reviews macroeconomic theory in terms of its relevance to policies to fight inflation.

Over a decade has passed since the standard remedy of demand restraint was first urged to combat inflation. By the mid-1960s, many economists, including those at the Council of Economic Advisers, believed war expenditures were pushing the economy into the inflationary, excess-demand zone and recommended tax increases to help restrain aggregate demand. We cannot know how different subsequent economic performance would have been if that advice had been heeded. But it was not. Unemployment continued to decline into 1969, and the inflation rate in consumer prices rose above 5 percent. Inflation, by then, had become firmly entrenched in economic decisionmaking. When demand finally fell and unemployment rose in the recession of 1970, the inflation rate scarcely budged. Both average hourly earnings and the private nonfarm price deflator rose faster during 1970–71 than in any year of the 1960s.

Many observers concluded that a recession deeper than that of 1970 would be needed to stop inflation. In summer 1971, the Nixon administration tried a different cure, imposing wage and price controls that lasted in modified form until April 1974. These controls slowed the inflation rate for most wages and prices. But by the time the controls expired, higher prices for food and fuel, which were largely unrelated to the state of demand, and for industrial raw materials, which reflected strong world demand and speculative buying, had created double-digit rates of overall inflation. Together with a nonaccommodating aggregate-demand policy, this price explosion also started a recession that was double the size of the average previous postwar recession and that lasted until spring 1975.

Note: I am grateful to Jesse M. Abraham for his extensive research assistance.

It is now three years since the trough of this deepest postwar recession. By the end of that recession, inflation had slowed sharply from its 1974 pace, but further improvement was slight once recovery began. From 1975 through 1977, all available measures of tightness in either labor markets or product markets registered ample slack. And no large upward movements have occurred in particular components of the price level since the Organization of Petroleum Exporting Countries increased oil prices in 1974. Yet despite all these disinflationary developments, the rate of inflation, by any broad measure, has continued at a historically high rate and now shows signs of creeping still further upward.

Table 1 summarizes the inflation in the economy since the Korean War as measured by four alternative indexes: compensation per hour, the hourly earnings index, and the price deflator, all of which are averages for the private nonfarm economy; and the consumer price index. Except in 1974 and 1975, when controls ended and oil prices soared, the three measures for the private nonfarm economy have moved closely together, with compensation per hour and the price deflator differing by approximately the trend rate of growth in labor productivity. The consumer price index is more volatile than the deflator. They have differed noticeably when the relative prices of food or imports changed a great deal, although the inclusion of these prices is not the only difference between the indexes. By any of these measures, inflation has been noticeably faster in the 1970s than in previous periods. It has been faster since 1975 than in the early 1970s. And it has been faster over the most recent four quarters than in previous years of the present recovery.

Inflation is unpopular. It hampers policymaking and inhibits the pursuit of high employment. This paper provides a basis for evaluating alternative approaches to slowing it.

TABLE 1

Wage and Price Inflation in the United States, Selected Periods, 1954-78 (average annual percent change)

Period	PRIVATE NONFARM ECONOMY			Consumer price index
	Compensation per hour	Hourly earnings index	Price deflator	
Post-Korean War (1954-59)	4.6	4.1	2.4	1.4
Early 1960s (1960-65)	4.0	3.1	1.1	1.3
Late 1960s (1966-69)	6.4	5.6	3.7	3.8
Precontrol 1970s (1970-71)	6.7	6.8	4.7	5.1
Controls (1972-73)	6.8	6.5	3.6	4.8
Food-fuel explosion (1974-75)	9.5	8.5	10.7	10.1
1976	8.7	7.2	5.2	5.8
1977	8.8	7.3	5.4	6.5
1978:1[a]	9.1[b]	8.0[b]	6.3	6.6

Source: U.S. Bureau of Labor Statistics.
a. Percent change from the first quarter of 1977 to first quarter of 1978.
b. Without the large increase in the minimum wage in January 1978, the increases would have been an estimated 8.9 percent for compensation and 7.6 percent for hourly earnings.

THE MAINLINE MODEL

In this section I briefly outline what I perceive to be the important characteristics of the U.S. economy that have led to the present stubborn inflation.
Unlike many journalists describing the stagflation period, I do not conclude that
economists fail to understand the economy. And unlike some professional writers of this period, I do not conclude that the Keynesian revolution got everything wrong. However, we have learned during the past ten years that the
Keynesian analysis stops short of adequately modeling the inflation process.

Let me begin by describing the essential features of what I call the mainline
model of the U.S. macroeconomy. It offers a description of macroeconomic
behavior that is compatible with a broad range of more specific models that
would have similar policy implications. . . .

In the mainline model, wage and price behavior are closely linked, and
there is at least some mutual causality between them. Because the effect of
wages on prices is more predictable and better established, it is useful to begin
analyzing the inflation problem by describing the macroeconomics of labor
markets.

Wages respond to the tightness of labor markets but not enough to avoid
fluctuations in employment brought about by corresponding fluctuations in
demand. Thus, something like a Phillips curve exists, at least for periods that
are relevant to policymakers and to the conduct of economic affairs, and for the
range of unemployment actually experienced. Within this framework, average
wages begin to rise at an inflationary rate while unemployment is still well
above frictional levels.

Wages also respond to what has been happening to wages, prices, profit
margins, or all three, or to what is expected to happen to them. All these
alternatives are accommodated in the mainline model and are discussed further
below. What is important is that they all predict considerable inertia in wage
inflation. The response of wages to variations in demand is characteristically
sluggish.

Some prices are sensitive to demand, particularly prices of industrial raw
materials and goods whose costs include a large component of costs for raw
materials. Agricultural prices are sensitive to world crop conditions, and prices
of tradable goods respond to competition from goods produced abroad. But
prices in most of the private sector are closely related to variable costs, the most
important of which are labor costs. Given wages, these prices are only slightly
affected by demand, and consequently their movement in response to demand
variations is also sluggish.

With the possible exception of situations in which unemployment is exceptionally low or industrial operating rates are exceptionally high, variations in
aggregate demand lead primarily to variations in output, employment, and
unemployment. There can be sustained unemployment arising from inadequate
demand. At the aggregate level, the response to variations in demand is similar
whether the variation comes from fiscal policy, monetary policy, an unex-
plained change in velocity, or from some shift in demand from the private sector
or from foreign demand for exports.

Within this general description, a number of issues that are important to
the design of anti-inflation policy remain open. What is the response of inflation
to alternative paths of real activity? Are wages affected by past wages, past

living costs, past price margins or profitability, or all three? Is the inertia of inflation essentially backward looking or forward looking; and to the extent that expectations matter, how can they be affected? These are difficult questions that are not easily settled by empirical evidence. . . .

ALTERNATIVE VIEWS

The mainline model . . . provide[s] a fairly general description of the macroeconomy and the inflation process. Although [it] leave[s] room for alternative views about the microeconomic underpinnings of inertia and for further research on quantitative questions, [it] do[es] provide a basis for discussing anti-inflation policies. The blame for inflation or the remedies for it, however, are often argued along lines that are not predicted by the mainline model or from views of the economy that are incompatible with it. Before examining what there is to learn from the mainline model about strategies for slowing inflation, I review some of these dissenting views.

Budget Deficits

If a poll were taken to sample opinions on the causes of inflation, most votes would probably go to government deficits. An economist would grant the effects of deficits on aggregate demand and would be hard pressed to find causal links between deficits and inflation over and above their effects on demand. He would also be aware that historically most deficits have come from the operation of automatic stabilizers during periods of underemployment.

Although to my knowledge no serious model predicts that actual deficits will explain inflation [Perry estimated two equations and found either a negative or a zero correlation], the actual relationship between budget deficits and economic performance is complicated, and [usual econometric equations do not] summarize that relationship in any meaningful way. . . .

The lack of a causal connection between budget deficits and inflation does not deny possibly important linkages between government programs and the current inflation. . . . Government programs have contributed to inflation by pursuing goals through means that raise the price level rather than through means that show up in the budget deficit. If the costs took the form of federal expenditures or tax credits and thus appeared in the deficit, they would not affect the price level, providing that the level of aggregate demand remained the same. Paradoxically, excessive anxiety about deficits can itself be inflationary.

Excessive Growth of Money

Besides deficits, a close contender in public opinion polls on the causes of inflation would be excessive growth of money. Unlike the deficit explanation, a positive connection between money growth and inflation is acknowledged widely by the professional community. What divides economists is the issue of whether or not a causal role can be assigned to money in addition to its role as a determinant of aggregate demand. The mainline view acknowledges the role of aggregate demand in inflation and the role of money in aggregate demand. It denies any additional, special role of money in causing inflation. . . .

TABLE 2
Unemployment Benefits and Minimum Wage Relative to Average Earnings,
Selected Periods, 1951-77 (in percent)

Description	1951–55	1956–60	1961–65	1966–70	1971–75	1976–77
Unemployment compensation replacement ratio (net)[a]	39.4	42.9	44.4	46.0	47.3	47.1
Relative minimum wage [b]	45.4	47.6	48.3	51.1	47.2	44.3

Sources: Average weekly unemployment compensation benefits, *Economic Report of the President, January 1978*, table B-33, and updates from U.S. Department of Labor, Employment and Training Administration; spendable earnings (worker with 3 dependents), U.S. Bureau of Economic Analysis, *Business Statistics, 1975* (Government Printing Office, 1976) and *Survey of Current Business*, various issues; straight-time earnings in manufacturing, U.S. Bureau of Labor Statistics, *Employment and Earnings, United States, 1909–75*, Bulletin 1312–10 (GPO, 1975), and *Employment and Earnings*, various issues.
a. Unemployment compensation benefits as a percentage of spendable weekly earnings.
b. Minimum wage as a percentage of straight-time hourly earnings in manufacturing.

Social Welfare Programs

Government programs of income maintenance would also be high on a list of popular explanations of inflation. Unemployment compensation and the minimum wage are the two programs that are most clearly related to wage behavior. Both have been studied carefully by economists and have at least potentially significant effects on labor markets.

Table 2 shows the percentage of after-tax earnings that was replaced by unemployment benefits and the minimum wage as a percentage of average earnings during recent periods. Both measures rose gradually during the post-war period until the last half of the 1960s. Between 1966–70 and the present, the net replacement ratio under unemployment compensation increased slightly, while the relative minimum wage declined sharply.

. . . Gramlich estimated that average wages rise by about 0.03 percent for each 1 percent change in the minimum.[1] A substantial rise in the minimum [wage], such as the 15 percent increase of January 1978, will have a noticeable effect on aggregate wages. However, during the period that inflation was worsening, the relative minimum wage was falling. And as the disaggregated results showed, wages in low-wage industries (where increases in the minimum wage have their principal effect) were falling behind other wages. The coverage of the minimum wage was substantially expanded in the mid-1960s, adding to its impact on average wages at that time. But that episode is too remote to have any relevance to the inflation of the 1970s. Finally, by reducing the employment prospects of young workers, the minimum wage may add to their unemployment and thus have a modest effect in shifting the Phillips curve. . . .

Unemployment compensation has a potential effect on wage inflation by reducing the willingness of recipients to accept available job offers. Together

[1]Edward M. Gramlich, "Impact of Minimum Wages on Other Wages, Employment, and Family Incomes," *Brookings Papers on Economic Activity*, 2:1976.

with other programs of income maintenance, it provides a disincentive to work compared with a situation in which no support is provided or one in which support does not depend on unemployment. However, such programs are not new to the recent years of rapid inflation. And as table 2 shows, the benefits have not become much more generous during the period when inflation has worsened.[2]

In the majority of cases, workers receiving unemployment compensation benefits have been laid off from jobs to which they expect to return. Wages in those jobs are inflexible because of the formal and informal relations binding employers and employees, not because workers who have been laid off are holding back their services waiting for better wages. While unemployment compensation may have some effect on the response of wages to unemployment, it is doubtful that the effect is large. The outcome might be different if most of unemployment among those who receive benefits were well described by simple search models and if wage offers were varied by firms in response to short-run variations in labor market tightness. But this is not the case.

Misperception, Perfect Markets, and Rational Expectations

The most serious conceptual challenge to the mainline model I have outlined comes from a view that attributes all of inflation and unemployment to misperceptions on the part of workers and firms: workers are led into more or less employment than they would normally want by their incorrect reading of wage or price trends. In a related set of models, "rational" expectations and extreme price and wage flexibility are assumed to characterize the macroeconomy. Workers are assumed to make market-clearing wage and price changes continuously, based on the best information available and constrained only by existing contracts. Except for information lags and delays until existing contracts expire, wages and prices are always adjusted to provide equilibrium levels of output and employment. Both these models have an important common feature: in contrast to the mainline model, they have variations in inflation causing variations in unemployment rather than the reverse. Without inflation surprises, unemployment would always be at a "natural rate."

The search models fail to explain the widespread phenomenon of layoffs or the cyclical pattern of quits. To the extent they predict that wages must accelerate if unemployment is to be maintained below its natural rate—their central implication—they predict wages must decelerate if unemployment is to stay above the natural rate for any sustained period. Alternatively, they may assume that misperceptions about available wage offers take a long time to be corrected. On the basis of this argument, the persistence of unemployment and inflation since the mid-1970s is understood as a continued overoptimism about available wage offers. Because most periods of unemployment have a duration

---

[2]In a series of articles providing many constructive suggestions for reforming the unemployment compensation system, Martin Feldstein has pointed out that replacement ratios for certain workers can rise above the averages shown in table 2. See Martin Feldstein, "Unemployment Compensation: Adverse Incentives and Distributional Anomalies," *National Tax Journal*, vol. 27 (June 1974), pp. 231–44. However, I doubt that such calculations could alter the verdict that there has been little change in the last decade in the relative benefits of the program.

measured in days or at most several weeks, it seems unrealistic to assume years of misperception to explain unemployment.

Models that combine wage and price flexibility with assumptions embodied in rational expectations about behavior have similar problems explaining persistence. Any deviation of unemployment from the natural rate can persist only until people become aware of the situation or renegotiate existing contracts. Except for three-year wage agreements negotiated with some large unions— agreements that cover only a small fraction of the work force—it is difficult to imagine price or wage arrangements in any important area of the economy that are bound by long-term contracts. Thus, when unemployment has deviated from past levels for any sustained period, the new unemployment level must be interpreted as a new natural rate. By contrast, the mainstream model that I have described recognizes sustained periods of underemployment and leaves open the possibility of changing unemployment through demand management.

SLOWING INFLATION: AGGREGATE DEMAND AND EXPECTATIONS

The inflation of the 1970s does not change the conclusion that slowing the economy and raising unemployment can slow and eventually eliminate inflation. The evidence is, however, that inflation would slow only gradually in response to holding back aggregate demand, and that the cost in lost employment and output per point of disinflation would be large. [Econometric analysis] generally predict[s] inflation will be less than one point slower in the third year of a policy that holds the unemployment rate one point higher. And the additional unemployment implies a loss of $50 billion to $60 billion a year in output in today's economy.

A different specification might alter the numerical estimates, but it could not reverse the verdict that the anti-inflation gains from restraining aggregate demand are disappointingly small. Arthur Okun recently summarized the estimates from six different econometric models and came to a similarly pessimistic conclusion.[3] Whatever view is held on the urgency of slowing inflation today, it is unrealistic to believe that the public or its representatives would permit the extended period of high unemployment required to slow inflation in this manner.

Stabilization strategy since 1975 may be interpreted as an attempt to find an output path that would gradually reduce unemployment and at the same time slow inflation. The evidence of the past few years provides little hope for such a possibility. After the hourly earnings index slowed in the early quarters of recovery, it began to accelerate gradually in 1977. Equations based on the level of tightness in the labor market predicted a continuing deceleration given the slack labor markets of 1976–77. But the predicted unwinding of inflation in response to unemployment is so gradual that it is easily offset by other inflationary developments. Food and import prices rose faster in 1977 than in 1976, although the effect on wages of their speedup in 1977 should have been slight. Unemployment declined noticeably during 1977, and this could help explain the

---

[3]Arthur M. Okun, "Efficient Disinflationary Policies," *American Economic Review*, vol. 68 (May 1978), pp. 348–52.

wage speedup if the change in unemployment as well as its level has an effect on wage inflation that is not captured in estimates using annual data.[4] But whatever the explanation is for recent wage changes, such developments further dramatize the difficulty of slowing the present inflation with demand management alone.

SLOWING INFLATION: EXPECTATIONS

William Fellner has articulated the principal challenge to the pessimistic verdict on using aggregate demand to slow inflation.[5] He views the inertia of inflation as a consequence of generalized expectations of inflation. According to Fellner, in recent years contracts governing wages and prices have been formulated with the expectation that inflation will continue into the future.[6] So long as these expectations are maintained, they become a self-fulfilling prophecy. To stop inflation, policy must change these expectations. In Fellner's view, the only way to change them is through a convincing demonstration that monetary and fiscal policies will not accommodate the expected inflation rate.

An example will serve to illustrate this point. Assume that 4 percent real growth is the desired path for output and that 6 percent is the expected inflation rate. A 10 percent growth rate of aggregate demand would be accommodating. If aggregate-demand growth were held to 8 percent, the econometric evidence predicts that real growth the first year would slow by nearly 2 percent while inflation would slow only slightly. After two years, real output would be more than 3 percent below the 4 percent growth path, and prices would be about 1 percent below that path. Fellner reasons that, by making the decision to slow aggregate demand convincing, expectations would change and the division between real growth and inflation would improve. The coefficients of the model that yield pessimistic projections today would be changed by the clear determination of the authorities to adopt a nonaccommodating policy.

How plausible is this remedy for inflation? The 1973–75 recession apparently did not change the coefficients. It could be argued, however, that this period did not demonstrate nonaccommodation convincingly because policies promptly turned to aiding recovery once unemployment increased. Let me bring together the scattered evidence presented earlier for questioning Fellner's optimism.

First, the evidence is that the inertia process is expectational but to only a limited extent. That does not mean that people do not have expectations about inflation, but simply that current wage and price decisions, as opposed to decisions in other spheres such as lending or investing, are not governed by

[4]An effect from such changes appears in [wage] equations estimated with quarterly data. The insignificance of lagged unemployment when added to . . . wage equations . . . argues against any important effects from a change in unemployment over a period as long as a year. I regard the correct specification as an open question in light of the differing results with quarterly and annual data.

[5]William J. Fellner, *Towards a Reconstruction of Macroeconomics: Problems of Theory and Policy* (American Enterprise Institute, 1976).

[6]Martin Neil Baily, in "Stabilization Policy and Private Economic Behavior," *BPEA, 1:1978,* pp. 11–50, has recently explored the idea that the generalized expectation of prosperity has influenced the behavior of firms in a stabilizing way. Believing that the government will avoid the deep slumps of the past, firms themselves respond with hiring, stocking, and investment decisions that are more stabilizing than in the past. I interpret Fellner's views on inflationary expectations as analogous to this model of changing real behavior.

those expectations. Even in the area of long-term labor contracts, in which expectations could be important, the analysis presented above shows that wage developments are better explained as backward looking and that escalators are used to avoid predicting the future. For most questions regarding inflation it is not crucial to know whether the inertia process is forward looking or backward looking. It does matter here.

Second, even if the econometric coefficients from Phillips curves are interpreted as expectational rather than backward looking, how much will an announced policy of demand restraint affect those expectations? If a nonaccommodating aggregate-demand policy is totally convincing, it will lead people to expect that unemployment will rise. But why should this affect their expectations about inflation by more than the short-run Phillips curve predicts? If inflation responds weakly to actual unemployment, why should expected inflation respond so strongly to expected unemployment?

This leaves room for a small gain in Fellner's scheme. If there are some wage contracts made with a view to the unemployment rate anticipated in the future, expecting more unemployment should modify such contracts by the amount predicted by the Phillips curve. If a restrictive nominal GNP path is to be pursued, there is thus some gain from announcing it ahead of time. My only question is whether there is reason to expect more than the improvement predicted by the Phillips curve as applied to the expected *future* course of unemployment. And if even that effect is confined to a small subset of contracts that are actually forward looking, the total benefits would be limited. On the price side, there are depletable resources whose price depends on expectations of prospective demand, but these are not important in the overall price level.

If wage and price setting were sufficiently concentrated in this economy, the possibilities for affecting inflation through Fellner's route would be greatly enhanced. A roomful of private decisionmakers who recognized that their inflationary behavior would directly affect their level of output and employment would be expected to respond favorably to a government policy of nonaccommodation. That is not what occurs in the U.S. economy.

Linking an incomes policy to an announced nonaccommodating policy on aggregate demand would help achieve Fellner's result. As discussed below, an effective incomes policy would produce a more favorable prospective split between real growth and inflation for any given path of nominal demand growth. Thus, expectations of inflation would change by more than the Phillips curve predicts. And to the extent that expectations do affect current wage decisions—which is still an open question—they would complement an incomes policy. Although it is an incomes policy that changes the immediate trade-off, the nonaccommodating demand policy is a necessary complement. Without it, the reduced inflation promised by the improved trade-off could be dissipated by a movement along the new trade-off curve.

SLOWING INFLATION: TAX-BASED INCOMES POLICIES*

Although there are several variations of tax-based incomes policies (TIPs), their differences are primarily important in determining their acceptability, the ease

---

*EDITOR'S NOTE: For a fuller discussion of TIP proposals and alternatives to TIP, see Part 4.

of their implementation, and their effectiveness in altering individual wage and price decisions. . . . At the macroeconomic level, the main impact of alternative TIPs affecting wages will be similar. And TIPs that act on prices primarily ensure that price restraint parallels wage restraint, which is what the macroeconomic model predicts without such policies.

It is simplest to integrate TIP effects into the macroeconomic model by assuming that the same path of real output is pursued with and without the program. Starting from the present state of the economy, a TIP that causes individual wages to rise more slowly than they otherwise would can be represented simply as a reduction in the constant term of the wage equation. Whether TIP will alter the slope of the short-run Pillips curve or whether it will reduce permanently the unemployment rate that represents full employment are separate issues that are briefly considered below. With a downward shift in the constant term of the wage equation, nominal aggregate demand must be reduced by an amount that is proportional to the shift in order to maintain the desired output path. This necessitates an appropriate combined adjustment in fiscal and monetary policies. This relatively simple procedure is all that is needed to integrate TIP and aggregate demand policies in the first year; a similar adjustment is required in subsequent years if the shift caused by TIP each year could be specified. But the macroeconomic analysis does raise some questions about the size of that shift in subsequent years and the difficulty of attaining it.

Lagged Effects

In most views of the inflation process, the slower average wage increases resulting from TIP in the first year will reduce wage pressures in the second year. If prices slow correspondingly, as would be expected, this favorable lagged effect would be predicted by [econometric analysis]. Because the estimated lags are short, a major fraction of the first year's improvement in inflation will be perpetuated into the second year. In actual experience, however, some of the complications introduced by TIPs might lead to lagged effects that are different from these estimates.

Any TIP program may alter slightly the distribution of wages. The possibilities are numerous and the likely outcomes differ according to whether a penalty or reward TIP is employed. The main possibility for obtaining lagged effects that are noticeably smaller than the macromodel predicts probably arises in the case of a reward TIP that is employed for only one year. On the one hand, without a reward in the second year, workers whose wages had been restrained would tend to increase their wage demands to catch up with those that had not. On the other hand, firms that had not participated would be at a competitive cost disadvantage relative to firms that had, and that would put downward pressure on their wage offers. If these two influences cancel each other, the lagged effects from the economic equations should hold.

If the lagged wage effects in the macroeconomic model represent generalized expectations, the TIP program can be viewed in two ways. First, expectations that are based on actual experience should be favorably influenced by the initial slowdown in average wages and prices under TIP. This influence can be expected to grow if TIP effects are present over successive years. Second, expectations should be influenced by the existence of TIP as a specific and acceptable anti-inflation program. It should enhance the effects on inflationary expectations that Fellner looks for through policies of nonaccommodating aggregate demand. I have argued that these policies may be weak because their primary effect would be to change expectations of unemployment. Together with TIP, a greater part of any change in nominal demand expectations would be changes in expectations of the price level.

Changing the Structure

TIPs are sometimes espoused as a means of shifting the Phillips curve in a favorable direction. . . . There is little basis, however, for judging whether such a favorable shift would be maintained in a period of substantially tighter labor markets. Because excess demand in the labor market now appears to develop gradually, TIP might make the Phillips curve more nearly L-shaped. In moderately tight markets, wages might be restrained, producing an improved trade-off; but in extremely tight labor markets, TIP might be relatively ineffective and the short-term trade-off might be the same as before.

TIPs do not have to reduce the unemployment rate that represents full employment in order to be useful. They would be a valuable tool if they were simply a shortcut to price stability and slowed the present wage-price spiral without a period of sustained high unemployment. If they were also an indirect remedy for structural problems in the labor market that produce inflation while involuntary unemployment still exists, that would be a bonus.

MEASURES TO CUT COSTS AND PRICES

What effect can we expect on the ongoing inflation rate from one-time increases or reductions in prices or costs? We can rely on cost changes to be reflected in prices. Beyond that, the empirical evidence is unfailingly ambiguous. The price shocks of the mid-1970s affected wages, but not proportionately. Consumer prices appear to have some persistent effect on wages, but it is modest once the effects of lagged wages themselves are allowed for. On the basis of the evidence, it appears that only a minor fraction of any shock to prices would filter through into average wage changes and thus have some multiplied effect. That still makes measures to cut prices and costs worth pursuing and their opposites worth avoiding. Even if only one-quarter of any price change influences wages, 1 percent removed from the CPI reduces wage inflation by about as much as 1 percentage point more unemployment for one year.

Measures to cut prices and costs can be effectively included as part of a larger anti-inflation strategy. In any such strategy, success will be self-perpetuating. Failure in the aggregate will almost surely cause the pieces to come apart. If the government can point to direct price-cutting measures of its own, it would stand a better chance of obtaining support from the private sector, either for voluntary restraint or for TIP. And if the government could accomplish that, it could change the inertia equations in a favorable way.

II/SOLUTIONS WITH A MONETARIST LEANING

The substitution of paper money for metallic currency is a national gain; any further increase of paper beyond this amount is a form of robbery.

JOHN STUART MILL

Inflation is always and everywhere a monetary phenomenon; this is the rallying call for a group of economists called monetarists. Their argument is powerful: Looking at the relationship between money and inflation, one finds that the two have always moved in rough correspondence. All economists now agree with this statement, thanks in large measure to monetarists' consistent reminders. The present differences between the monetarist and nonmonetarist positions are much more subtle. Oversimplifying, the difference is that to a monetarist, increases in money cause increases in the price level,

$$\Delta M \longrightarrow \Delta P$$

whereas a nonmonetarist sees the causation the other way around:

$$\Delta P \longrightarrow \Delta M$$

In the article "Money and Inflation" (which appeared in his regular *Newsweek* column), Milton Friedman beautifully states the simplest monetarist position.

The subtler arguments are not to be found in the popular writings; they are generally reserved for more academic articles. In 1976 William Fellner wrote a book, *Towards a Reconstruction of Macroeconomics*, that serves as a classic statement of the highest level monetary theory. Fellner's reasoning is compelling. Turning the tables on the critics of monetarism, he accepts the antimonetarist arrow of causation as part of the story. That, he argues, is not the whole story, however. *Prices lead money only because people rationally expect the money supply to increase*, an expectation built in through years of experience with the government increasing money whenever unemployment threatened. This theory and the reasoning behind it have made strong impressions on government policy and have been the spearhead of a debate designed to dethrone Keynesian economics. According to Fellner, the inflation we are now suffering is nothing but the after-effects of Keynesian excesses. Keynes said, in the long run we are all dead. He is, but we are not, and it is the children who must pay for the excesses of their parents. The end result of this argument is a compelling metaphysic: No matter which way the arrow of causation goes, money is still the cause of inflation. In the one case it is the expectation of the money supply rising, and in the other it is the actual money supply rising.

The policy prescription follows immediately: Monetarism, Fellner argues, has not failed in the postwar period; it has never even been tried. Expansive monetary and fiscal policies have become so taken for granted and engrained into the U.S. economy that no one takes the government seriously when it suggests that it will slow the growth of the money supply. The only way to break this expectation-inflation cycle is to choose a monetary rule (often called the Friedman-Fellner monetary rule) governing the growth of the money supply, and to stick to it regardless of the short-term consequences. Yes, the result will be unemployment, but unemployment is the necessary suffering that we must pay for the sins of the past decades.

In terms of implementing the theory, the monetarists are anything but a unified group; their theory encompasses a broad range of divergent policy prescriptions. In the next pair of articles we see some of those differences. In "Using Escalators to Help Fight Inflation" Friedman argues that "the political will to accept such a recession, without reversing policy and restimulating inflation, is simply not present." The only way to make it politically feasible to end inflation is to adopt measures that will reduce the side effects of anti-inflation measures. This is the role of escalator clauses or indexation, which Friedman favors. Fellner, on the other hand, has his doubts about indexation, as we see in his assessment titled "The Controversial Issue of Comprehensive Indexation."

In the writings of Friederich A. Hayek, we see yet another monetarist position. Drawing on an almost unequaled wealth of historical experience, Hayek gives a slightly different version of the story told by Friedman and Fellner. Again, it is Keynes who draws the flak, but this time it is heavy flak: ". . . John Maynard Keynes [was] a man of great intellect but limited knowledge of economic theory. . . . [It has been] proposed that we call the third quarter of this century . . . the age of Keynes, as the second quarter was the age of Hitler. I do not feel that the harm Keynes did is really so much as to justify *that* description."

As with Fellner and Friedman, it is the problem of controlling governments that is foremost in Hayek's mind; his distrust, however, goes much deeper than Friedman's or Fellner's, and he calls for a more radical cure. According to Hayek, authorities will never be able to resist the demand for inflation; therefore, a new method of protecting the money supply from the politician must be found. The answer at which he arrives is to remove the government monopoly of money. Why not let the people choose freely what money they want to use? He concludes: "It seems to me that if we could prevent governments from meddling with money, we would do more good than any government has ever done in this regard. And private enterprise would probably have done better than the best they have ever done."

As you read the various monetary solutions, consider carefully their relation to one another and to the other solutions presented in this volume. Which is the most logical conclusion? Are they all reasonable? How do they differ from the mainline view? Could one have developed an argument for other types of solutions, perhaps even an incomes policy in a monetarist framework? Are monetarist views necessarily conservative? Could they be held by a liberal?

Money and Inflation

MILTON FRIEDMAN

Milton Friedman is presently a Senior Research Fellow at the Hoover Institution. Long considered the "economic guru" of the right, his *Capitalism and Freedom* (1962) and his *Monetary History of the U.S.* (1963) are regarded as classics in the literature. He was the recipient of the Nobel Prize for Economics in 1976. In the following short article reprinted from his regular *Newsweek* column, he demonstrates the power of his pen.

In 1863, a famous British economist, W. Stanley Jevons, published a pamphlet analyzing the effect of the California and Australian gold discoveries. One conclusion was that "an expansion of currency occurs one or two years prior to a rise of prices."

PRICES LAG . . .

On July 13, 1976, The Times of London published an article by its editor, William Rees-Moog, with the provocative heading "How a 9.4% Excess Money Supply Gave Britain 9.4% Inflation." In his article, Rees-Mogg erroneously attributes to me rather than to Jevons the demonstration that "there was a time lag, normally of about two years, between changes in the money supply and consequential changes in prices." Accordingly, he compares the increase in money supply each year in excess of the increase in output with the increase in prices two years later. For individual years, there is wide variation. But for 1964 to 1973 as a whole, the excess money supply rose at the average rate of 9.4 per cent per year; and for 1966 to 1975, prices rose at the average rate of 9.4 per cent.

Of course, the identity of these two numbers is a coincidence. Many factors other than changes in money supply affect the precise rate of inflation. But rough agreement between the two numbers—and even more important, their tendency to rise and fall together—is no coincidence. For example, the corresponding numbers for the U.S. are 4.2 per cent for money and 5.8 per cent for prices. For the prior decade, 1954 to 1964, they are 0.6 per cent for money and 1.8 per cent for prices, so both went up together by roughly the same amount.

For the U.S., as for Britain, this relationship is of long standing. Our own money-supply estimates go back to 1867. Throughout that period, changes in prices have tended to follow changes in money supply by roughly two years.

More recently, Congressman Stephen Neal, chairman of a House subcommittee on domestic monetary policy, reported that staff studies indicate that

---

*For the U.S., these figures are for money supply defined by M_2 (currency plus all commercial bank deposits), and for output defined by GNP at constant prices. The corresponding money figures for M_1 (currency plus demand deposits) are 1.7 for 1964 to 1973 and −1.5 for 1954 to 1964.

Milton Friedman, "Money and Inflation," *Newsweek*, September 20, 1976, p. 77. Copyright © 1976 by Newsweek, Inc. All rights reserved. Reprinted by permission.

"the rate of inflation rises and falls in the wake of increases and decreases in the supply of money," with the peak effect taking place after a lag of 23 months.

A lag of two years is *not* a natural constant that will prevail under all circumstances. It has characterized countries that, like the U.S. and Britain, have generally experienced only moderate rates of inflation during peacetime. In countries like Israel, Brazil, Chile or Argentina that have experienced much higher and more variable rates of inflation, the lag is only a few months.

The close relation between money and prices has persisted despite major changes in the determinants of the supply of money. When Jevons wrote, and for the next half-century, changes in the supply of money were produced mainly by gold discoveries or improvements in the methods of extracting gold from ore or developments in private banking. Today, gold no longer plays any monetary role and banking developments only a minor one. The money supply is controlled by the government—through the Federal Reserve in the U.S., the Bank of England in the U.K.

... SO DOES UNDERSTANDING

Rees-Moog's article aroused a storm of controversy. In the ten days after it was published, the Times printed some 25 letters denouncing, praising or amplifying the article. The controversy is understandable. As Rees-Moog wrote, "These figures have changed further my own attitude to incomes policy [i.e., wage and price control]. If the Excess Money Supply determines the rate of inflation equally closely in years subject to incomes policy and in years without, there seems to be no evidence left that incomes policy has any significant influence on inflation." Yet the current British Labor government is pinning most of its hopes for curbing inflation on a form of incomes policy—the so-called "social contract" with the unions whereby they agree to accept a low limit on wage increases.

The old chestnut goes: "What is a share of Penn Central worth?" Answer: "Together with a quarter, it will get you a cup of coffee." Similarly, the social contract, together with low monetary growth, will curb inflation. With rapid monetary growth, it will be another unsuccessful experiment.

Towards a Reconstruction of Macroeconomics

WILLIAM FELLNER

Currently a resident scholar at the American Enterprise Institute for Public Policy Research, William Fellner has served both as a member of the President's Council of Economic Advisers and as a consultant to the U.S. Treasury Department. He is a highly regarded theorist and has published numerous books, including *Monetary Policies and Full Employment* (1946) and *Competition Among the Few* (1949). The following is excerpted from his most recent book, *Towards a Reconstruction of Macroeconomics* (1976).

Macroeconomic theory, which owes a huge debt to Keynes's work of 1936, has a deficiency from which it should be freed to be useful for more than an analysis of the policy requirements of a past period with very special characteristics—the 1930s. A theory of macroeconomic equilibrium can easily be developed into a theory of equilibrium growth paths, and as such can serve as a valuable frame of reference, but only if it clearly recognizes that in the neighborhood of such a growth path there cannot occur significant and sustained deviations of actual movements of the price level from expected movements. The employment policy results and other economic and social consequences of major unexpected movements of the price level are exceedingly damaging, even if it takes a short while for the damage to be clearly observable. Keynes and the Keynesians have paid little attention to what this implies for economic theory as well as for policy. Their monetarist critics, who have shown awareness of the problem, have not placed it in the center of the debate on the fundamentals of macroeconomics and have not worked it out or clarified it sufficiently. The fact that the world has recently suffered the consequences of significant inflationary disturbances, which in the United States have by now lasted for about ten years and have grown exceedingly difficult to cope with, has much to do with the influence of a macroeconomic theory that has not been adequately reconstructed.

If demand management policies will not succeed in *conditioning* market expectations to a reasonably predictable behavior of the price level—that is, if the public's expectations will not be formed according to credible price-level targets of the authorities—then we shall be heading for comprehensively controlled societies, administered with reliance on significantly enlarged police power. The issue has by now become a dramatic one, and it is wrong to talk around such a crucial issue by using evasive terminology on controls. Implied in the conditioning effort that is required for avoiding a transition into such a state is the need to recognize that the relation of the authorities to the public has an essential *game-of-strategy* aspect.

The authorities must act on assumptions about the public's responses, and

William Fellner, *Towards a Reconstruction of Macroeconomics* (Washington, D.C.: American Enterprise Institute for Public Policy Research, 1976), pp. 1–4, 13–18, 135–139. Reprinted by permission.

members of the public must act on their assumptions about the responses of other members of the public and on assumptions about the reactions of the authorities to these. It is not enough to recognize that "rational expectations" are formed in view of the presumptive future behavior of the authorities rather than simply on the basis of the past behavior of the variables to which the expectations relate. A further essential fact is that the public attaches probability judgments to the way the behavior of the authorities may become influenced by the behavior of the public itself.[1] This is why credibility is of utmost importance—a fact that has gradually become clearer to at least some policy makers, but that has not been recognized as an essential element of a usable macroeconomic theory.

In their behavior in such a strategy situation, the authorities must be aware that no demand management policy can be successful in trying to validate an expectational system such as develops in markets without regard to the price level objectives of the policy makers. To try to validate an internally inconsistent and unstable expectational system is a hopeless effort. Nor will the effort to condition the markets to sustainable price-level expectations be successful if the determination of the authorities lacks sufficient credibility, because in that case the effort will lead to protracted "stagflation" that, in turn, is apt to lead the authorities to give up. Lack of credibility is self-justifying.

This position involves rejecting recent policy procedures based on the idea that we should take for granted money-wage and price-setting practices that developed in view of the public's past price experience during an inflationary period; and that we should aim for the money GNP that corresponds to an acceptable real GNP and to an acceptable employment level, given such pricing behavior by the public. Except for a short-term payoff to policy makers which is provided by the temporary fooling effect of unanticipated inflation, such an "accommodating" policy has proved self-defeating. It is self-defeating because it renders the expectational system that is so accommodated unstable upward, thereby destabilizing the economy and giving rise subsequently to the high costs of suppressing an accelerating inflationary process. The so-called Phillips trade-off between inflation and unemployment is a purely short-run phenomenon that must not be allowed to serve as a basis for demand management policy.

Demand management through monetary and fiscal policy can prove successful only if it succeeds in conditioning the public's price level expectations by creating an environment of appropriate restraint to which decision makers in the markets must adjust to avoid heavy losses. To imply that markets will continue for long to be guided by the past price behavior observed during a period of lax policies, and will do so regardless of how firmly convinced the

---

[1]The position developed in this [article] about expectations overlaps significantly with the views underlying the "rational expectations" hypothesis, but the analysis I shall present implies also that the problems we need to face contain a crucial element of games strategy. The games-strategy element derives from a justified suspicion on the part of the public that it depends on the public's behavior whether the authorities will persist in their mode of behavior. Further, it will be explained why I consider it inadvisable to . . . [connect] the hypothesis of rational expectations with the hypothesis of the "natural rate of unemployment" [as others have done]. In my view the hypothesis of the natural rate of unemployment cannot be carried over from the theory of perfect competition to "given imperfections" of actual markets (on some implied and inevitably arbitrary definition of a state in which these imperfections remain "given").

public is that there has been a change in policy, means building on assumptions that are not borne out by historical experience; these are the assumptions that provide excuses for postponing again and again the changeover from lax to sustainable policies. It is, of course, inevitable that the transition from a period in which the expectational system was allowed to "run wild" to a period of conditioned price-level expectations should involve uncomfortable adjustments; but the more the adjustments are postponed, the costlier they become. . . .

Macro-equilibrium requires that the output decisions in the markets should be guided by price-level expectations to which the decision makers have become conditioned by those in charge of demand management policies (monetary and fiscal policies) and it requires that the behavior of the price level to which expectations have become geared should be a sustainable behavior that can in fact be validated by the appropriate policies. To repeat: it is hopeless to try to validate by means of policy measures a fluid expectational system that develops independently in the markets and is not grounded outside itself. If the economy is to move in the neighborhood of an equilibrium path, the expectational system needs to be anchored in consistently pursued objectives of demand management policy. . . .

UNCONVINCING OBJECTIONS

I will end these introductory remarks with a brief presentation of the reasons I am unconvinced by two objections frequently encountered in discussions with my professional colleagues.

In the first place, it is often said there is little hope that wage and price behavior will adjust to demand policy objectives. This would suggest that the blocking of a reasonable policy effort would last long enough to make adoption of effective direct controls inevitable. But, as I said before, I am convinced that if this diagnosis should prove realistic, the reason would be the lack of consistency and credibility of the demand management policy declaring its determination to persist in creating no more aggregate demand than is called for by price level objectives and by the output movements compatible with these. It is essential to keep in mind that after all major inflationary interludes in economic history it is precisely the consistency and credibility of demand management efforts that made stabilization possible. It is equally essential to keep in mind that in the postwar United States until the second half of the 1960s the dismal view that the markets could and would keep sabotaging a price-level oriented demand-management policy would have been regarded as pure phantasy.

Try to visualize an environment in which it would again be fully believed that upward deviations from the known price-level targets of the authorities would impose a heavy penalty on all employers and a significant deterioration in the job outlook for workers. Each individual employer and worker or workers' representative would then have to tell himself: If in my small area I behave inconsistently with the general policy objective and many other individuals do the same in their areas, then business conditions will deteriorate greatly, and I will then regret my behavior; my main goal should then have been to avoid commitments that would make me share the exceedingly poor sales or employment outlook of the rest of the community. Alternatively, if while behaving inconsistently with the general policy objectives, I keep the possibility in mind that the others will not behave in the same way, then, too, I will regret my behavior because it will have led to a restriction of my sales volume *beyond* any degree that might (in some cases) reflect my increased market power. This latter consideration derives its justification from the fact that shifts in market power would come through even if the price level targets of the authorities were observed. To deny that the market environment can be shaped along these lines means to assert that the now relevant part of American economic history began in 1965. *Yet, what changed demonstrably about 1965 was the behavior of the policy makers, with no consistent or sufficiently pronounced signs of disillusionment on their part until very recently, and market behavior changed in response to policy changes.* This will become clear as we go along.

Needless to say, one must be prepared to encounter hurdles on the way back from an accelerating inflation to a sustainable behavior of the price level, where "sustainable behavior" presumably means near-horizontality of the general price trend (though . . . this specific interpretation of a viable price-level target does not follow cogently from basic economic analysis). Hurdles are encountered because at the start of the transition back to normalcy the determination of the authorities to persist may not yet be credible, but this is not the only reason. The other reason is that at the beginning of the transition process past commitments create for the sellers of goods and services a problem of trade-offs between (1) charging the costs developing from the past commitments and therefore losing sales volume and (2) not charging these costs in full for the sake of maintaining their sales volume at a more satisfactory level. Either choice is uncomfortable, and in some circumstances an economy on the way back to normalcy will indeed have to go through a period in which continued steep price increases are temporarily combined with a cyclical contraction of output. But if the policy effort is consistent, tomorrow's "past commitments" will cause the sellers smaller difficulties than today's and the transition period will not last long.

The more narrow-minded technicians—in contrast to the many who know how to blend their techniques with common sense—have a tendency to deny the validity of considerations such as these because they pretend that expectations depend on the lagged past behavior of variables without regard to the credibility of future policy action. But this view disregards the fact that the past behavior of all variables was also significantly influenced by expectations about the behavior of policy makers and thus by the credibility of the authorities' avowed objectives. For some time now the credibility of the authorities' anti-inflationary assertions has been extremely low in the United States as in the rest of the world. In 1973 and 1974 inflationary expectations and the corresponding pricing practices were further strengthened by the widely held belief that by additional demand creation the authorities would and should "accommodate" inevitable burdens arising from partly natural and partly man-made supply limitations. Thereby the authorities would and should *ease* a "pass-through" of specific price changes with inflationary consequences for the general price level—as if such monetary accommodation could improve the position of those sectors on which the burden was imposed by a binding constraint. The obstinacy of inflationary money-wage and price-setting practices had a great deal to do with the known lack of obstinacy of the authorities in their pursuit of anti-inflationary objectives.

Another frequently heard objection to the position I take is that it over-dramatizes the difference between a system that does and one that does not rely on direct wage and price controls. Between the comprehensive controls of the police state and abstention from the use of direct wage and price controls, it is argued, there is a large intermediate area. There does indeed exist a large intermediate area, but it is practically certain to prove an area of demoralization and low performance. It is possible to threaten with wage and price controls and not to adopt them, or to adopt them in form but not to enforce them; it is possible to enforce them haphazardly on rare occasions more or less at random; last but not least, it is possible to enforce them against those who are unpopular with the average voter or with the press, but not against others. But if demoralization of the society is to be avoided, one should surely be careful about when and how the penal system is used and against whom and how its use is threatened. The intermediate area between comprehensive wage and price controls and reliance on demand management policies without direct controls is highly objectionable, even if not objectionable in precisely the same sense as a well-organized and thoroughly policed system of political and economic control. It is remarkable how many euphemisms—ranging from "jawboning" to "social consensus"—have cropped up in recent years for hiding the true character of that large intermediate area. We have here the latest version of George Orwell's "Newspeak" for describing spotty and haphazard interferences by which uncertainty can be raised to an exceedingly high level throughout the economy.

With respect to economic efficiency, the main difficulty with direct wage and price controls under democratic political institutions is that, to the extent that the controls are enforced, the wage and price structure is regulated with a view to the next elections and the decisions about the "appropriate" profits on successful but often very risky innovations are likewise politically inspired. In such circumstances market forces play a much smaller role in determining the outcome than is the case in a reasonably well functioning market economy. Occasionally proposed tax incentives or tax penalties for preventing inflationary money-wage increases are vulnerable to the same criticism, since such incentives or penalties must postulate a desirable wage and price *structure*, with substantial economic or legal penalties imposed on those who behave differently under the influence of market forces.

Unless market power is made or allowed to grow very large, its ability to distort the forces of competition is significantly smaller than that of governments that engage in the regulation of the wage and price structure. Democratic political institutions create no safeguards in this respect because deciding highly complex technical matters with vote-getting objectives in mind must lead to bad results. Only by undue stretching of any acceptable concept of equity could it be claimed that such politically inspired results represent a sacrifice of efficiency for the sake of equity—all the less so because, in a large country living under democratic institutions, spottiness of the enforcement effort can be taken for granted. In some small countries the difficulties may be reduced by the fact that, given reasonably free trade, the forces generated across the borders play a decisive role and these forces cannot be distorted by the domestic political process. Nor is the enforcement problem as difficult in small as in large countries. But the fate of the world will not be decided by the small countries, and this [article] was written in one that is large.

Basically, we have the choice between (1) conditioning market expectations to a behavior of the price level which, when it comes to be anticipated by the public, can be enforced by demand management policy, and (2) quite thoroughly changing the characteristics of our economic and political system. Macroeconomic theory will gradually have to be reconstructed in such a way as to take this into account. This [article] represents a move in that direction, and I hope that it will not remain the only move.

I hope also that the analysis of these problems will recognize two facts reflecting the elements of strategy in the relations between the authorities and the population. One of these is that, while recessions resulting from the required demand-policy restraint in times of inflationary wage-price behavior will become rarer if the willingness of the authorities to resort to such restraint is generally anticipated, occasions will nevertheless recur when that willingness will have to be demonstrated at the cost of a cyclical setback. The other fact is that any manageable method of subsidizing the needy by guaranteed (or quasi-guaranteed) subsistence requires safeguards against misuse. Therefore, in the strategy situation that must be taken for granted, a government's ability to live up to "guaranteed" subsistence as a general rule requires determination not to live up to it in individual cases in which there is a sufficient presumption that the alleged need has developed because the individual was planning to rely on the guarantee. There is no way of formulating detailed prescriptions for a reasonable application of these principles, but this same negative statement can be made about most relevant problems of strategy—problems that have nevertheless often been faced successfully once their essential properties were recognized. . . .

THE ALTERNATIVE

. . . Transition to a system of administrative wage and price controls is the alternative to a credible demand-management policy directed to the highest activity levels consistent with reasonable price-level targets. . . .

"Reasonable price-level targets" should in all probability be interpreted as involving a gradual return to a practically horizontal general price trend. In a debate in which we are trying to come to grips with one of the most essential problems of our times there is no justification for talking around the subject by avoiding the term "wage and price controls" and substituting for it such words as "jawboning," "social contract," "social consensus," "incomes policy," and so on. These expressions have begun to proliferate, but either they represent mere political sugar-coating or they describe no more than the spotty and arbitrary use of governmental powers under the influence of political group pressures. They do not describe ways of improving the results that develop from a market system. Nor is there reason for expecting viability of the wage and price *structures* that are inevitably implied in tax-subsidy schemes occasionally proposed for preventing "undesirable" wage-price behavior by means of democratically legislated "carrots and sticks." It is, of course, possible to get lost for a long time in a region of ineffective selective interferences inspired by vote-getting considerations, and it is possible thereby to weaken greatly a country internationally. But even if history could take that turn in some countries, it would be morbid to try to construct a theory of how best to achieve *that* result.

A system of comprehensive direct wage and price controls *is* an alternative to be taken seriously. Given the present political structure of the Western world, transition to direct controls would not be smooth, since the required institutions and the required willingness to obey unconditionally are lacking. Comprehensive controls call for heavy reliance on police power, and the number of would-be violators with whom Western law-enforcement apparatus can cope is very limited. We are not doing particularly well about mugging in the streets, and the impulse to sell one's goods and services on the most favorable terms acceptable to buyers has so far remained much more generally characteristic of our population than the impulse to mug.

Not even a comprehensively controlled political and economic system could, of course, reconcile a full employment program with a program greatly reducing the disadvantages suffered by persons when they are out of work. On the other hand, such a system could directly or indirectly force many more people onto payrolls. Further, it might be able to keep a regulated price level constant, and it could regulate income differentials. What goods would be available at those wages and prices is another question. In particular, it is practically impossible to develop criteria for the appropriate profits "permissible" to investors engaging in risky innovations in circumstances where the unsuccessful are not compensated for their losses. The incentive to innovate would in all probability be greatly reduced in those circumstances.

But there is a sense in which rigorously controlled systems can be made workable, while a policy designed to guarantee full employment regardless of the supply price of labor and regardless of the demand for labor at given real wages must prove unworkable. Trying to make such a policy workable for a short period by generating inflationary movements of unexpected steepness has led us into profound difficulties, and it is imperative that we rid ourselves of these. Whether a system of generalized subsistence guarantees can prove viable depends on the characteristics of the population and on how such a system is constructed and administered. Thus, we may be hopeful about the future but we have a much better chance of overcoming our difficulties if we remain aware of the uncertainties and thereby of the dangers against which we must guard.

THE FUTURE OF MACROECONOMICS

It does seem clear that in some essential respects the macrotheoretical systems of the future will have to possess different properties from those in which our students have been trained. When we try to visualize future developments in the area of economic theory, it is advisable not to take into account the possibility that the United States (or any other major Western country) will for a long time be lost and demoralized in an area of haphazard and ineffectual interferences under partial government controls administered with a view to the next election. If that possibility should turn out to be the case, its intellectual counterpart is likely to be represented by bizarre and basically uninteresting variants of Keynesianism. The possibility cannot, of course, be entirely disregarded, but for our present purposes we may leave it aside.

A rigorously controlled economic and political system needs a demand management theory whose role is much less central in the general analytical structure than has been the role of our demand theories in recent decades. In such a system demand management becomes a handmaiden of comprehensive administrative planning, probably with subsidies as well as rigorous price controls included in the planning operations, and thus with inflation and deflation much less a problem. In these systems the difficulties to which the population is exposed develop mainly from a very high degree of dependence of the individual on those in charge politically. It is this power structure that, in the specific area of economic affairs, reflects itself in a low level of innovating activity and in a lack of adjustability of the product mix to the desires of the public.

If we are to prove successful in avoiding these developments, we must rely on a macro-theoretical framework that clearly recognizes the price level implications of the concept of macro-equilibrium. To do so will require recognition of the dependence of workable demand policy on a strategy by which price level expectations are conditioned to policy targets. In addition, the effect of widely spreading subsistence guarantees must be recognized much more clearly. In other respects, too, it will be necessary to pay more attention to the bearing of institutional rigidities on achievable employment policy goals. One may favor some of these rigidities—all of us probably favor some and take some others for granted even if we do not favor them—but in that case one must accept their consequences and leave room for them in one's macro-theory and employment policy. Other institutional rigidities exist largely because the bulk of the public misunderstands their consequences and has not been made properly aware of the harm they do.

If we are to succeed in avoiding unpalatable political and economic alternatives, we shall need a macro-theory assigning the proper role to the problems [of inflation and unemployment]. Differently expressed: *unless* we develop our analysis in a framework recognizing the significance of these problems, we shall before long witness basic changes in our economic and political environment, and these changes will have become acceptable only because we shall by then have moved into an area of low performance and demoralization.

Using Escalators to Help Fight Inflation

MILTON FRIEDMAN

Besides being one of the strongest advocates of a monetary rule as the best
solution to inflation, Milton Friedman has also championed the cause of indexation
as a policy that would make it easier to bring inflation under control. In the following
selection he gives the reasons for his support.

The real obstacles to ending inflation are political, not economic. Ending inflation would deprive government of revenue that it now obtains without legislation. Ending inflation would also produce a temporary, though perhaps fairly
protracted, period of recession or slowdown and relatively high unemployment.

These obstacles to ending inflation can be substantially reduced through
what has come to be called "indexation"—the widespread use of price-
escalator clauses in private and governmental contracts. Such arrangements
are not a good thing in and of themselves. They are simply a lesser evil than a
badly managed money. The widespread use of escalator clauses would not by
itself either increase or decrease the rate of inflation. But it would reduce the
revenue that government acquires from inflation—which means that government would have less incentive to inflate. More important, it would reduce the
adverse side effects that effective measures to end inflation would have on
output and employment.

From time immemorial, the major source of inflation has been the
sovereign's attempt to acquire resources to wage war, to construct monuments,
or for other purposes. Inflation has been irresistibly attractive to sovereigns
because it is a hidden tax that at first appears painless or even pleasant, and
above all because it is a tax that can be imposed without specific legislation. It is
truly taxation without representation.

The revenue yield from inflation takes three major forms:

- *Additional fiat money.* Since ancient times, sovereigns have debased coinage
  by replacing silver or gold with base metals. (Current examples include U.S.
  dimes and quarters, formerly silver but now copper coated with a nickel
  alloy.) Later, paper currency supplemented token coins. More recently still,
  book entries at central banks (misleadingly called deposits) have been added
  to the repertory. Governments use the fiat money they issue to finance expenditures or repay debts. In addition, the fiat money serves as a base on
  which the banking system creates additional money in the form of bank
  deposits. In calendar 1973, the U.S. government realized around $8 billion
  from these sources.

- *Windfall tax yield.* Inflation increases the yield of the personal and corporate
  income tax by pushing individuals into higher income brackets; generating

Milton Friedman, "Using Escalators to Help Fight Inflation." Reprinted from the July 1974 issue of
Fortune Magazine, pp. 94–97, 174, 176, by special permission; ©1974 Time Inc.

paper capital gains on which taxes must be paid; and rendering depreciation allowances inadequate to replace capital, so that a return of capital is taxed as if it were a return on capital. Estimates by the economist George Terborgh of the effect of inflation on the reported profits of nonfinancial corporations imply that the inflation yield from the corporate tax alone amounted to nearly $13 billion in 1973.

- *Reduction in the real amount of outstanding debt.* Much of the federal government's debt was issued at yields that did not allow for current rates of inflation. On a conservative estimate, the government must have realized in 1973 something like $5 billion from this source.

All told, then, the government's revenue from inflation came to more than $25 billion in 1973. Ending inflation would end these sources of revenue. Government would have to reduce expenditures, increase explicit taxes, or borrow additional funds from the public at whatever interest rate would clear the market. None of these courses is politically attractive.

An even more serious political obstacle to ending inflation is the reluctance of the public to tolerate the transitory rise in unemployment that ending inflation would currently entail. To avoid misunderstanding, let me stress that I am not saying an increase in unemployment is a cure for inflation. It is not. There are many ways to increase unemployment that would exacerbate rather than cure inflation. I am saying something very different: that unemployment is today an inevitable *side effect* of curing inflation—just as the need to stay in bed is a side effect of a successful operation for appendicitis but is not itself a cure.

Ending inflation requires a slowing down in the growth rate of total dollar spending. In my opinion, a reduction in the growth rate of the quantity of money is the only reliable instrument available to government for slowing down the growth rate of total dollar spending. But what follows is independent of that proposition. If there is some other way to slow spending growth, the side effects will be essentially the same. Hence this analysis of side effects of ending inflation is relevant even if you do not accept my monetarist view.

THE LONG LAG IN EXPECTATIONS

When total spending slows down, each producer separately tends to regard the reduction in the demand for his product as special to him, and to hope that it is temporary. He is inclined to meet it primarily by reducing output or accumulating inventory, not by shading prices. Only after a time lag will he start to shade prices. Similarly, any of his workers who are laid off are likely to react by waiting to be recalled or by seeking jobs elsewhere, not by moderating wage demands or expectations.

A slowdown in total spending will therefore tend to be reflected initially in a widespread slowdown in output and employment and an increase in inventories. It will take some time before these lead in turn to widespread reductions in the rate of increase in prices and the rate of increase in wages. It will take still more time before *expectations* about inflation are revised and the revised expectations encourage a resumption of employment and output.

Different activities, moreover, have different speeds of adjustment. Some prices, wages, and production schedules are fixed a long time in advance; others can be adjusted promptly. Accordingly, a slowdown of total spending produces substantial shifts in *relative* prices, which will sooner or later have to be corrected. The corrections, in turn, cause economic disturbances.

For the U.S. the time delay between a change in the rate of monetary growth and a corresponding change in the rate of growth of total spending and total output has averaged six to nine months. The further delay until a braking effect on prices is evident has averaged twelve to eighteen months. Accordingly, the total delay between a change in monetary growth and a change in the rate of inflation comes to about two years.

AN OPPORTUNITY CAST ASIDE

After inflation has continued for a time, inflationary expectations are reflected in interest rates, union contracts, and other long-term arrangements. Then a drop in the inflation rate imposes severe strains and hardships. The employer who granted very large wage increases in the expectation of continued inflation finds his real wage costs higher than he bargained for. The borrower who agreed to pay a very high interest rate finds his real borrowing cost higher than he expected. For example, a homeowner who took out a mortgage at 10 percent would be in a bad fix if the prevailing rate dropped to 5 percent, while the lender on that 10 percent mortgage would have received a bonanza.

Such side effects constitute, I believe, the most important political obstacle to ending inflation, given the commitment on the part of most modern governments to "full employment," the failure of the public at large to recognize the inevitable if temporary side effects of ending inflation, and the unwillingness or inability of political leaders to persuade the public to accept these side effects.

Some years back, when the rate of inflation was much lower than now, I believed that the readjustment required was sufficiently mild and brief to be politically feasible. But, unfortunately, the opportunity was cast aside on August 15, 1971, when President Nixon reversed economic policy by imposing a price and wage freeze and encouraging expansive monetary and fiscal policy.

A MASOCHISTIC EXERCISE

At the time, we were well on our way to ending inflation without severe side effects. At the cost of the mild 1970 recession, the annual rate of inflation had been reduced from over 6 percent to 4.5 percent and was still declining. The economy was slowly recovering from that recession. Had the nation had the will—for President Nixon was reflecting a widespread national consensus when he reversed policy—another year of continued monetary restraint and of slow expansion would probably have turned the trick. As it was, the 1970 recession was a masochistic exercise rather than a side effect of a successful cure.

As everyone certainly knows, inflation is now far worse than in August, 1971. The very high rate in the first half of 1974 was doubtless a temporary bubble, but even on the most optimistic view, inflation is not likely to fall below 6 percent during the next twelve months. Starting from that level, and with inflationary expectations ever more deeply entrenched, an effective policy to end inflation would entail as a side effect a considerably more severe and protracted recession than we experienced in 1970. The political will to accept such a recession, without reversing policy and restimulating inflation, is simply not present.

What then? If we do nothing, we shall suffer ever higher rates of inflation—not continuously, but in spurts as we overreact to temporary recessions. Sooner or later, the public will get fed up, will demand effective action, and we shall then have a really severe recession.

How can we make it politically feasible to end inflation much sooner? As I see it, only by adopting measures that will reduce the side effects from ending inflation. These side effects fundamentally reflect distortions introduced into *relative* prices by *unanticipated* inflation or deflation, distortions that arise because contracts are entered into under mistaken perceptions about the likely course of inflation. The way to reduce these side effects is to make contracts with prices, wages, or interest rates stipulated in *real* terms, not nominal terms. This can be done through the widespread use of escalator clauses.

Indexation is not a panacea. It is impossible to escalate all contracts (consider, for example, currency in circulation), and widespread escalation would be cumbersome. A great advantage of using money is precisely the ability to carry on transactions cheaply and efficiently, and universal escalator clauses reduce this advantage. Far better to have no inflation and no escalator clauses. But that alternative is not now available.

AN IDEA WITH ANCESTORS

Let me note also that the use of escalator clauses is not a new idea or an untried idea. It dates back to at least 1707, when a Cambridge don, William Fleetwood, estimated the change in prices over a six-hundred-year period in order to get comparable limits on outside income that holders of fellowships should be permitted to receive. The use of escalator clauses was explicitly suggested a hundred years later by an English writer on money, John Wheatley. In 1886 the concept was spelled out in considerable detail, and enthusiastically recommended, by the great English economist Alfred Marshall.

The great American economist Irving Fisher not only favored the "tabular standard"—as the proposal for indexation was labeled nearly two centuries ago—but also persuaded a manufacturing company that he had helped to found to issue a purchasing-power security as long ago as 1925. Interest in the tabular standard was the major factor accounting for the development of index numbers of prices. In recent years, indexation, as the tabular standard is now called, has been adopted by Brazil on a wider scale than I would recommend for the U.S. It has been adopted on a lesser scale by Canada, Israel, and several other countries.

ABOLISHING HIDDEN TAX INCREASES

For the U.S., my specific proposal has two parts, one for the federal government, one for the rest of the economy. For the federal government, I propose that escalator clauses be legislated; for the rest of the economy, that they be voluntary, but that any legal obstacles be removed. The question of which index number to use in escalator clauses is important but not critical. As Alfred Marshall said in 1886, "A perfectly exact measure of purchasing power is not only unattainable, but even unthinkable." For convenience, I would use the cost-of-living index number calculated by the Bureau of Labor Statistics.

The U.S. government has already adopted escalation for social-security payments, retirement benefits to federal employees, wages of post-office employees, and perhaps some other items. Taxes that are expressed as fixed percentages of price or other value base are automatically escalated. The government should now proceed to adopt escalator clauses in the personal and corporate income tax and in government securities. . . .

The Personal Income Tax

Minor details aside, four changes are called for:

- The personal exemption, the standard deduction, and the low-income allowance should be expressed not as a given number of dollars, but as a given number of dollars multiplied by the ratio of a price index for the year in question to the index for the base year in which indexation starts. For example, if in the first year prices rise by 10 percent, the base amounts should be multiplied by 1.10.

- The brackets in the tax tables should be adjusted similarly, so that, in the example given, $0-500 would become $0-550, and so on.

- The base for calculating capital gains should be multiplied by the ratio of the price index in the year of sale to the price index in the year of purchase. This would prevent the taxing of purely paper capital gains.

- The base for calculating depreciation on fixed capital assets should be adjusted in the same way.

The Corporate Tax

- The present $25,000 dividing line between normal tax and surtax should be replaced by that sum multiplied by a price index number.

- The cost of inventories used in sales should be adjusted to eliminate book profits (or losses) resulting from changes in prices between initial purchase and final sale.

- The bases for calculating capital gains and depreciation of fixed capital assets should be adjusted as for the individual income tax.

Government Securities

Except for short-term bills and notes, all government securities should be issued in purchasing-power form. For example, Series E bonds should promise a redemption value equal to the product of the face value (calculated at an interest rate of, say, 3 percent per year) and the ratio of the price index in the year of redemption to the price index in the year of purchase. Coupon securities should carry coupons redeemable for the face amount multiplied by the relevant price ratio, and bear a maturity value equal to the face amount similarly multiplied by the relevant price ratio.

THE ETHICAL ASPECT

These changes in taxes and in borrowing will reduce both the incentive for government to resort to inflation and the side effects of changes in the rate of inflation on the private economy. But they are called for also by elementary principles of ethics, justice, and representative government, which is why I propose making them permanent.

As a result largely of inflation produced by government, personal income taxes are today heavier than during the peak of World War II financing, despite several legislated "reductions" in tax rates. Personal exemptions in real terms are at an all-time low. The taxes levied on persons in different economic circumstances deviate widely from the taxes Congress explicitly intended to levy on them. Congress has been in the enviable position of actually imposing higher taxes while appearing to reduce taxes.

As for government borrowing, the savings-bond campaigns of the Treasury have been the largest bucket-shop operation ever engaged in. This is not a recent development. In 1951, in responding to a questionnaire of the Joint Economic Committee of Congress, I wrote:

> I strongly favor the issuance of a purchasing-power bond on two grounds: (a) It would provide a means for lower- and middle-income groups to protect their capital against the ravages of inflation. These groups have almost no effective means of doing so now. It seems to me equitable and socially desirable that they should. (b) It would permit the Treasury to sell bonds without engaging in advertising and promotion that at best is highly misleading, at worst, close to being downright immoral. The Treasury urges people to buy bonds as a means of securing their future. Is the implicit promise one that it can make in good faith, in light of past experience of purchasers of such bonds who have seen their purchasing power eaten away by price rises? If it can be, there is no cost involved in making the promise explicit by adding a purchasing-power guaranty. If it cannot be, it seems to me intolerable that an agency of the public deliberately mislead the public.

Surely the experience of the nearly quarter century since these words were written reinforces their pertinence. Essentially every purchaser of savings bonds (or, indeed, almost any other long-term Treasury security) during that period has paid for the privilege of lending to the government. The supposed "interest" he has received has not compensated for the decline in the purchasing power of the principal, and, to add insult to injury, he has had to pay tax on the paper interest. And the inflation that has sheared the innocent lambs has been produced by the government that benefits from the shearing!

It is a mystery to me, and a depressing commentary on either the understanding or the sense of social responsibility of businessmen (note that I say of *businessmen*, not of business), that year after year eminent and honorable business leaders have been willing to participate in this bucket-shop operation by joining committees to promote the sale of U.S. savings bonds, or by providing facilities for payroll deductions for that purpose.

Private use of escalator clauses is an expedient that has no permanent role if government manages money responsibly. Hence I favor keeping such private use voluntary in order to promote its self-destruction if that happy time arrives.

No legislation is needed for the private adoption of escalator clauses, and such clauses are now widespread. More than five million workers are covered by union contracts with automatic escalator clauses, and there must be many nonunion workers who have similar implicit or explicit agreements with their employers. Many contracts for future delivery of products contain provisions for adjustment of the final selling price either for specific changes in costs or for general price changes. A great many rental contracts for business premises are expressed as a percentage of gross or net receipts, which means that they have an implicit escalator clause. This is equally true for percentage royalty payments and for automobile-insurance policies that pay the cost of repairing actual damage. Some insurance companies issue fire-insurance policies under which the face value is automatically adjusted for inflation. No doubt there are many more examples of which I am ignorant.

It is highly desirable that the practice of incorporating escalator clauses be extended to a far wider range of wage agreements, contracts for future delivery of products, and financial transactions involving borrowing and lending. The first two are entirely straightforward extensions of existing practices. The third is more novel.

HEDGED BOTH WAYS

The arrangements suggested for government borrowing could apply equally to long-term borrowing by private enterprises. Instead of issuing a security promising to pay, say, interest of 9 percent per year and to repay $1,000 at the end of ten years, XYZ Corp. could promise to pay 3 percent plus the rate of inflation each year, and to repay $1,000 at the end of ten years. Alternatively, it could promise to pay each year 3 percent times the ratio of the price index in that year to the price index in the year the security was issued, and to repay at the end of ten years $1,000 times the corresponding price ratio for the tenth year.

One question has invariably been raised when I have discussed this kind of arrangement with corporate executives: "Is it not too risky for us to undertake an open-ended commitment? At least with fixed nominal rates we know what our obligations are." This is a natural query from businessmen reared in an environment in which a roughly stable price level was taken for granted. But in a world of varying rates of inflation, the fixed-rate agreement is the riskier agreement. The dollar receipts of most businesses vary with inflation. If inflation is high, dollar receipts are high, and business can afford to pay the escalated rate of interest. If inflation is low, dollar receipts are low, and they will find it easier to pay the low rate with the adjustment for inflation than a fixed but high rate. And similarly at the time of redemption.

What is crucial is the relation between assets and liabilities. For many enterprises, their assets, including goodwill, are real in the sense that the dollar value will rise or fall with the general price level. But their liabilities tend to be nominal, i.e., fixed in dollar terms. Accordingly, these enterprises benefit from inflation at a higher rate than was anticipated when the nominal liabilities were acquired, and they are harmed by inflation at a lower rate than was anticipated. Match assets and liabilities, and such enterprises would be hedged against either event.

A related yet somewhat different case is provided by financial intermediaries. Consider savings-and-loan associations and mutual-savings banks. Both their assets (primarily home mortgages) and their liabilities (due to shareholders or depositors) are expressed in nominal terms. But they differ in time duration. The liabilities are in practice due on demand; the assets are long term. The mortgages now in the portfolios were mostly issued when inflation and therefore interest rates were much lower. If the mortgages were revalued at current yields—i.e., at the market prices they could be sold for in a free secondary market—every savings-and-loan association would be technically insolvent.

THE DISINTERMEDIATION MENACE

So long as the thrift institutions can maintain their level of deposits, no problem arises because they do not have to liquidate their assets. But if inflation speeds up, interst rates on market instruments will rise further. Unless the thrift institutions offer competitive interest rates, their shareholders or depositors will withdraw funds to get a better yield (the process inelegantly termed disintermediation). But with their income fixed, the thrift institutions will find it difficult or impossible to pay competitive rates. (This situation is concealed but not altered by the legal limits on the rates they are permitted to pay.)

Further acceleration of inflation threatens a major crisis for this group of financial institutions. And the crisis is no minor matter. Total assets of these institutions approach $400 billion. As it happens, they would be greatly helped by a deceleration of inflation, but some of their recent borrowers who are locked into high rates on mortgages would be seriously hurt.

Consider how different the situation of the thrift institutions would be with widespread escalator clauses. The mortgages on their books would be yielding, say, 5 percent plus the rate of inflation; they could afford to pay their shareholders or depositors 3 or 4 percent plus the rate of inflation (assuming that legal limits were removed or modified). They, their borrowers, and their shareholders or depositors would be fully protected against changes in the rate of inflation.

Similarly, an insurance company could afford to offer an inflation-protected policy if its assets were in inflation-protected loans to business or mortgages or government securities. A pension fund could offer inflation-protected pensions if it held inflation-protected assets.

A TEMPERING OF HARDSHIPS

To repeat, none of these arrangements is without cost. It would be far better if stable prices made them unnecessary. But they seem to me far less costly than continuing on the road to periodic acceleration of inflation, ending in a real bust.

Note that the suggested governmental arrangements will stimulate the private arrangements. Today one deterrent to issuance of private purchasing-power securities is that the inflation adjustment would be taxable to the recipient along with the real interest paid. The proposed tax changes would in effect exempt such adjustments from taxation, and aso make purchasing-power securities more attractive to lenders. In addition, government issuance of purchasing-power securities would offer effective competition to private borrowers, inducing them to follow suit.

How would widespread adoption of the escalator principle affect economic policy? Some critics say that indexation would condemn us to perpetual inflation. I believe that, on the contrary, indexation would enhance the government's ability to act against inflation.

To begin with, indexation will temper some of the hardships and distortions that now follow from a drop in the rate of inflation. Employers will not be stuck with excessively high wage increases under existing union contracts, for wage increases will moderate as inflation recedes. Borrowers will not be stuck with excessively high interest costs, for the rates on outstanding loans will moderate as inflation recedes. Indexation will also partly counteract the tendency of business to defer capital investment once total spending begins to decline— there will be less reason to wait in expectation of lower prices and lower interest rates. Businesses will be able to borrow funds or enter into construction contracts knowing that interest rates and contract prices can be adjusted later on in accord with indexes of prices.

STEELING THE POLITICAL WILL

Most important, indexation will shorten the time it takes for a reduction in the rate of growth of total spending to have its full effect in reducing the rate of inflation. As the deceleration of demand pinches at various points in the economy, any effects on prices will be promptly transmitted to wage contracts, to contracts for future delivery, and to interest rates on outstanding long-term loans. Accordingly, producers' wage costs and other costs will go up less rapidly than they would without indexation. This tempering of costs, in turn, will encourage employers to keep more people on the payroll, and produce more goods, than they would without indexation. The encouragement of supply, in turn, will work against price increases, with additional moderating feedback on wages and other costs.

With widespread indexation, in sum, firm monetary restraint by the Federal Reserve System would be reflected in a much more even reduction in the pace of inflation and a much smaller transitory rise in unemployment. The success in slowing inflation would steel the political will to suffer the smaller withdrawal pains, and so might make it possible for the Fed to persist in a firm policy. As it became credible that the Fed would persist, private reactions could reinforce the effects of its policy. The economy would move to noninflationary growth or high levels of employment much more rapidly than now seems possible.

The major objection to indexation is the allegation that escalators have an inflationary impact on the economy. In this form, the statement is simply false. An escalator goes into effect only as the result of a prior price increase. Whence came that? An escalator can go down as well as up. If inflation slows, and hence so do wage increases, do escalators have a deflationary impact?

Escalators have no direct effect on the rate of inflation. They simply assure that inflation affects different prices and wages alike, and thus they moderate distortions in relative prices and wages. With widespread use of escalators, inflation will be *transmitted* more quickly and evenly, and hence the harm done by inflation will be less. But why should that raise or lower the rate of inflation?

On a more sophisticated level, it has been argued that by reducing the revenue yield from any given rate of inflation, indexation would induce the government to speed up the rate of inflation in order to recoup the lost revenue. Furthermore, it has been suggested that the general public would interpret the adoption of escalator clauses to mean the government has given up the fight against inflation, and is seeking only to live with it—which in turn would reinforce inflationary expectations. To me, these objections do not seem weighty. If the public does not wish to stop inflation, but is content to have the government use inflation as a regular source of revenue, the sooner we adapt our institutions to that fact the better.

A BENEFICIAL TRADE-OFF

On a still more sophisticated level, it can be argued that, by removing distortions in relative prices, indexation will make it easier for the public to recognize changes in the rate of inflation, will thereby reduce the time lag in adapting to such changes, and so will make the nominal price level more sensitive and variable. It is certainly possible that indexation would have this effect, though it is by no means demonstrated. But if so, the *real variables* would be less sensitive and more stable—a highly beneficial trade-off. Moreover, it is also possible that by making accurate estimates of the rate of inflation less important, indexation will reduce the attention devoted to such estimates, and thereby provide greater stability.

An objection of a very different kind is that inflation serves the critical social purpose of resolving incompatible demands by different groups. In this view, the participants in the economy, to put it crudely, have "non-negotiable demands" for more than the entire output. These demands are reconciled because inflation fools people into believing that their demands have been met when in fact they have not been. Escalator clauses, it is argued, would bring the inconsistent demands into the open. Workers who would accept a lower real wage produced by unanticipated inflation will not be willing to accept the same real wage in explicit negotiations. If this view is correct on a wide enough scale to be important, I see no other ultimate outcome than either runaway inflation or an authoritarian society ruled by force. Perhaps it is only wishful thinking that makes me reluctant to accept this vision of our fate.

A MAJOR SOURCE OF UNREST

The conventional political wisdom holds that the citizenry may mutter about inflation but votes on the basis of the level of unemployment. Nobody, it is said, has ever lost an election because of inflation; Hoover in 1932 and Nixon in 1960 lost because of unemployment. But as we leave the Depression decade further and further behind, and as we experience more and more inflation, this conventional wisdom becomes increasingly questionable. Edward Heath surely lost an election because of inflation. [While he was in office] Prime Minister Tanaka's popularity [reached] an all-time low because of inflation. Throughout the world, inflation is a major source of political unrest.

Perhaps indexation is not the best expedient in this time of trouble. But I know of no other that holds out as much promise of both reducing the harm done by inflation and facilitating the ending of inflation. If inflation continues to accelerate, the conventional political wisdom will be reversed. The insistence on ending inflation at whatever cost will lead to a severe depression. Now, before that has occurred, is the time to take measures that will make it politically feasible to end inflation before inflation ends not only the conventional wisdom but perhaps also a free society.

The Controversial Issue of Comprehensive Indexation

WILLIAM FELLNER

Monetarists are not united in their support of indexation, as can be seen in the following article by William Fellner, who looks at some of the problems inherent in this solution.

THE NATURE OF THE CURRENT DEBATE

The usual argument for comprehensive indexation implies assumptions which I consider unrealistic. To my knowledge no contributor to the professional debate has suggested that indexation—and the periodic revisions of payment obligations that it entails—would provide adequate protection against the harmful effects of accelerating inflation on resource allocation and on welfare in general. The proponents of comprehensive indexation usually do argue, however, that the system would make it easier to get inflation under control.

It is sometimes implied that a government which is relying on inflation to divert output away from the private economy will stop applying this kind of hidden taxation if, in consequence of the rapid and automatic wage-price revisions occurring under indexation, any given degree of inflation becomes a less effective means of diverting resources. I think the contrary is much more likely to be true: a government engaged in this kind of hidden taxation is much more apt to step up its inflationary moves than to abandon them, if more money is needed to achieve the same result in real terms.

However, we should pay attention not merely to cases in which the authorities "initiate" inflation in order to acquire resources without taxation but also (and, at present, perhaps mainly) to cases in which the authorities are known to "accommodate" steep cost trends at high levels of resource utilization for fear that failure to do so would lead to a cyclical setback. In *this* context, the argument in support of indexation deserves more careful analysis. Yet I believe (1) that at the stage of the process at which the United States finds itself now the indexation argument is nevertheless outright misleading and (2) that on assumptions which would be "ideal" for its validity the argument cannot be brushed aside but is quite a bit weaker than most of its proponents would lead one to think.

I will not distinguish a third category of inflationary processes—so-called commodity inflations—which are supposedly explained by a rise in specific prices in relation to others. According to the popular discussion that has developed mainly since 1973, food and energy prices are cases in point. Yet a steepened increase in specific prices does not itself explain why demand-

William Fellner, "The Controversial Issue of Comprehensive Indexation," in *Essays on Inflation and Indexation*, Domestic Affairs Study 24 (Washington, D.C.: American Enterprise Institute for Public Policy Research, October 1974), pp. 63–69. Reprinted by permission.

management policies fail to use sufficient restraint to achieve a correspondingly lesser rate of increase in the other components of the GNP deflator.

ACTUAL AND EXPECTED INFLATION

From informal exchanges of views I have concluded that a meeting of minds on the indexation problem—at least a meeting of minds on the nature of the differences—is made easier by using terminology that fits into a simple and by now more or less conventional model. For most purposes this simple model has all along seemed too "aggregative" to me. But it is easy to make adjustments for its shortcomings and to grasp its implications.

In the terminology I shall be using, a state described by the proposition that "the expected rate of inflation" falls short of the actual rate of inflation should be visualized as a state in which policies are adopted that lead to more inflation than was expected by private decision makers when they entered contracts involving payment obligations for the period. The contrary is true of a state described by the proposition that "the expected rate of inflation" exceeds the actual rate.

We may regard the state in which the expected rate falls short of the actual as one in which (1) the typical wage earner underestimates the future rise of the consumer price index (CPI) and (2) the typical employer underestimates the prices that will be charged by those from whom he buys, that is, he overestimates his own future *relative prices*. When actual inflation is thus kept running ahead of inflationary expectations and a very large part of the public has in each phase entered into obligations expecting more real income than will prove to be available, comprehensive indexation of deferred payments would increase the difficulties that need to be faced. The authorities would have two options: (1) they could accommodate a further acceleration of the actual rate and also of the lagging expected rate of inflation, or (2) they could rely on monetary and fiscal restraint in an effort to reduce the actual rate to or below the current expected rate. But if they chose the second of these two options, they would probably have to carry out their policy of restraint in even more cumbersome circumstances than those in which such a policy would have to be put into effect in the absence of indexation.

OUR RECENT INFLATION

I believe that in the United States we have been living for some time in an environment that can be described by an excess of the actual over the expected inflation rate in the sense here explained. Real wage and profit trends strongly suggest that inflation has been kept steep enough to disappoint most decision makers, ex post facto, concerning the real incomes they will be earning at the levels of activities which were being maintained. This is another way of saying that, in successive phases, obligations were entered into which implied the availability of a larger total real income than has in fact accrued to the typical parties accepting the obligations. In these circumstances the excess of actual over expected inflation keeps steepening the inflationary expectations. As a result, the whole process shows a pronounced tendency to accelerate.

In any country in which this kind of discrepancy between the actual and the expected rate continued to be generated, comprehensive indexation would lead to additional acceleration. Under indexation, money wages and other costs would be adjusted upward more rapidly because the fact that price inflation was proceeding more rapidly than had been expected would have a prompter effect on costs and hence also a prompter feedback on prices. Moreover, in the individual sectors decision makers expecting a faster rate of increase in the price measure used for indexation will probably *try* to move their prices even faster than the rate at which they expect the index to rise. The reason for this is that the hitherto existing relation between the typical seller's own prices, on the one hand, and the wage rates and the prices he *pays*, on the other, has been disappointing to him. Not being satisfied with his relative prices, he will try to raise them. Such a self-defeating inflationary process can be "beaten down" by monetary-fiscal restraint. However, comprehensive indexation would be apt to increase the resistance of the price trend to such restraint, and hence to increase the underutilization and the resulting hardships of the required adjustment period. This is so because of the existence of an initial tendency toward steepened inflation.

ASSUMPTIONS MORE FAVORABLE TO THE INDEXATION ARGUMENT

By pointing out that indexing would have harmful consequences in the type of disequilibrium we were considering, we have admittedly not met the issue of comprehensive indexation in general. What if the actual rate of inflation has already been reduced to the expected rate and the problem is that of stabilizing this lower rate? In response to this question, it may be suggested that if the authorities should be successful in establishing such an inflationary equilibrium, the markets would make allowances for the roughly predictable rate of general price increase without formal indexation. On the other hand, it may be argued that formal indexation of payment obligations, *even with reliance on some inevitably deficient index*, would have advantages as well as disadvantages in this case. However, the question of "promoting indexation" would be reduced to minor importance because of the allowances which the markets would make anyway for the roughly foreseen inflation rate.

But what if we are already in a condition in which the actual rate of inflation just about equals the initially given expected rate and we then seek a transition to a condition in which the actual rate will equal a *lowered* expected rate—say, a zero rate or at least a significantly reduced one? I think most proponents of comprehensive indexation have *this* problem in mind, or problems which in simplified terminology can be similarly described.

For example, assume that at the present writing we conclude from wage trends, interest rates, and other variables that "the expected rate of inflation" in the United States is somewhere around 7 percent a year, and assume further that we have reduced the actual rate to this number but want to reduce it to 3 percent or less, possibly to zero. Comprehensive indexation would then have the result that when general price increases successively decelerated to 5 percent, 4 percent, and so forth, the money wage rates earlier agreed upon would automatically follow suit. This is at least a potential advantage because it may promote further relatively painless price deceleration at the right time. But even when the argument becomes narrowed to the situation we are now considering, qualifications need to be added. It is easy to overestimate the strength of the argument because potential disadvantages must be set against the potential advantage rightly claimed.

I will limit myself here to calling attention to a complication developing from an inevitable time lag, one that makes it very likely that a reduction of a high equilibrium rate of inflation to a low one would be accompanied by a cyclical setback with or without indexation. Even with comprehensive indexing, individual decision makers must be willing to sell their goods at decelerating prices *before* indexing has led to a deceleration of their wage and other costs and without knowing *when* (or even *whether*) the cost deceleration will take place—because that deceleration, after all, depends on how other sellers of goods will behave and thus on how the price index will move. Only in an environment having the output and employment characteristics of a cyclical setback will price deceleration take place, *whether there is indexation or not.*

Furthermore, not only is it true that even under indexation the weakness of markets must force price deceleration prior to any wage deceleration brought about by indexing—the indexing of wages being presumably based on the CPI—but empirically it is also true that the timing of the CPI's deceleration relative to any individual seller's sale-and-price decision is quite uncertain. The proponents of indexing argue that under indexing wage deceleration follows an assumed price deceleration "automatically." The argument is valid but, as we shall see in a moment, no individual seller and no policy maker can make a reasonably dependable guess as to when the CPI would decelerate as a result of a policy of general monetary restraint. The individual seller knows only that this does not depend on his own sale-and-price decisions.

Factual statements on when price deceleration has started in some period are not clear-cut unless the spans over which prices are averaged as well as the spans over which price changes are measured are clearly stated, and it is uncertain how the technique of comprehensive indexation would be applied in these respects. Nevertheless, on the basis of the available data, it seems safe to suggest that the CPI decelerated during the recession of 1953–54, but did not decelerate at all *during* the recession of 1957–58 or *during* that of 1960–61. It is doubtful whether, even when we consider the special problem of reducing a higher equilibrium rate of inflation to a lower equilibrium rate, mechanical reliance on inevitably deficient index numbers is to be recommended, since the initial response of the price index to demand restraints and hence the induced wage response may well be forthcoming after a recession that has run its full course. This is illustrated by the recessions of 1957–58 and 1960–61 but not by that of 1969–70, *during* which the CPI did indeed start decelerating. There *is* a presumption that in the recession of 1969–70, as well as in that of 1953–54, indexing would have made the feedback of initially price-induced wage deceleration on prices more pronounced. Yet, taking the case of the recession of 1969–70, it is hard to imagine that wage agreements based on indexation would not have caused substantial difficulties of a different kind because it is hard to conceive of wage agreements stipulating so low a rise in *real* wage rates as the one which took place in that recession period.

CONCLUSIONS, POSITIVE AND NEGATIVE

While my appraisal of indexing has not turned me into a "fan," I am not as unbending in my negativism as some of the proponents are in their advocacy. As the reader has seen, I am aware of pros as well as cons when the problem is defined as that of reducing the actual rate of inflation from some currently expected rate to a lower expected *and* actual level. Also, I recognize that some of the allowances which markets would make for general price increases in any future, more or less stabilized "inflationary equilibrium" could be considered the equivalents of indexing. Indeed, in such a situation formula indexation itself might prove the smoothest method of incorporating the allowances into contracts of *some types*, despite the obvious inadequacies of all the available indices. However, I am firmly convinced that where we are faced with the consequences of the actual inflation rate having been kept above the expected rate and with the resulting tendency of inflation to accelerate, comprehensive indexing would create significant additional difficulties. It would do so *both* on the pessimistic assumption that the same policy attitudes continue *and* on the more hopeful assumption that policy makers are at long last determined to put an end to a state of disequilibrium in which inflation is accelerating.

Even at the cost of a cyclical setback, policy makers must show this determination unless they are willing to stage a transition into a much more regimented economic and political system in which merely the symptoms of inflation would be suppressed. If they wake up to this danger, they will stop using their monetary and fiscal tools to generate increasingly steep inflation. Instead, they will use these tools with sufficient restraint so as to create an environment in which, after an unavoidable period of adjustment, the bulk of the private decision makers *becomes and remains aware of the risks of entering into obligations on terms and on a scale implying the unrealistic real-income expectations that develop under a lax policy*. To predict that such a change of policy attitudes would miscarry because the adjustment period would last too long and would be intolerably harsh means giving up on our society at a stage of its development where playing it always safe in one direction has proved an unsuccessful political strategy but the society itself has shown a great deal of staying power and vitality.

I should add two remarks. The first is that I do not extend my skepticism about indexing proposals to matters of taxation—that is, to the question of periodic adjustments of exemption limits, of deductions, of tax brackets, and to the determination of amounts on which capital gains taxes are levied. These matters involve political rather than market decisions, and it is clear that in a world where the general price level is rising, earlier decisions on tax provisions lead to unintended results. My second and final remark is that I have not tried to analyze a situation in which a significant reduction in a steep inflation rate is carried out with what essentially is effective regulation of wage rates, combined with restrained demand-management policies and supplemented by indexation. This is not the context relevant to the present American indexation debate, although adequate comparative analysis of specific problems arising in alternative political environments is, of course, of substantial interest.

Choice in Currency: A Way to Stop Inflation[1]

F. A. HAYEK

Friederich A. Hayek is one of the most famous economists in the world. His contributions extend far beyond economics, and his *Road to Serfdom* (1944) is considered one of the most insightful books ever written on the political philosophy of capitalism. In 1974 he was awarded the Nobel Prize in Economics for his many contributions. His latest works include collections of his writings under the titles *Studies in Philosophy, Politics and Economics* and *Law, Legislation and Liberty* as well as numerous shorter essays on the role of money in the economy. This selection is based on an address he gave to the Geneva Gold and Monetary Conference, September 25, 1975.

MONEY, KEYNES, AND HISTORY[2]

The chief root of our present monetary troubles is, of course, the sanction of scientific authority which Lord Keynes and his disciples have given to the age-old superstition that by increasing the aggregate of money expenditure we can lastingly ensure prosperity and full employment. It is a superstition against which economists before Keynes had struggled with some success for at least two centuries.[3] It had governed most of earlier history. This history, indeed, has been largely a history of inflation; significantly, it was only during the rise of the prosperous modern industrial systems and during the rule of the gold standard, that over a period of about two hundred years (in Britain from about 1714 to 1914, and in the United States from about 1749 to 1939) prices were at the end about where they had been at the beginning. During this unique period of monetary stability the gold standard had imposed upon monetary authorities a discipline which prevented them from abusing their powers, as they have done at nearly all other times. Experience in other parts of the world does not seem to have been very different: I have been told that a Chinese law attempted to prohibit paper money for all times (of course, ineffectively), long before the Europeans ever invented it!

Keynesian Rehabilitation

It was John Maynard Keynes, a man of great intellect but limited knowledge of economic theory, who ultimately succeeded in rehabilitating a view long

---

[1] Based on an Address entitled "International Money" delivered to the Geneva Gold and Monetary Conference on 25 September, 1975, at Lausanne, Switzerland.

[2] [The main section and sub-headings have been inserted to help readers, especially non-economists unfamiliar with Professor Hayek's writings, to follow the argument; they were not part of the original lecture.—ED.]

[3] [This observation is amplified by Professor Hayek in a note, "A Comment on Keynes, Beveridge and Keynesian Economics," page 23.—ED.]

F. A. Hayek, *Choice in Currency: A Way to Stop Inflation* (London: Institute of Economic Affairs, 1976), pp. 9–24. This paper was first published by the Institute of Economic Affairs, London, as their Occasional Paper 48, under the title "Choice in Currency: A Way to Stop Inflation."

the preserve of cranks with whom he openly sympathised. He had attempted by a succession of new theories to justify the same, superficially persuasive, intuitive belief that had been held by many practical men before, but that will not withstand rigorous analysis of the price mechanism: just as there cannot be a uniform price for all kinds of labour, an equality of demand and supply for labour in general cannot be secured by managing *aggregate* demand. The volume of employment depends on the correspondence of demand and supply *in each sector* of the economy, and therefore on the wage structure and the distribution of demand between the sectors. The consequence is that over a longer period the Keynesian remedy does not cure unemployment but makes it worse.

The claim of an eminent public figure and brilliant polemicist to provide a cheap and easy means of permanently preventing serious unemployment conquered public opinion and, after his death, professional opinion too. Sir John Hicks has even proposed that we call the third quarter of this century, 1950 to 1975, the age of Keynes, as the second quarter was the age of Hitler.[4] I do not feel that the harm Keynes did is really so much as to justify *that* description. But it is true that, so long as his prescriptions seemed to work, they operated as an orthodoxy which it appeared useless to oppose.

Personal Confession

I have often blamed myself for having given up the struggle after I had spent much time and energy criticising the first version of Keynes's theoretical framework. Only after the second part of my critique had appeared did he tell me he had changed his mind and no longer believed what he had said in the *Treatise on Money* of 1930 (somewhat unjustly towards himself, as it seems to me, since I still believe that volume II of the *Treatise* contains some of the best work he ever did). At any rate, I felt it then to be useless to return to the charge, because he seemed so likely to change his views again. When it proved that this new version—the *General Theory* of 1936—conquered most of the professional opinion, and when in the end even some of the colleagues I most respected supported the wholly Keynesian Bretton Woods agreement, I largely withdrew from the debate, since to proclaim my dissent from the near-unanimous views of the orthodox phalanx would merely have deprived me of a hearing on other matters about which I was more concerned at the time. (I believe, however, that, so far as some of the best British economists were concerned, their support of Bretton Woods was determined more by a misguided patriotism—the hope that it would benefit Britain in her post-war difficulties—than by a belief that it would provide a satisfactory international monetary order.)

THE MANUFACTURE OF UNEMPLOYMENT

I wrote 36 years ago on the crucial point of difference:

> It may perhaps be pointed out that it has, of course, never been denied that employment can be rapidly increased, and a position of "full employ-

---

[4]John Hicks, *The Crisis in Keynesian Economics*, Oxford University Press, 1974, p. I.

ment" achieved in the shortest possible time, by means of monetary expansion— least of all by those economists whose outlook has been influenced by the experience of a major inflation. All that has been contended is that the kind of full employment which can be created in this way is inherently unstable, and that to create employment by these means is to perpetuate fluctuations. There may be desperate situations in which it may indeed be necessary to increase employment at all costs, even if it be only for a short period— perhaps the situation in which Dr. Brüning found himself in Germany in 1932 was such a situation in which desperate means would have been justified. But the economist should not conceal the fact that to aim at the maximum of employment which can be achieved in the short run by means of monetary policy is essentially the policy of the desperado who has nothing to lose and everything to gain from a short breathing space.[5]

To this I would now like to add, in reply to the constant deliberate misrepresentation of my views by politicians, who like to picture me as a sort of bogey whose influence makes conservative parties dangerous, what I regularly emphasise and stated nine months ago in my Nobel Memorial Prize Lecture at Stockholm in the following words:

The truth is that by a mistaken theoretical view we have been led into a precarious position in which we cannot prevent substantial unemployment from re-appearing: not because, as my view is sometimes misrepresented, this unemployment is deliberately brought about as a means to combat inflation, but because it is now bound to appear as a deeply regrettable but *inescapable* consequence of the mistaken policies of the past as soon as inflation ceases to accelerate.[6]

Unemployment via "Full Employment Policies"

This manufacture of unemployment by what are called "full employment policies" is a complex process. In essence it operates by temporary changes in the distribution of demand, drawing both unemployed and already employed workers into jobs which will disappear with the end of inflation. In the periodically recurrent crises of the pre-1914 years the expansion of credit during the preceding boom served largely to finance industrial investment, and the over-development and subsequent unemployment occurred mainly in the industries producing capital equipment. In the engineered inflation of the last decades things were more complex.

What will happen during a major inflation is illustrated by an observation from the early 1920s which many of my Viennese contemporaries will confirm: in the city many of the famous coffee houses were driven from the best corner sites by new bank offices and returned after the "stabilisation crisis," when the banks had contracted or collapsed and thousands of bank clerks swelled the ranks of the unemployed.

---

[5]F. A. Hayek, *Profits, Interest and Investment,* Routlege & Kegan Paul, London, 1939, p. 63n.
[6]F. A. Hayek, "The Pretence of Knowledge," Nobel Memorial Prize Lecture 1974, reprinted in *Full Employment at Any Price?*, Occasional Paper 45, IEA, 1975, p. 37.

The Lost Generation

The whole theory underlying the full employment policies has by now of course been thoroughly discredited by the experience of the last few years. In consequence the economists are also beginning to discover its fatal intellectual defects which they ought to have seen all along. Yet I fear the theory will still give us a lost of trouble: it has left us with a lost generation of economists who have learnt nothing else. One of our chief problems will be to protect our money against those economists who will continue to offer their quack remedies, the short-term effectiveness of which will continue to ensure them popularity. It will survive among blind doctrinaires who have always been convinced that they have the key to salvation.

The 1863 Penny

In consequence, though the rapid descent of Keynesian doctrine from intellectual respectability can be denied no longer, it still gravely threatens the chances of a sensible monetary policy. Nor have people yet fully realised how much irreparable damage it has already done, particularly in Britain, the country of its origin. The sense of financial respectability which once guided British monetary policy has rapidly disappeared. From a model to be imitated Britain has in a few years descended to be a warning example for the rest of the world. This decay was recently brought home to me by a curious incident: I found in a drawer of my desk a British penny dated 1863 which a short 12 years ago, that is, when it was exactly a hundred years old, I had received as change from a London bus conductor and had taken back to Germany to show to my students what long-run monetary stability meant. I believe they were duly impressed. But they would laugh in my face if I now mentioned Britain as an instance of monetary stability.

THE WEAKNESS OF POLITICAL CONTROL OF MONEY

A wise man should perhaps have foreseen that less than 30 years after the nationalisation of the Bank of England the purchasing power of the pound sterling would have been reduced to less than one-quarter of what it had been at that date. As has sooner or later happened everywhere, government control of the quantity of money has once again proved fatal. I do not want to question that a very intelligent and wholly independent national or international monetary authority *might* do better than an international gold standard, or any other sort of automatic system. But I see not the slightest hope that any government, or any institution subject to political pressure, will ever be able to act in such a manner.

Group Interests Harmful

I never had much illusion in this respect, but I must confess that in the course of a long life my opinion of governments has steadily worsened: the more intelligently they try to act (as distinguished from simply following an established rule), the more harm they seem to do—because once they are known to aim at particular goals (rather than merely maintaining a self-correcting spontaneous order) the less they can avoid serving sectional interests. And the demands of all organised group interests are almost invariably harmful— except only when they protest against restrictions imposed upon them for the benefit of other group interests. I am by no means re-assured by the fact that, at least in some countries, the civil servants who run affairs are mostly intelligent, well-meaning, and honest men. The point is that, if governments are to remain in office in the prevailing political order, they have no choice but to use their powers for the benefit of particular groups—and one strong interest is always to get additonal money for extra expenditure. However harmful inflation is in general seen to be, there are always substantial groups of people, including some for whose support collectivist-inclined governments primarily look, which in the short run greatly gain by it—even if only by staving off for some time the loss of an income which it is human nature to believe will be only temporary if they can tide over the emergency.

Rebuilding the Resistances to Inflation

The pressure for more and cheaper money is an ever-present political force which monetary authorities have never been able to resist, unless they were in a position credibly to point to an absolute obstacle which made it impossible for them to meet such demands. And it will become even more irresistible when these interests can appeal to an increasingly unrecognisable image of St. Maynard. There will be no more urgent need than to erect new defences against the onslaughts of popular forms of Keynesianism, that is, to replace or restore those restraints which, under the influence of his theory, have been systemat- ically dismantled. It was the main function of the gold standard, of balanced budgets, of the necessity for deficit countries to contract their circulation, and of the limitation of the supply of "international liquidity," to make it impossible for the monetary authorities to capitulate to the pressure for more money. And it was exactly for that reason that all these safeguards against inflation, which had made it possible for representative governments to resist the demands of powerful pressure groups for more money, have been removed at the instigation of economists who imagined that, if governments were released from the shack- les of mechanical rules, they would be able to act wisely for the general benefit.

I do not believe we can now remedy this position by *constructing* some new international monetary order, whether a new international monetary author- ity or institution, or even an international agreement to adopt a particular mechanism or system of policy, such as the classical gold standard. I am fairly convinced that any attempt now to re-instate the gold standard by international agreement would break down within a short time and merely discredit the ideal of an international gold standard for even longer. Without the conviction of the public at large that certain immediately painful measures are occasionally necessary to preserve reasonable stability, we cannot hope that any authority which has power to determine the quantity of money will long resist the pressure for, or the seduction of, cheap money.

Protecting Money from Politics

The politician, acting on a modified Keynesian maxim that in the long run we are all out of office, does not care if his successful cure of unemployment is bound to produce more unemployment in the future. The politicians who will be blamed for it will not be those who created the inflation but those who stopped it. No worse trap could have been set for a democratic system in which the government is forced to act on the beliefs that the people think to be true. Our only hope for a stable money is indeed now to find a way to protect money from politics.

With the exception only of the 200-year period of the gold standard, practically all governments of history have used their exclusive power to issue money in order to defraud and plunder the people. There is less ground than ever for hoping that, so long as the people have no choice but to use the money their government provides, governments will become more trustworthy. Under the prevailing systems of government, which are supposed to be guided by the opinion of the majority but under which in practice any sizeable group may create a "political necessity" for the government by threatening to withhold the votes it needs to claim majority support, we cannot entrust dangerous instruments to it. Fortunately we need not yet fear, I hope, that governments will start a war to please some indispensable group of supporters, but money is certainly too dangerous an instrument to leave to the fortuitous expediency of politicians—or, it seems, economists.

A Dangerous Monopoly

What is so dangerous and ought to be done away with is not governments' right to issue money but the *exclusive* right to do so and their power to force people to use it and to accept it at a particular price. This monopoly of government, like the postal monopoly, has its origin not in any benefit it secures for the people but solely in the desire to enhance the coercive powers of government. I doubt whether it has ever done any good except to the rulers and their favourites. All history contradicts the belief that governments have given us a safer money than we would have had without their claiming an exclusive right to issue it.

CHOICE OF MONEY FOR PAYMENT IN CONTRACTS

But why should we not let people choose freely what money they want to use? By "people" I mean the individuals who ought to have the right to decide whether they want to buy or sell for francs, pounds, dollars, D-marks, or ounces of gold. I have no objection to governments issuing money, but I believe their claim to a *monopoly*, or their power to *limit* the kinds of money in which contracts may be concluded within their territory, or to determine the *rates* at which monies can be exchanged, to be wholly harmful.

At this moment it seems that the best thing we could wish governments to do is for, say, all the members of the European Economic Community, or, better still, all the governments of the Atlantic Community, to bind themselves mutually not to place any restrictions on the free use within their territories of one another's—or any other—currencies, including their purchase and sale at any price the parties decide upon, or on their use as accounting units in which to keep books. This, and not a utopian European Monetary Unit, seems to me now both the practicable and the desirable arrangement to aim at. To make the scheme effective it would be important, for reasons I state later, also to provide that banks in one country be free to establish branches in any of the others.

Government and Legal Tender

This suggestion may at first seem absurd to all brought up on the concept of "legal tender." Is it not essential that the law designate one kind of money as the legal money? This is, however, true only to the extent that, *if* the government does issue money, it must also say what must be accepted in discharge of debts incurred in that money. And it must also determine in what manner certain non-contractual legal obligations, such as taxes or liabilities for damage or torts, are to be discharged. But there is no reason whatever why people should not be free to make contracts, including ordinary purchases and sales, in any kind of money they choose, or why they should be obliged to sell against any particular kind of money.

There could be no more effective check against the abuse of money by the government than if people were free to refuse any money they distrusted and to prefer money in which they had confidence. Nor could there be a stronger inducement to governments to ensure the stability of their money than the knowledge that, so long as they kept the supply below the demand for it, that demand would tend to grow. Therefore, let us deprive governments (or their monetary authorities) of all power to protect their money against competition: if they can no longer conceal that their money is becoming bad, they will have to restrict the issue.

The first reaction of many readers may be to ask whether the effect of such a system would not according to an old rule be that the bad money would drive out the good. But this would be a misunderstanding of what is called Gresham's Law. This indeed is one of the oldest insights into the mechanism of money, so old that 2,400 years ago Aristophanes, in one of his comedies, could say that it was with politicians as it is with coins, because the bad ones drive out the good.[7] But the truth which apparently even today is not generally understood is that Gresham's Law operates *only* if the two kinds of money have to be accepted at a prescribed rate of exchange. Exactly the opposite will happen when people are free to exchange the different kinds of money at whatever rate they can agree upon. This was observed many times during the great inflations when even the most severe penalties threatened by governments could not prevent people from using other kinds of money—even commodities like cigarettes and bottles of brandy rather than the government money—which clearly meant that the good money was driving out the bad.[8]

---

[7]Aristophanes, *Frogs*, 891–898, in Frere's translation:
Oftentimes we have reflected on a similar abuse
In the choice of men for office, and of coins for common use,
For our old and standard pieces, valued and approved and tried,
Here among the Grecian nations, and in all the world besides,
Recognised in every realm for trusty stamp and pure assay,
Are rejected and abandoned for the trash of yesterday,
For a vile adulterated issue, drossy, counterfeit and base,
Which the traffic of the city passes current in their place.
About the same time, the philosopher Diogenes called money "the legislators' game of dice"!

[8]During the German inflation after the First World War, when people began to use dollars and other solid currencies in the place of marks, a Dutch financier (if I rightly remember, Mr. Vissering) asserted that Gresham's Law was false and the opposite true.

Benefits of Free Currency System

Make it merely legal and people will be very quick indeed to refuse to use the national currency once it depreciates noticeably, and they will make their dealings in a currency they trust. Employers, in particular, would find it in their interest to offer, in collective agreements, not wages anticipating a foreseen rise of prices but wages in a currency they trusted and could make the basis of rational calculation. This would deprive government of the power to counteract excessive wage increases, and the unemployment they would cause, by depreciating their currency. It would also prevent employers from conceding such wages in the expectation that the national monetary authority would bail them out if they promised more than they could pay.

There is no reason to be concerned about the effects of such an arrangement on ordinary men who know neither how to handle nor how to obtain strange kinds of money. So long as the shopkeepers knew that they could turn it instantly at the current rate of exchange into whatever money they preferred, they would be only too ready to sell their wares at an appropriate price for any currency. But the malpractices of government would show themselves much more rapidly if prices rose only in terms of the money issued by it, and people would soon learn to hold the government responsible for the value of the money in which they were paid. Electronic calculators, which in seconds would give the equivalent of any price in any currency at the current rate, would soon be used everywhere. But, unless the national government all too badly mismanaged the currency it issued, it would probably be continued to be used in everyday retail transactions. What would be affected mostly would be not so much the use of money in daily payments as the willingness to *hold* different kinds of money. It would mainly be the tendency of all business and capital transactions rapidly to switch to a more reliable standard (and to base calculations and accounting on it) which would keep national monetary policy on the right path.

LONG-RUN MONETARY STABILITY

The upshot would probably be that the currencies of those countries trusted to pursue a responsible monetary policy would tend to displace gradually those of a less reliable character. The reputation of financial righteousness would become a jealously guarded asset of all issuers of money, since they would know that even the slightest deviation from the path of honesty would reduce the demand for their product.

I do not believe there is any reason to fear that in such a competition for the most general acceptance of a currency there would arise a tendency to deflation or an increasing value of money. People will be quite as reluctant to borrow or incur debts in a currency expected to appreciate as they will hesitate to lend in a currency expected to depreciate. The convenience of use is decidedly in favour of a currency which can be expected to retain an approximately stable value. If governments and other issuers of money have to compete in inducing people to *hold* their money, and make long-term contracts in it, they will have to create confidence in its long-run stability.

"The Universal Prize"

Where I am not sure is whether in such a competition for reliability any government-issued currency would prevail, or whether the predominant preference would not be in favour of some such units as ounces of gold. It seems not unlikely that gold would ultimately re-assert its place as "the universal prize in all countries, in all cultures, in all ages," as Jacob Bronowski has recently called it in his brilliant book on *The Ascent of Man*,[9] if people were given complete freedom to decide what to use as their standard and general medium of exchange—more likely, at any rate, than as the result of any organised attempt to restore the gold standard.

The reason why, in order to be fully effective, the free international market in currencies should extend also to the services of banks is, of course, that bank deposits subject to cheque represent today much the largest part of the liquid assets of most people. Even during the last hundred years or so of the gold standard this circumstance increasingly prevented it from operating as a fully international currency, because any inflow or outflow in or out of a country required a proportionate expansion or contraction of the much larger superstructure of the national credit money, the effect of which falls indiscriminately on the whole economy instead of merely increasing or decreasing the demand for the particular goods which was required to bring about a new balance between imports and exports. With a truly international banking system money could be transferred directly without producing the harmful process of secondary contractions or expansions of the credit structure.

It would probably also impose the most effective discipline on governments if they felt immediately the effects of their policies on the attractiveness of investment in their country. I have just read in an English Whig tract more than 250 years old: "Who would establish a Bank in an arbitrary country, or trust his money constantly there?"[10] The tract, incidentally, tells us that yet another 50 years earlier a great French banker, Jean Baptist Tavernier, invested all the riches he had amassed in his long rambles over the world in what the authors described as "the barren rocks of Switzerland"; when asked why by Louis XIV, he had the courage to tell him that "he was willing to have something which he could call his own!" Switzerland, apparently, laid the foundations of her prosperity earlier than most people realise.

Free Dealings in Money Better than Monetary Unions

I prefer the freeing of all dealings in money to any sort of monetary union also because the latter would demand an international monetary authority which I believe is neither practicable nor even desirable—and hardly to be more trusted than a national authority. It seems to me that there is a very sound element in the widespread disinclination to confer sovereign powers, or at least

[9] Jacob Bronowski, *The Ascent of Man*, BBC Publications, London, 1973.
[10] Thomas Gordon and John Trenchard, *The Cato Letters*, dated 12 May, 1722 and 3 February, 1721 respectively, published in collected editions, London, 1724, and later.

powers to command, on any international authority. What we need are not international authorities possessing powers of direction but merely international bodies (or, rather, international treaties which are effectively enforced) which can prohibit certain actions of governments that will harm other people. Effectively to prohibit all restrictions on dealings in (and the possession of) different kinds of money (or claims for money) would at last make it possible that the absence of tariffs, or other obstacles to the movement of goods and men, will secure a genuine free trade area or common market—and do more than anything else to create confidence in the countries committing themselves to it. It is now urgently needed to counter that monetary nationalism which I first criticised almost 40 years ago[11] and which is becoming even more dangerous when, as a consequence of the close kinship between the two views, it is turning into monetary socialism. I hope it will not be too long before complete freedom to deal in any money one likes will be regarded as the essential mark of a free country.[12]

You may feel that my proposal amounts to no less than the abolition of monetary policy; and you would not be quite wrong. As in other connections, I have come to the conclusion that the best the state can do with respect to money is to provide a framework of legal rules within which the people can develop the monetary institutions that best suit them. It seems to me that if we could prevent governments from meddling with money, we would do more good than any government has ever done in this regard. And private enterprise would probably have done better than the best they have ever done.

A Comment on Keynes, Beveridge, and Keynesian Economics

Lord Keynes has always appeared to me a kind of new John Law. Like Law, Keynes was a financial genius who made some real contributions to the theory of money. (Apart from an interesting and original discussion of the factors determining the value of money, Law gave the first satisfactory account of the cumulative growth of acceptability once a commodity was widely used as a medium of exchange.) But Keynes could never free himself from the popular false belief that, as Law expressed it, "as the additional money will give work to

[11]*Monetary Nationalism and International Stability*, Longmans, London, 1937.
[12]It may at first seem as if this suggestion were in conflict with my general support of fixed exchange rates under the present system. But this is not so. Fixed exchange rates seem to me to be necessary so long as national governments have a monopoly of issuing money in their territory in order to place them under a very necessary discipline. But this is of course no longer necessary when they have to submit to the discipline of competiton with other issuers of money equally current within their territory.

people who were idle and enabled those already working to earn more, the output will increase and industry will prosper."[13]

It was against this sort of view that Richard Cantillon and David Hume began the development of modern monetary theory. Hume in particular put the central point at issue by saying that, in the process of inflation, "it is only in this interval or intermediate situation between the acquisition of money and the rise of prices, that the increasing quantity of gold and silver is favourable to industry."[14] It is this work we shall have to do again after the Keynesian flood.

In one sense, however, it would be somewhat unfair to blame Lord Keynes too much for the developments after his death. I am certain he would have been—whatever he had said earlier—a leader in the fight against the present inflation. But developments, at least in Britain, were also mainly determined by the version of Keynesianism published under the name of Lord Beveridge for which (since he himself understood no economics whatever) his scientific advisers must bear the responsibility.

I have been blamed for charging Lord Keynes with a somewhat limited knowledge of economic theory, but the defectiveness of his views on the theory of international trade, for example, have often been pointed out. And the clearest proof seems to me to be the caricature of other theories which he presented, presumably in good faith, in order to refute them.

F.A.H.

---

[13]John Law, *Money and Trade Considered with a Proposal for Supplying the Nations with Money*, W. Lewis, London, 1705. [*A Collection of Scarce and Valuable Tracts* (the Somers Collection of Tracts, Vol. XIII), John Murray, London, 1815, includes John Law's tract (1720 edition) at pp. 775–817; an extract from p. 812 reads: "But as this addition to the money will employ the people that are now idle, and those now employed to more advantage, so the product will be increased, and manufacture advanced."—ED.]

[14]David Hume, *On Money* (Essay III).

III / WAGE-PRICE CONTROLS, GUIDELINES, GUIDEPOSTS, JAWBONING, AND SUCH

It is the task of superior man to adjust demand and supply so as to keep prices on a level.

CONFUCIUS

The monetarist position that any real anti-inflation policy must entail a decrease in the growth of the money supply has now been fairly well accepted by all economists.

Robert Solow, commenting on Milton Friedman's numerous mentions of the money supply, quipped that everything seems to remind Milton of the money supply. Solow went on to say that everything reminded *him* of sex; the only difference was that he did not write about it all the time. The point behind his comment is fundamental to assessing the position of advocates of wage and price controls; while they agree that any anti-inflation policy must include controlling the money supply, the important question for the nonmonetarist is whether controlling the money supply is sufficient.

There are two reasons why it might not be: The first is political and is the one the monetarists emphasize. *Does* the government have the gumption necessary to implement a sufficiently restrictive monetary policy? The answer is unclear from the monetarists' writings. Fellner has his doubts but believes it is the only way. Friedman does not believe it is sufficient and favors indexation to make restrictive policy actions politically more acceptable. Hayek believes that the government will never have the willpower and that the only real solution lies in taking the money supply out of government's hands.

The second reason, one of equity and efficiency, is the one the incomes policy proponents emphasize. *Should* the government have the gumption to institute restrictive monetary policy? Their equity argument goes something like this: Restrictive monetary policy does not affect all groups equally; the burden falls heavily on certain groups of people, specifically the lowest paid workers and those businesses that are credit intensive. Why should these groups have to bear most of the burden? If we are a just society, we should design a program that shares the burden more equally. Incomes policies, they argue, constitute precisely such a program.

The efficiency argument is subtler, but the essence of the argument goes as follows: In today's society money affects prices, but only with a long time lag. Thus the connection between money and prices is not direct ($\Delta M \longrightarrow \Delta P$); it goes from money to to unemployment to prices ($\Delta M \longrightarrow \Delta U \longrightarrow \Delta P$). This intermediate step is inefficient. If we can establish a direct tie between money and prices, we can channel the power of restricting money directly into prices, thereby avoiding the inefficient unemployment.

$$\Delta M \longrightarrow\!\!\!/\;\; U \longrightarrow\!\!\!/\;\; \Delta P$$

Income policies fulfill this role; they are, therefore, a necessary complement to monetary policy.

The monetarists' answer to these arguments is one of practicality; there are simply too many variables out there. We can control some prices and wages some of the time, but we cannot control all prices and wages all of the time. If we try to do so, we will create a situation in which the market is not free to operate, and government control will be required to a degree that threatens the liberty of individuals.

According to the monetarists, society is far better off with the inequities and inefficiencies of monetary policy than it would be if government could say when one can and cannot raise prices and wages. Government control always leads to one thing—even more government control.

Proponents of wage and price controls dispute these claims in varying degrees. They believe either that the monetarists have overemphasized the fears or that safeguards against the difficulties can be built into the program. To accomplish this end, some suggest temporary rather than permanent controls, while others support rough guidelines rather than direct controls. At this point the issues become hazy; there is no right or wrong, only gray areas that must be judged from one's perception of past experience.

A final note: One criticism that is often made of incomes policies does not apply to the arguments presented here. Since the pro-incomes policy argument accepts that supply must equal demand, the comparisons sometimes made between general wage and price controls and price control in only one market are not relevant. Price control in one market tries to invalidate the market, holding the price below the market clearing price. The results are shortages and black markets. General price controls, used in conjunction with general monetary policy, need cause no aggregate shortages. Used in this way they are not a replacement for the market; they are merely an aid to help it work more efficiently.

The readings in this section are designed both to give you a flavor of the history of wage and price controls and to enable you to see the arguments for and against them. The first two readings are historical.

Craufurd D. Goodwin's introduction to *Exhortation and Controls* gives an excellent historical perspective on the role of controls, broadly interpreted in the postwar period. One of the most interesting insights he offers is how the same issues arise again and again, only to be lost in the archives of the period, so that the issues must be faced anew the next time around.

In the second selection, Arnold R. Weber suggests four models of wage-price policy implementation. We learn that an incomes policy is not always an incomes policy; generally, in fact, it has not been. He concludes the first section of the article with the statement, "If the purpose of wage-price policy has been to regulate the flow of economic events in the economy, it has been more analogous to sandbag embankments thrown up to resist flash floods than to dams built for the systematic control of the stream of wage and price decisions." These different objectives of incomes policies in the past have led proponents to the same defense that Fellner used for monetary policy (and which George Bernard Shaw used for Christianity): They haven't failed; they haven't even been tried. In the second section of his article, Weber outlines the deficiencies of past wage-price policies.

The next two selections are by two well-known advocates of incomes policies. In "Inflation and How to Overcome It," Leon H. Keyserling recounts the history of unemployment and inflation in the postwar period and then, referring to the historical record, argues against the "trade-off" theory that unemployment can be used as a weapon against inflation. Not only is the trade-off cruel and indefensible, it does not work; a healthy growing economy has always led to less inflation, not more. What we need is more planning and less reliance on monetary policy, and if these policies lead to inflation, "we should not shy away from . . . controls." The controls, however, should not only be designed to restrain inflation, they "should also be applied flexibly and fairly in pursuit of defined goals for full employment and production, priorities, and social justice."

In his afterword to *Money: Whence It Came, Where It Went,* John Kenneth Galbraith echoes Keyserling in chastising monetary policy. He begins: "If anything is evident from . . . history, it is that the task [of managing money] attracts a very low level of talent." According to Galbraith, we must not rely on monetary policy to fight inflation; instead, he argues, "direct wage and price control where there is market power is inevitable." Used together with planning, controls provide a reasonable policy for the government to follow. He concludes with a thoughtful historical insight: "Nothing . . . lasts forever. That is true of inflation. It is true of recession. Each stirs the attitudes, engenders the action which seeks to bring itself to an end—and eventually does. . . . If anything is certain from this history, it is that those who see themselves as the strongest defenders of the system . . . will be the most fearful of measures designed to conserve the system."

The next two articles specifically concern the 1971–1974 controls. Both articles agree that the controls failed, but their conclusions are quite different. Herbert Stein in "Why Controls Failed" draws very narrow conclusions, cautioning the reader about the political realities in which controls must be administered. C. Jackson Grayson, Jr., draws much stronger conclusions, stating seven ways in which "controls interfere (negatively) with the market system."

Though many economists have been hesitant about advocating direct controls, they still believe that some government involvement is necessary. Thus a whole group of weaker forms of controls have been devised. These partial controls go under many names: Guidelines, jawboning, and moral suasion are a few that have been used. But whatever the name, the issues are the same.

The next two selections in this part are excerpts from a classic exchange over the issue of guideposts between Milton Friedman and Robert Solow. Although they were written in 1968 and concerned the 1966–1967 controls, the questions they raise have not changed. In "What Price Guideposts?" Friedman condemns controls of any type, arguing against them on practical and theoretical grounds.

Solow takes a position in favor of controls. The title of Solow's piece, "The Case Against the Case Against the Guideposts," gives a good synopsis of his argument. Rather than arguing in favor of guidelines, he takes a defensive position, arguing that guidelines are "a far cry from wage and price control" and serve as "a device for the education and mobilization of public opinion." Moreover, they can influence only those wage and price decisions that are not made in the free market. Thus, even though they might be somewhat inequitable, under the appropriate circumstances they offer a little help at even less cost. Solow believes that, given the alternatives, guidelines have a role to play.

In October 1978 the United States once again turned to guidelines, an outline of which is presented in "Fact Sheet on Inflation." Although the program is voluntary, if an industry does not comply, certain government actions are "triggered" that transform the voluntary controls into "enforcible voluntary" controls. The report card of these latest proposals is not yet in. Labor immediately rejected the program as inequitable and called for mandatory controls on all income, while business took a cautious wait-and-see approach. It is likely that the program will be subject to continuous modification as the government attempts to find a compromise acceptable to all.

The issues raised by wage-price controls have been raised many times in the past, and they will be raised again many times in the future. As you read these selections, carefully consider the following questions: Are the administrative problems of controls surmountable? If they are, are they worth the costs? Must controls affect relative prices? What other forms could controls take? Do guidelines avoid the problems posed by direct controls? Do they do any good at all? Is the decision about controls a political or an economic question?

Exhortation and Controls:
The Search for a Wage-Price Policy

CRAUFURD D. GOODWIN

Craufurd D. Goodwin, a specialist in economic history, is currently a professor of economics at Duke University. A member of the Brookings Institution associated staff, he has made penetrating and objective analyses of the history of wage and price controls. In this article, excerpted from the introduction of a book of the same name that he edited, he briefly reviews the history of anti-inflation policy in the United States.

Every president from Truman on has faced inflation as a major problem of his administration and has had to construct a policy for its solution. Truman was compelled initially to administer and then to dismantle a complex system of controls during the first few months after World War II. He returned to controls at the time of the Korean outbreak. In between, he and his advisers wrestled with threats of both recession and secular inflation, conditions that they saw as lingering clouds on the American horizon. Of the five presidents [through Nixon] only Truman faced a full three-pronged inflation caused by excess demand, cost-push, and worldwide shortages of food and raw materials, although Nixon in 1973 saw the deadly trilogy reappear. Eisenhower enjoyed a term of office during which prices were relatively stable and no specific tools of wage and price control were required. In this period, however, economists inside and outside government perceived what they took to be a new phenomenon, inflation and unemployment occurring together—the worst fears of the Truman years borne out. Even without excess demand, prices had a tendency to inch upward. The abbreviated Kennedy administration brought a new level of involvement of professional economists to the top ranks of the executive branch of government, as well as the reappearance of an inflationary threat and the formulation of a new "guidepost" strategy to deal with it. Under Johnson, guideposts and the vigorous presidential "jawboning" that accompanied them were put fully to the test, as provided by the Vietnam War. The Nixon administration in its early years responded to the policies of its predecessors by rejecting direct wage-price intervention and returning to exclusive dependence on fiscal and monetary policy and improvements in market efficiency. This approach ended abruptly with the unexpected announcement on August 15, 1971, of a mandatory system of controls....

A number of generalizations about the development of wage-price policy during the [postwar period are possible].[1] ... First, it is clear that as early as

[1] Editor's note: These generalizations were suggested by other essays in the book for which this selection serves as an introduction.

1945 and intermittently thereafter economists in and out of government were persuaded that inflation more than the prewar bogeys of unemployment and maldistribution of income could become the Achilles' heel of a free-price economy. Price stability, they concluded, simply might not be consistent with the economic and social institutions that characterize a modern democracy, especially strong trade unions, oligopolistic industries, and a public commitment to full employment. Predictably, concern about the dangers of secular inflation fluctuated directly with changes in the price level, but after extended periods of price increases such as the late 1940s and late 1960s attention turned seriously to systemic explanations. That moderate inflation might be permanently consistent with substantial levels of unemployment was clearly perceived by the late 1950s. Because of America's self-image throughout the period as the economic as well as the political leader of the noncommunist world, secular inflation was seen to be perilous not only for the domestic economy but for the entire international economic order as well.

The weight given to various ill effects of inflation varied over the three decades. Truman perceived the main danger as being the depression that had always before followed inflation, and could be expected to do so again. He and members of his administration did discuss and worry about the hardships imposed on segments of society by inflation, but his chief worry continued to be that what goes up too rapidly must come down with a crash. During the next three presidents' administrations the effects of inflation on international competitiveness and the balance of payments joined its other costs at center stage. During the latter part of the Nixon administration, when inflation at near-record peacetime rates had been sustained for some time, concern about massive citizen unrest occasioned by real or imagined hardships was uppermost.

Matching the perception of the profound dangers of inflation was abiding faith in the capacity of reasonable men to do something about it. This faith found expression in three directions. First, from the beginning of the thirty-year period until the end presidents were advised to bring together leaders of those segments of the economy that allegedly contributed to the inflation problem—above all, big business and big labor—so that in some sort of cooperative fashion they could solve this public problem. The repeated failure of labor-management conferences and committees under both Democratic and Republican administrations did not dampen the enthusiasm for this device (the most recent example being the conference on inflation of September 1974). Second, the power of public opinion was widely believed to be an effective restraint on "irresponsible" agents of inflation. If only the people were aware of the potentially inflationary impact of key decisions, this argument ran, they would rise in righteous wrath and smite the transgressor. The frequent proposals for advance notification of price increases was predicated mainly on this belief in the power of public opinion. Third, though in different degrees under different presidents, presidential advisers had firm faith in the capacity of economic science to find answers to this as to other economic problems. Confidence was probably greatest during the administrations of Kennedy and Johnson, but [what is striking throughout this period] is the persistent optimism of both economists and consumers of economics despite the seeming intractability of the problems with which the science dealt.

A wide range of explanations and solutions for inflation were advanced within the government. To some extent the weight attached to each depended on the doctrinal convictions and political persuasions of the proponents. Keynesian, or "liberal," economists tended to lean toward cost-push explanations and advocated various techniques of threat and persuasion to restrain noncompetitive industrial sectors from raising their prices. They roundly rejected an increase in unemployment as a cure for inflation, but they did favor tax increases and see controls as a last-choice alternative. "Neoclassical," or conservative, economists, on the other hand, were more inclined to blame labor than business, and they tended to favor monetary and fiscal policy, especially a reduction of government expenditures, as a means of reducing effective demand; except during the aberration of the first Nixon administration they vigorously opposed all controls. This distinction among "types" of economists according to their views on wage-price policy is by no means neat and clear. As time went on and all devices and explanations were found to have their weaknesses, the distinction became more a matter of emphasis than of firm conviction.

During periods when monetary and fiscal policy seemed incapable of halting inflation, not only were controls seriously contemplated but earnest discussions took place about whether systemic changes had occurred in the American and world economies that made inflation inevitable. It was feared that changes of at least four types might have taken place: a growth of monopolistic elements' power so great that prices were flexible only upward; a commitment of governments to full employment (and the related "fine tuning") so strong that resistance to price and wage restraints in key markets had been weakened; a shift in production toward services in which improvements in efficiency were few; and a new ethos among workers that demanded rising money wages and declining effort regardless of changes in productivity. To the extent that analysts accepted systemic explanations for inflation they tended to turn toward such long-run alternatives as antitrust action, labor market reform, and education or reinvigoration of the work force.

Unexpected developments in foreign affairs repeatedly had a marked effect on the evolution of wage-price policy. In most cases international conflicts or fear of involvement therein brought sharp increases in military expenses. These developments led repeatedly to use or serious contemplation of direct controls in the face of inadequate monetary and fiscal policies, such as prevailed during the Korean War and in the aftermath of Vietnam. The sudden end of World War II, of course, was the reverse of the other situations. Then public relief at the conclusion of hostilities led to premature abandonment of controls. In at least one case—the Berlin crisis of 1961—President Kennedy was able to take advantage of the public sense of emergency to turn away from direct controls and make informal restraints more effective.

Perhaps the single most controversial element of wage-price policy in the postwar period has been the practice of direct intervention by the executive in pricing decisions. Arguments against this practice were proffered early and were often repeated. Above all, critics noted, such arbitrary actions by the government were inconsistent with a competitive economic system; if competition was inadequate the correct approach was antitrust action or regulation, not hectoring of the monopolies.

Moreover, presidential intervention, or "jawboning" as it came to be called, seemed manifestly inequitable on several counts. Usually a few very visible "key" industries of high concentration were singled out for special attention. Labor complained that collective bargaining was especially vulnerable while the pricing of many goods on which workers depended remained inviolate. Moreover, pressure was almost always against the price-raiser, seldom against those who failed to lower prices. Above all, the critics said, it was paradoxical that "public-spirited" price-makers in the economy who responded cooperatively to executive intervention should suffer by receiving lower prices for their goods while "unpatriotic" price-makers gained from their lack of cooperation.

Despite the obvious weaknesses of and objections to jawboning, it was used in varying degrees by every administration examined here. Certain sectors of the economy were selected for special attention either because they were the focus of consumer interest (e.g., automobiles and meat), because they seemed to be a determinant of national growth (e.g., steel or petroleum), or because they exhibited low elasticity of supply (e.g., housing). In labor markets, to preserve equity, the concept of average productivity gains as a basis for awards was developed under Truman and grew into the celebrated wage "guideposts" of the Kennedy and Johnson years.

The place of economic growth in the fight against inflation presented yet more uncertainties for presidential advisers. It seemed that upward pressures on prices increased at near full capacity and this provided one argument against excessive stimulation of the economy. On the other hand, average costs could be expected to decline in the long run with economies of scale and growth in output. Moreover, in the short run there was danger that too much restraint, as well as too little, would be inflationary by forcing producers into uneconomic small runs. All administrations reached the conclusion that, other things being equal, a level of economic activity near to full capacity but not quite at it was most conducive to price stability. Some Council members, such as Leon Keyserling under Truman, became known especially for their emphasis on full employment and growth as the best conditions for fighting inflation.

A subtheme [found in this period] is the increasing use of professional economists in government, not only in the Council of Economic Advisers but as presidential aides, specialists throughout the executive branch, and even as cabinet officers. At times, the evolving role of the CEA was closely tied to the development of wage-price policy. In offering advice about the control of inflation the Council often found itself at a great disadvantage because of limited or false information about defense or foreign policy. Moreover, in the implementation of guidepost restraints and jawboning the Council was drawn away from its staff advisory function toward the tasks of an administrative agency or, as suggested by one Council chairman, an economic "general staff." The hope of some members was that the Council would deal with strategy rather than with tactics, but this distinction was never clearly drawn. The varying styles of the several councils must be noted, the result in part of differences in presidential preference and in part of the differences of the Council members themselves. Relations with leaders of the economics profession were one indication of Council style; these varied from distant during the Truman years to remarkably close under Kennedy. As the years went on it became increasingly difficult for any president to contemplate economic policy formation seriously without professional advice. But whether he took it from a single source or many, direct or in digested form through a nonprofessional filter, had a marked influence on the result. The Councils' relations with the public also varied. In general it appears that the Councils that enjoyed the greatest intimacy with their presidents found it most difficult to serve other constituencies. Candor with the public became impossible when policy adviser became policy determiner.

A striking feature of the whole story recorded here is the short institutional memory of the economic advisory arms of government. Repeatedly, circumstances and policy measures, whether labor-management conferences or productivity rules, were discussed as if they had never occurred or been proposed before. The phenomenon is largely the result of the presidential form of government wherein each new chief executive brings in his own advisers and sweeps out the old. Nevertheless the observer cannot help wondering if more provision for the accumulation of wisdom and experience might not be valuable. To an important degree this function was performed in an informal way by a dozen or so prominent persons who appeared to deal with wage-price problems in several administrations: for example, Gardner Ackley, Arthur F. Burns, Gerhard Colm, John T. Dunlop, Kermit Gordon, Walter W. Heller, John P. Lewis, Paul W. McCracken, Arthur M. Okun, Walter S. Salant, Charles L. Schultze, Herbert Stein, Robert C. Turner, and Henry C. Wallich. But should an important social system have to depend on such accidents of fate?

It is common for historians to experience acute feelings of *déjà vu* when working through an extended period of years. [A study of postwar wage-price policy] is not an account of human reason progressively discerning more clearly, understanding more completely, and conquering more effectively the complex problems of wage-price policy that face society. Rather, a repetitive cyclical development seems more accurately to characterize the story. Problems were discovered and then rediscovered. Solutions were tried and tried again, with varying degrees of success. "Guideposts" accompanied by jawboning are one example: they had roots in the Truman era, flowered under Kennedy and Johnson, and seem fated now for rebirth under President Ford. It would be hard for anyone to argue that wage-price policy at the end of [Nixon's] administration was demonstrably more enlightened than at the end of the first, or that the executive's understanding of the problems was a great deal more profound.

Humility may be an unfamiliar mask for economic advisers to wear. But an optimist may hope that the sobering experience of the past three decades will lay the basis for far greater progress in the next.

The Continuing Courtship
[Models and Limits of Wage-Price Policy]

ARNOLD R. WEBER

Arnold R. Weber, provost of Carnegie-Mellon University and dean of its Graduate School of Industrial Administration, served as executive director of the Cost of Living Council in 1971 in addition to his many other high-level government positions. He was later appointed a public member of the Pay Board. Professor Weber is the author of numerous articles and two books about the 1971–1974 controls, including *In Pursuit of Price Stability: The Wage-Price Freeze of 1971* and *The Pay Board's Progress: Wage Controls in Phase II* (together with Daniel J. B. Mitchell). In the following excerpt from his article "The Continuing Courtship," he recounts the various models and limits of wage-price policy.

MODELS OF WAGE-PRICE POLICY IMPLEMENTATION

... Four models of wage-price policy can be identified. These models link together objectives, elements of coverage, organizational arrangements, the nature of the standard, and sanctions. It cannot be said that the models are "rational" in the sense that they represent some efficient combination of variables to achieve the objective of controlling inflation. They do have a retrospective logic, however, in that they describe a consistent relationship between objectives, organization, and the other elements of wage-price policy.

The Decoy Model

The first model may be characterized as the "decoy model." Wage-price policies are articulated to divert political pressure for government action rather than as part of a serious effort to influence wage and price behavior. The objective of the program is stated in the most general terms so that they apply to every economic unit while having relevance for none. There is comprehensive coverage in principle but no effective coverage in fact, except when some egregious incident takes place. The standard is formulated in the broadest possible terms and may embrace slogans such as "responsibility," "discipline," or "restraint." Normally, a cabinet committee symbolizes the administration's dedication to price stability, although in some instances special organizations are established to "monitor and review" price and wage developments. Sanctions are limited to exhortation and expressions of concern. To a large degree, the decoy model is an anti–wage-price-policy model.

The decoy model was unveiled during the Eisenhower administration, refined in the early part of the Nixon administration, and revived by President

Ford. In each case, the President and his economic advisers were reluctant to go beyond expressions of concern and calls for responsibility. No specific targets for government intervention or criteria for such actions were identified. Well-publicized organizations were established, such as the Cabinet Committee on Price Stability, the National Commission on Productivity, and the Council on Wage and Price Stability. There was no hint of pressure other than presidential brow-lifting.

The Defensive Model

The second combination of elements may be called the "defensive model." Here the general objective is to provide a reserve capability to intervene in particular wage and price decisions that are highly visible or identified as engendering inflationary pressures. The defensive model is especially suited to circumstances in which wage-price policy is used to support expansionist policies. Coverage is universal in principle, but in fact the policies are applicable primarily to large economic units in basic industries. A criterion for responsible behavior is defined but left in imprecise form, allowing the executive to use discretion in determining when to intervene and when not to. In implementing the program, the President will call on the existing agencies of government whose efforts will be coordinated on an ad hoc basis by some central unit, normally the Council of Economic Advisers. The sanctions employed may encompass the full range of government influence and authority, such as threats of prosecution under the antitrust laws, stockpile disposal, and so on.

The defensive model was used during the Kennedy administration and, with a few modifications, properly characterizes Phases III and IV during the Nixon administration. The Nixon case is especially interesting because here a formal regulatory system was turned into a defensive program by executive action. Although the stabilization program was founded on statutory authority, Phase III was unveiled as an exercise in self-regulation. Firms and unions were expected to conform to the existing regulations, but the "stick in the closet" was substituted for an assertive enforcement procedure. Since there was some friction between the underlying philosophy of Phases III and IV and the statutory framework within which the program was administered, an accelerated schedule of decontrol was pursued in an effort to ease it.

The Offensive Model

The third model is the "offensive model." In this case, wage-price policy is viewed as part of a serious effort to contain inflation even though it is not part of a legally based system. Coverage is broadly defined and the policy applied to sectors with a significant impact on price levels. Special administrative units are organized to link the process of review with the exercise of influence and sanctions. An effort is made to define a standard in more precise terms so that it establishes a trip point setting off government action. In effect, the executive branch is committed to act when decisions in designated sectors of the economy exceed the standard. This approach was employed during the Johnson administration when wage-price policy became a substitute for fiscal and monetary policies.

The Regulatory Model

The most robust variety of wage-price policy is the "regulatory model," in which there is an organized effort, supported by statutory authority, to directly regulate wage and price movements. Because it is founded on law, the model does not depend on positive intervention by the government. Instead, general compliance with the published standards and regulations is expected. Coverage tends to be broad and formal adjustments may be made from time to time in response to changing economic circumstances. The program is administered by self-contained agencies that usually enjoy independent status. Conventional legal sanctions for compliance, such as fines, injunctions, and criminal penalties, are available. The regulatory model has traditionally been most closely associated with wartime.

The only peacetime use of such a model was during Phases I and II of the Nixon administration, when it dealt with the consequences of extraordinary events and policies that transformed the position of the United States in the world economy. To the extent that there was a specific objective, it was to protect a highly stimulative policy and to suppress inflationary pressures as they built up in the economy. When the true test of the system of controls came at the beginning of 1973, the administration retreated to the defensive model before many shots had been fired.

These models are not of course prescriptive. Rather, they describe the various efforts that have been made to carry out wage-price policy. The primary impression is one of improvisation, with the blending of short-term economic requirements and political pressures, and resort to jerry-built organizational arrangements. If the purpose of wage-price policy has been to regulate the flow of economic events in the economy, it has been more analogous to sandbag embankments thrown up to resist flash floods than to dams built for the systematic control of the stream of wage and price decisions.

THE LIMITS OF WAGE-PRICE POLICY

Wage-price policy in the United States has now undergone thirty years of trial and error, and it is fair to say that there has been as much of the latter as the former. Even without a systematic (if not econometric) assessment of this policy's effectiveness, several deficiencies have been cast into sharp relief by this review.

First, there has been a consistent failure to develop a national consensus on the objectives of and rules governing wage-price policy. The preferred technique has been some variant of a labor-management committee. On more venturesome occasions, broadly constituted one-time conferences have been convened, bringing together representatives of diverse interest groups. The 1974 Summit Conference on Inflation was perhaps the most sophisticated of these endeavors.[1] Unfortunately, there is no evidence that these advisory committees or pseudo-parliamentary conclaves achieved anything approaching a durable

---

[1] The conference was held in Washington on September 27 and 28, 1974, and was attended by representatives of special interest groups, such as organized labor, agriculture, finance, and housing, and economists, all of whom had participated earlier in separate "mini conferences." No formal program was adopted.

consensus. Indeed, the record indicates that they have emphasized differences in interest rather than creating a common framework within which the interests could be harmonized. Nor can there by any optimism about the likelihood of defining such a consensus in the foreseeable future. Where the economy is organized on market principles of self-interest and these principles are extended into the political process, there is little prospect of agreement on the operational goals of wage-price policy except in wartime or when there is universal concern over impending catastrophe.

Second, wage-price policy has been unable to achieve an even-handed treatment of wages and prices. The imbalance has not been deliberate but rather a consequence of the particular administrative arrangements for the implementation of the policy. And though economic objectives may not require even-handedness, political factors make any deviation from uniformity perilous.

Wages have been most severely restrained under formal systems of control, and prices have borne the brunt of government actions under informal programs. The political consequences of this asymmetry have been magnified by the fact that wage-price policy has usually been cast in broad national terms, although no one realistically expects it to be applicable to all situations. Thus each instance of different treatment is viewed as evidence of class oppression rather than as an effort to deal with economic power or market deficiencies in particular cases. Different treatment may be accepted when it is related to "surgical" efforts to deal with problems in individual industries, but not when it is viewed as part of some national scheme for shifting power relations among economic groups.

Third, the quest for a standard that is comprehensive, equitable, and sufficiently precise for effective administration has been less than successful. The productivity concept serves a useful purpose in establishing the goals of wage-price policy, but it affords only limited guidance for their attainment and may even be mischievous in individual cases. By fastening on productivity as the dominant standard, price restraint has frequently been linked to wage restraint, although the relation between them should not be determinate. Aside from problems of measurement, the relevance of productivity as a sensible basis for wage and price decisions in the short run is diminished as one moves from the economy as a whole to untidy markets for specific goods and categories of labor. To a large extent, productivity has been an attractive operational standard because of its convenience in casual systems of administration rather than its applicability in specific cases.

Fourth, there has never been a sensible theory of coverage. Presumably, wage-price policy emerged as an attractive alternative because it could bridge the gap between the macroeconomic policies that would sustain high levels of growth and employment for the economy as a whole and wage-price decisions in particular cases. These links have never been carefully identified. Consequently, wage-price policy administrators have turned almost as a reflex to the same set of industries. If the steel industry had not existed, it probably would have been invented for the convenience of the chairman of the Council of Economic Advisers. Wage-price policy has invariably been brought to bear on steel and automobiles, although the health services industry may now have a more consequential effect on the general price level.

Last, the organizational arrangements for carrying out wage-price policy have had all the continuity of a pickup volleyball team. For the most part, wage-price policy has been administered by a cast of thousands drawn from different agencies at different times. Because the objectives, coverage, and legal authority associated with wage-price policy have never been clearly established on a continuing basis, the organizational arrangements have had a consistent quality of improvisation.

Inflation and How to Overcome It

LEON H. KEYSERLING

Leon H. Keyserling, chairman of the Council of Economic Advisers under President Truman, is currently president of the Conference on Economic Progress. He has been extremely active in "behind the scenes" politics in Washington and deserves primary responsibility for the passage of the Humphrey-Hawkins Bill. Long critical of the use of monetary policy to fight inflation, he argues that growth, long-term planning, and controls, if necessary, are the answer. The following selection is excerpted from his pamphlet "Recession, Inflation, and How to Overcome Both."

GROWTH, EMPLOYMENT, AND INFLATION

. . . During 1947–1953, the average annual rate of real economic growth was 4.9 percent. Average annual unemployment was 4.0 percent, but it was reduced to 2.9 percent in the last year, compared with 3.9 percent in the first year. Average annual inflation was only 3.0 percent, and it was reduced from 7.8 percent in the first year to 0.8 percent in the last year, with the help of moderate price controls during the Korean war. (To allow for the momentum of policy effects, the first year of any new Administration is also treated as the last year of its predecessor.)

During 1953–1961, the average annual rate of real economic growth, punctuated by three recessions, was only 2.4 percent. The average annual unemployment rate was 5.1 percent, and rose from 2.9 percent in the first year to 6.7 percent in the last. The very poor record with respect to production and unemployment would have been far too high a price to pay for an average annual rate of price inflation of 1.4 percent. Be this as it may, with recessions and high unemployment becoming an almost chronic state of affairs, the rate of price inflation was about two and a half times as high in 1961 as in 1953.

During 1961–1969, the average annual rate of real economic growth was 4.8 percent. Due to the 6.7 percent unemployment inherited in the first year, the average annual unemployment rate was 4.7 percent, but it was reduced to 3.5 percent in the last year. The average annual rate of price inflation during 1961–1966, years averaging vigorous real economic growth, was only 1.5 percent. Thereafter through 1969, the average annual rate of real economic growth was only 3.3 percent, and only 2.7 percent from 1968 to 1969, while price inflation accelerated greatly, and price inflation reached 5.4 percent in 1969. Besides the slowdown in growth, other factors in this inflation were large tax reductions in 1964, the intensification of the Vietnam war in 1965 and 1966, and sharp but temporary increases in grain prices due to huge shipments to India in response to severe drought there. But even so, the average annual rate of inflation was only 2.6 percent for the period 1961–1969 as a whole.

Leon H. Keyserling, "Inflation and How to Overcome It," from *Recession, Inflation, and How to Overcome Both*, a study prepared for the Coalition for a Democratic Majority, pp. 5–13. Reprinted by permission of the author.

The period from the start of 1969 through 1974 witnessed the practical application of the atrocious thesis that the way to restrain inflation is to direct hammerblows against employment and production. In consequence of two planned recessions, the average annual rate of real economic growth was only 2.5 percent. The average unemployment rate was 5.1 percent, and rose from 3.5 percent in the first year to 5.6 percent in 1974 and 8.2 percent in January 1975. The average annual rate of price inflation was 6.1 percent, and rose from 5.9 percent in the first year to 12.2 percent in 1974.*

THE "TRADE-OFF" THEORY MUST BE ABANDONED

[With respect to inflation] there is a *dilemma* which really exists only in consequence of confused thinking and cross-purposes. It is said that more vigorous actions cannot be taken to restraain inlation because that would increase unemployment still more and reduce production still more. Simultaneously, it is said that more vigorous and effective measures cannot be taken to reduce unemployment and increase production, to meet our domestic needs and to do social justice, because this would increase inflation. Impaled upon the horns of this dilemma, national economic policy is not moving decisively on either front.

There are three basic reasons why the entire concept of this dilemma, the concept of the "trade-off" between inflation and unemployment, is as wrong as it can be.

In the first place, for empirical reasons already set forth fully, measures to curb inflation should not involve the terrible risks of skating for another year or longer on the thin ice of aggravated recession and increased unemployment. Nobody can be wise enough to forecast that this course might not lead to a breakthrough of depressionary rather than recessionary magnitudes, though nothing equal to the Great Crash.

Second, the attempt to accomplish a different trend in prices at the expense of real economic growth, employment and production, and domestic priorities and social needs, is egregiously unmindful of the true function of prices. No particular range of price trends should be our overwhelming objective to the neglect of all else. Those price trends—whether up or down or stable—are desirable which optimize real economic growth, production, and employment, attend to priorities, and do social justice through the impact of prices (along with money income trends) upon income distribution, and thus upon resource allocation.

If the actual amount of price inflation which we averaged annually during 1969–1974 (6.1 percent) had been accompanied by successful programs to maintain full employment and production, distribute income equitably, and meet our priority needs, we would have been infinitely better off than we are now, even though not as well off as if we had achieved these other purposes with less inflation. But the *same* amount of price inflation, abetted by policies deliberately contrived to defeat all of these great purposes in the name of curbing inflation, has been cruel, stupid, and indefensible.

*The period 1974–1978 gave much further empirical support for the position I take based upon 1947–1974. LHK, January 1979.

Third, and most important of all, the long experience of the U.S. economy, as detailed above, proves conclusively that *a fully healthy and/or advancing U.S. economy nets tremendously less price inflation in the long run than a weak and faltering American economy, moving downward instead of upward.*

The reasons for this are also clear. In the "administered price" sectors of the economy, there is a pronounced and persistent attempt to compensate, through higher prices, for inadequate volume of sales. Stagnation and recession greatly reduce productivity or output per man-hour; the resultant increases in *per unit* costs foment price increases. The shortages, selective and general—induced or aggravated by contrived restraints on growth—augment inflation, excellent examples being housing and medical care. Both the ups and downs of a roller-coaster economic performance spawn business uncertainties which release "protective" or "anticipatory" price increases.

The implications for immediate and long-range national economic and social policies and programs are equally clear. We must move at once toward full economic restoration *and* much greater price stability. Both are necessary, and neither is feasible without the other.

The foregoing analysis, in its entirety, points up the need for the following . . .

GOALS, GROWTH, AND THE ENVIRONMENT

The President,* in the very nature of our political system and traditions, should set forth, for consideration by the Congress and the people, *an immediate and long-range program, comprehensive in nature, and directed toward restoration of maximum employment, production, and purchasing power by the end of 1976, or shortly thereafter.* This should consist of:

1. Establishing quantitative goals for maximum employment and production, as required by the Employment Act of 1946, through 1976 at least. This should be accompanied by quantitative delineation of the broad allocations of resources and incomes or purchasing power which will bring the economy back into balance, meet priority needs, and do social justice. This is not an undoable task: it has been done successfully in the past in times of unusual stress and strain, such as during World War II and the Korean war.

2. Improvement of the environment is essential. *But the no-growth or low-growth thesis, advanced in some influential quarters on environmental and other grounds, should be rejected in its entirety.* Low-growth and no-growth brings economic and social evils (of which massive unemployment and immense production forfeitures are first among many) which tremendously exceed the allegedly undesirable byproducts of optimum growth. Environmental improvement, requiring immense amounts of new investment, is not feasible without optimum growth, or would be feasible without such growth only by further sacrifice of other high priority programs, including housing, education, and health.

*EDITOR'S NOTE: This study was made during Gerald Ford's administration.

MONETARY POLICY

3. Excessively tight credit and intolerably high interest rates should be resisted by all available means, because the current monetary policy has many inflationary impacts, is grossly discriminatory, and is highly inimical to production and employment. This change requires Congressional legislation and Presidential action, and even the initiation of such measures might bring much pressure to bear upon the Federal Reserve. The virtual "independence" of the Federal Reserve System violates every principle of ultimate responsibility to the elected representatives of the people. The Federal Reserve System should be mandated to increase the money supply in accord with the real economic growth required to restore maximum employment and production by the end of 1976, or shortly later, and to maintain it thereafter. During 1974–1976, the average annual growth in the money supply should be 8–10 percent. Such a monetary policy in itself would reduce all interest rates greatly. In addition, the Federal Reserve System should be required to achieve vastly more credit availability and vastly lower interest rates in areas of national priority need, including shortage areas, accompanied by relatively less expansion of credit and less reduction of interest rates with respect to less essential or postponable activities. This course would also be anti-inflationary.

TAXATION AND SPENDING

4. Earlier in the discussion, it was pointed out that the economy as a whole was operating at the start of 1975 at an annual rate of at least 125 billion dollars below full production, measured in fourth quarter 1974 dollars. Allowing for the continuous growth in the labor force and in productivity, it is estimated that to restore full employment and full production by the end of 1976 or shortly thereafter the annual rate of total national production, measured in fourth quarter 1974 dollars, should be about 302 billion dollars higher in fourth quarter 1976 than in fourth quarter 1974. This requires an average annual real economic growth rate of 9.1 percent during 1974–1976, and 4.7 percent during 1976–1980. Times in the past demonstrated this to be attainable.

Very powerful stimulants, injected at the Federal level, are now needed to open up any reasonable prospects for full economic restoration by the end of 1976, or shortly thereafter. If the public service employment program reached one million jobs, this would provide a stimulus somewhere in the range of 8 billion dollars, annual rate. It is recommended that an additional Federal stimulus of about 32 billion should be provided, bringing the total stimulus up to about 40 billion. Even using a very high "multiplier" of 3, this 40 billion stimulus would add somewhere in the neighborhood of 120 billion to GNP, a quite conservative effort in view of the 302 billion expansionary task and the prospect of further inflation. This additional stimulus should be divided reasonably between the right kind of tax cuts and the right kind of increases in spending. Perhaps 16 billion dollars of each might be a good starting point, but many other divisions between the two would be workable. *Excessive emphasis upon tax cuts, to the detriment of increases in spending for high priority purposes, would be extremely hurtful to many nationwide economic and social needs.* The

President's threat to veto all new increases in spending programs, and to cut back some existing programs, is dangerous beyond description.

5. The tax cuts should concentrate upon reducing the Federal tax burden on lower-middle and low-income families. This would help to relieve the worst victims of inflation and recession, and would have other equitable consequences. It would also be more efficient than other kinds of tax cutting toward expansion of production and employment, because those in the lower half of the income structure spend immediately a larger part of their tax incomes, and save relatively less, than those higher up in the income structure. Generally speaking, there is no large need for further general tax incentives to business investors, because adequate demand by private consumers and in the form of public outlays would assure at least adequate profits and investment at existing price levels. Some selective tax incentives, and low interest rate loans furnished or backed by the Federal Government, appear clearly desirable—for housing, the utilities, and bottle neck areas (such as production of drilling and coal mining equipment, and coal car production). As tax reductions of the type recommended are so immediately and urgently needed, they should not await simultaneous enactment of other types of tax reforms. As soon as feasible, however, vigorous efforts should be made to recoup revenuewise a part of the tax reductions, by closing glaring loopholes and, if need be, through increases in corporate rates and in the upper ranges of the personal income structure. These recoupments would tend to bring the economy into better balance, and therefore would not have repressive effects upon production and employment comparable to the stimulative impact of the tax reductions.

6. The increases in the spending side of the Federal Budget, beyond the increases in the President's 1976 Budget, should be directed toward meeting the priorities of our national needs and toward overcoming selective shortages, for it is manifest that this phase of the task cannot be accomplished by stimuli in the form of tax reduction. There may be room in the Budget to compensate for a substantial portion of this increased spending by safe and sound cuts elsewhere in the Budget, and such cuts would not have a repressive effect upon production and employment comparable to the stimulative effect of the increased spending. Greatly reduced interest rates, for example, could over time save tens of billions of dollars in the Federal Budget each year. The proposed changes in the Federal Budget would increase production and employment, improve the servicing of priority needs, and have anti-inflationary effects, especially by alleviating acute shortages.

A Budget balance, or even a surplus to reduce the national debt, is manifestly a desirable goal in the longer run. But reckless slashing of the wrong parts of the Budget, under current recessionary conditions, is both inflationary and hurtful to production and employment. The President estimates a Budget deficit of about 35 billion dollars in fiscal 1975, and about 52 billion in fiscal 1976. The safest and surest road toward reducing the then erasing the Federal deficit, as all experience cited herein shows, is vigorous movement toward the then achievement of full utilization of our ever-growing and now sorely underutilized production capabilities. This would balance the Budget, under the spending and tax proposals set forth herein, shortly after calendar 1976. If the altered fiscal program and other programs herein proposed should add to inflationary pressures—the reverse is more likely—additional taxes should be selectively imposed, along progressive lines, and unnecessary or postponable spending should be further reduced, instead of short changing priority domestic programs.

The spending side of the Federal Budget should always allocate to the national priorities, which the Budget should serve, *the proper portion of estimated total national production at maximum levels of production and employment.* When we are actually below such levels, such allocation will have the additional value of stimulating the economy. When we are at or above such levels, we should not reduce priority programs, but instead should use the tax side of the Federal Budget to combat inflation.

CONTROLS

7. The foregoing programs and policies, partly by virtue of the economic restoration which they would bring about and partly in the other ways cited, would be the best way to cut inflation by more than half within a year's time, and reduce it to 3.0 percent by the end of 1976. But if the viewpoint remains prevalent that essential economic restorative efforts would make more difficult the reduction of inflation in the short run, we should not shy away from adequate controls. When the need was great enough in the past to call for mandated controls, during some earlier Administrations, they were administered successfully. There is an understandable reluctance to entrust controls once again to the current Administration, which distrusts controls, and whose immediate predecessor used them so unwisely.

However, if controls were to be restored, they would need to be different in kind, and not merely in degree, from those recently used with deplorable effects. Under the immediately previous Administration, controls were used *only* in a vain endeavor to restrain inflation at the expense of production, employment, and social justice. They were thus so inequitable that they fed the fat and starved the lean, through restraining real wage-rate gains excessively and winking at price-profit extortion. They thus injured the economy severely and aggravated the burden of inflation by redistributing income in a grossly inequitable manner.

An approriate effort under mandated controls, if resorted to, should be administered not only to restrain inflation. It should also be applied flexibly and fairly in pursuit of defined goals for full employment and production, priorities, and social justice. And for reasons of equity and economic balance, any such controls, if adopted, should be across-the-board, including prices, wages, dividends, and rent. In addition to the controls, the program should include an excess profits tax, which in earlier times helped to prevent excessive price-profit surges. There should be no removal of such controls as now exist on some oil prices, and no deregulation of natural gas. Although mandated controls, if adopted, should leave reasonable room for Executive discretion, there should in any event be legislated ceilings on interest rates with respect to housing and some other high priority programs, along with selective credit instruments for such programs. This balanced and equitable approach to controls, and this only, can elicit the public support essential to their success in our democracy. Consideration should be given to whether such controls, if adopted, should be administered by the current Administration or by an independent agency, in either event with Congressional mandates and standards.

The power of concentrated industries works at many times to subvert the "ideal" and self-repairing operation of the price system. The unjustifiable raising of prices creates vast economic imbalances, and also brings on the "price-wage" spiral. Thus, a price-guided program with teeth in it, whether we have general controls or not, is needed throughout the "cycle" for a few hundred of our largest corporations. This calls for a permanent public system of price monitoring accompanied by *subpoena* powers, at least with respect to key industries of a quasi-monopolistic nature. This might be accompanied by the authority to impose selective price controls or at least deferral of price increases.

At the very least, public investigatory powers and hearings should be used to direct more immediate public attention to price practices and trends.*

*The Humphrey-Hawkins Full Employment and Balanced Growth Act of 1978 embodies the approaches I recommend, but President Carter's January 1979 Budget Message and Economic Report, in my view, categorically violate the law of the land and espouse once again a set of policies tried and failed several times since 1953. LHK, January 1979.

Money: Whence It Came, Where It Went

JOHN KENNETH GALBRAITH

John Kenneth Galbraith has been a professor of economics at both Harvard
University and Trinity College, Cambridge, and is probably the most famous
"internal" critic of the economics profession. It has often been suggested that he
cannot really be an economist because he writes too well! He is, in fact, an excellent
economist and has served as president of the American Economic Association.
Among his many books are *The Affluent Society* (1958), *The New Industrial State*
(1967), and *Money: Whence It Came, Where It Went* (1975). The following selection
is the afterword to the latter.

. . . If anything is evident from . . . history, it is that the task [of managing
money] attracts a very low level of talent, one that is protected in its highly
imperfect profession by the mystery that is thought to enfold the subject of
economics in general and of money in particular. Inadequacy is protected
further, we have seen, by the fact that failure is almost never at cost to those
responsible. More often it has been an interesting subject for discussion, something that has given an added dimension to personality.

Finally, in monetary matters as in diplomacy, a nicely conformist nature, a
good tailor and the ability to articulate the currently fashionable financial
cliché have usually been better for personal success than an excessively inquir-
ing mind. Effective action and associated thought provoke fear and criticism. It
is for these and not the result that the individual is likely to be remembered. So,
in the management of money, as in economic management generally, failure is
often a more rewarding personal strategy than success.

There is reluctance in our time to attribute great consequences to human
inadequacy—to what, in a semantically less cautious era, was called stupidity.
We wish to believe that deeper social forces control all human action. There is
always something to be said for tolerance. But we had better be aware that
inadequacy—obtuseness combined with inertness—is a problem. Nor is it
inevitable. In the past, economic policy has been successful. We must assume
that it was successful not by happy accident but because informed and energetic
people made it so.

It will be no easier in the future than in the past for the layman or the lay
politician to distinguish between the adequate individual and the others. But
there is no difficulty whatever in distinguishing between success and failure.
Henceforth it should be the simple rule in all economic and monetary matters
that anyone who has to explain failure has failed. We should be kind to those
whose performance has been poor. But we must never be so gracious as to keep
them in office.

None of this is to suggest that success will be easy. Among the lessons from this history two stand out. The first is that the problem of money has not become fully coordinate with that of the economy, even with that of the polity. The second is that economic performance which a hundred years ago would have been accepted as inevitable and fifty years ago as tolerable is no longer accepted. What was then misfortune is now failure.

Specifically, in the last century and before, money was important. Corporations had no general power to move prices. Unions effectively did not exist. The taxes and expenditures of national states were controlled by the exigencies of war and peacetime need, not by what was required for the right kind of economic performance. What was used as money and how much there was of it made a difference; the instinct of the men who followed [free-silver advocate William Jennings] Bryan (and of those who opposed him) was not wrong.

In modern times, we have seen, the national budget has become a decisive factor in economic performance. It extensively determines whether demand will expand, prices rise, unemployment increase and—in consequence of government borrowing and the resulting deposit creation—whether the supply of money will expand. And beyond the budget is the power of unions and corporations directly to affect prices and, more than incidentally, to negate the restrictive effect of monetary and budget policy. As we have sufficiently seen, it is well within the scope of union and corporate power and advantage to shove up costs and prices while demand in the economy is shrinking and unemployment rising. Thus the distinctly disenchanting tendency in the modern economy for recession to be combined with inflation.

Corporate and trade-union power raise the further question of the distribution of power as a whole in the modern state and of the sovereignty of modern governments. And implicit in the effort to exercise such power by the state is a decision as to how income will be distributed. Thus monetary policy has become but a minor part of the whole economic policy. And economic policy has become an aspect of politics—of the question of who exercises power, who controls the rewards.

Nor is this all. We have seen that currencies now accumulate in large agglomerations outside the country of issue—the Eurodollars and the Petrodollars being the recent cases in point. And the transnational bank and the transnational corporation which hold or own these accumulations can move them into other currencies and out again in a volume that is far beyond the remedial and stabilizing capacity of existing machinery for monetary stabilization. Thus the modern problem of monetary management has a much greater international dimension than ever before.

There is a yet further problem. As the recent examples of petroleum and food amply show, supply and demand in the modern economy are now brought into equilibrium only after large movements in prices and in income. These have an extensive, unstabilizing effect on domestic price levels and international exchange rates. So stable prices and stable international exchanges also require action to prevent disruptive movements in the prices of individual products of major importance. This task too transcends national boundaries, goes beyond the reach of national authority.

Finally, to repeat, what served as adequate performance in the past is acceptable no longer. After the Napoleonic Wars in Britain and the Civil War in the United States, steps were taken to restore monetary stability and re-establish specie payments. Farm prices fell sharply. There was some increase in unemployment. There was much complaint but it was not operative. Economic hardship was then far from unnatural. Low prices, low wages and loss of jobs were not precisely acts of God. But they were not yet acts of government. Now, needless to say, they are.

Nothing, or anyhow not much, lasts forever. But what is well established is likely to last for a long time. So the forces that have shaped past policy (or which past policy has resisted), if they have been correctly identified in this history, will, one may assume, continue to operate for at least a while in the future. They are, in the fullest sense, historical imperatives. This means that they are not matters for ideological preference as commonly imagined. To see economic policy as a problem of choice between rival ideologies is the greatest error of our time. Only rarely, and usually on matters of secondary importance, do circumstances vouchsafe this luxury. Far more often, institutions and historical circumstance provide the same straitjacket for liberals and conservatives, socialists and men of avowedly medieval mind. What works for one works for all. What fails for one is abysmal for all.

If the near future is an extension of the near and more distant past, there are six imperatives that will shape or control monetary policy and the larger economic policy of which it is now a lesser part. These are:

1. The perverse unusefulness of monetary policy and the frustrations and danger from relying on it. This is perhaps the clearest lesson of the recent past. The management of money is no longer a policy but an occupation. Though it rewards those so occupied, its record of achievement in this century has been patently disastrous. It worsened both the boom and the depression after World War I. It facilitated the great bull market of the 1920s. It failed as an instrument for expanding the economy during the Great Depression. When it was relegated to a minor role during World War II and the good years thereafter, economic performance was, by common consent, much better. Its revival as a major instrument of economic management in the late '60s and early '70s served to combine massive inflation with serious recession. And it operated with discriminatory and punishing effect against, not surprisingly, those industries that depend on borrowed money, of which housing is the leading case. To argue that it was a success may well be beyond even the considerable skills of its defenders. Only the enemies of capitalism will hope that, in the future, this small, perverse and unpredictable lever will be a major instrument in economic management.

The central bank remains important for useful tasks—the clearing of checks, the replacement of worn and dirty banknotes, as a loan source of last resort. These tasks it performs well. With other public agencies in the United States, it also supervises the subordinate commercial banks. This is a job which it can do well and needs to do better. In recent years the regulatory agencies, including the Federal Reserve, have relaxed somewhat their vigilance. At the same time numerous of the banks have been involved in another of the age-old spasms of optimism and feckless expansion. The result could be a new round of failures. It is to such matters that the Federal Reserve needs to give its attention.

These tasks apart, the reputation of central bankers will be the greater, the less responsibility they assume. Perhaps they can lean against the long wind—resist a little and increase rates when the demand for loans is persistently great, reverse themselves when the reverse situation holds. But, in the main, control must be—as it was in the United States during the war years and the good years following—over the forces which cause firms and persons to seek loans and not over whether they are given or not given the loans.

It should be noted, in fairness, that the ineffectiveness, if not the danger, of monetary policy is being recognized by men of candid mind within the System. The President of the Federal Reserve Bank of New York has noted that the quantity of money, the magnitude of primary concern to those who have placed their faith in monetary policy, cannot effectively be measured. He has noted also that its short-run movements cannot be controlled, and also that such movements are without significant economic effect.[1] Not much hope for monetary policy remains, especially when it is remembered that all action must be taken in the short run, that long-run change is the aggregation of short-run changes. Similarly a recent Governor of the Federal Reserve System has observed that "... good monetary policy depends upon admitting how much we do not know [about the management of money.]"[2] There is a strong case against relying on an instrument or an innovation of widespread but unknown effects. The examples of atomic energy, supersonic transport and even Freon gas come to mind.

Still, what happens when there is reliance on monetary policy is not all that unknown. The record has been made; it is adverse.

2. The balancing factor in economic management will have to be the national budget, and the decisive need here is to overcome its presently fatal inelasticity for dealing with excess demand. This imperative lacks both novelty and subtlety. If monetary policy is unavailable for regulating aggregate demand in the economy, only fiscal policy remains. This, we have seen, operates with greater certainty than monetary policy for expanding demand; it was for this reason that it replaced monetary policy in the economists' faith during the Great Depression. And it operates with greater predictability of effect and much greater fairness for limiting demand. There is no grievous political or other problem in reducing taxes or increasing public outlays to expand aggregate demand. The Congress of the United States is especially cooperative and prompt when tax reduction is called for. Similarly, a sizable group of liberal economists resort, homeopathically, to tax reduction as a remedy for all ailments—even, on occasion, inflation. However, no similar enthusiasm is evident when a tax increase is required. Expenditure reduction is equally difficult, except as it invokes the oral enthusiasm of conservatives. And it operates against the high probability, one strongly believed by the present author, that civilian public needs in the United States are less amply supplied than the private consumption at least of the more affluent. There is the further structural difficulty that there is often, as in the case of construction and weapons procurement, a long

[1] Alfred Hayes, "Testing Time for Monetary Policy." An address before the New York State Bankers Association in New York City on January 20, 1975. One problem, among others, in measuring money supply, as noted by Mr. Hayes, involves savings deposits. These, increasingly, are interchangeable with, or indistinguishable from, deposits subject to check.

[2] Sherman J. Maisel, *Managing the Dollar* (New York: W. W. Norton & Co., 1973), p. 311.

lag between the decision to reduce an expenditure and the actual curtailment of outlays with its consequent effect on demand.

The solution, one which anyone who is uneasy about the excesses of executive power must come to with reluctance, is to separate the budget of the national government from the fiscal policy.[3] Expenditures would be determined and taxes established as now. One would hope this would be with a full and civilized appreciation of the need for a proper balance between public expenditure and private expenditure, public consumption and private consumption. Revenues would be expected to cover outlays so established when the economy was operating at approximately full employment levels. The taxes so set would redistribute income as deemed socially and economically desirable between income groups. Then authority for increases or decreases in taxes—within specified limits—would be allowed to the Executive purely for reasons of fiscal, i.e., larger economic, policy. These changes would be so designed as not greatly to alter the incidence of taxation as between different income groups.

3. Direct wage and price control where there is market power is inevitable. It should not be used where such power does not exist—in agriculture, small enterprise, where there are no unions. There regulation of aggregate demand must suffice. Controls reflect a policy which few wish to accept but which, wishes to the contrary, will not go away. As we have sufficiently seen, at or near full employment the market power of strong corporations and strong unions can create an inflationary dynamic of its own. And, we have seen, it has repeatedly done so. Though it is possible to arrest this inflationary thrust, it requires a greater recession and more unemployment than either compassion or the simple dictates of political survival will tolerate. As this goes to press, yet another effort to arrest inflation by use of monetary and fiscal policy is coming to an end. The resulting unemployment and recession are severe—far more painful than politicians of either party are willing to accept. And these consequences have appeared well in advance of the end of the inflation they were designed to cure. Inflation, at least for a period, is being combined with severe recession.

The only alternative to these unpleasant effects is for the government to intervene directly where there is market power—where there is the power by private action to increase prices and wages well before full employment and equally in face of falling demand. This removes from the private corporation a deeply cherished power. Similarly from the union. It confesses the error of much past and present economic instruction.[4] But again the straitjacket of circumstance. And so, in face of all the reluctance, the question of controls returns and returns again.[5]

---

[3] See the outline of this proposal in James Tobin, *The New Economics One Decade Older* (Princeton: Princeton University Press, 1974), p. 76 et seq. Impairment of the legislative authority over taxation is not something to be taken lightly. What is lacking is an alternative.

[4] Specifically it is in conflict with the general microeconomic assumption of competition and the view that the monopoly or oligopoly is responsive to reduced demand and not appreciably influenced by related horizontal movements in wage costs. And, of course, it is in conflict with the generally optimistic macroeconomic conclusion that fiscal and monetary policy will provide not an ideal but at least a tolerable reconciliation between employment and output on the one hand and price stability on the other.

[5] It must be emphasized again that this policy is useful only for the areas of the economy where there is market power. Recalling the discussion of the World War II experience, it fixes only prices that are already fixed. It is not useful and is in fact damaging if applied to such competitive markets as those for agricultural products, services, small enterprise generally or retailing.

4. Monetary and economic management are inextricably a part of the larger problem of income distribution in the modern economy. This too will become increasingly evident. Nothing is so attractive to the individual of conservative instinct as the thought that economic policy is a purely technical matter. No questions of social class or social policy are involved. Given the right technique—the skilled fine-tuning of Mr. Nixon's craftsmen—the economy is put right; power and income and their enjoyment remain unaffected. Liberals also have not been immune to the thought that monetary and fiscal policy—including the control of prices and incomes—are socially neutral.

It is not so. A central feature of modern economic society, we have seen, is the rejection by subordinate social classes of the prescriptive limits on their income and consumption. With this rejection go claims on production that cannot be met; from these claims comes inflation. If wages and therewith the consumption of blue-collar workers must be restrained in the interest of preventing claims on the economy that are beyond its capacity, the claims of other income recipients will also come up for consideration. What is required for profits, other property income, executive salaries, professional income will also be under examination. Nor will it be an answer that the consumption of the rich, or anyhow of the very rich, is a small part of the total. The question of equity—of some approach to equal treatment for all—is not less important than the aggregate of income involved. So movement toward a more consciously egalitarian income distribution will become an indispensable aspect of successful economic policy. We have sufficiently seen that successful policy will require restraint on trade-union claims. But there can be no future for a policy that selects wage- and salary-earners for such restriction and, however conveniently, leaves other claimants untouched.

5. Planning for the supply and conservation of use of important products and services will, increasingly, be an aspect of monetary and economic management. As noted, the movements in prices that are necessary to bring supply and use of important products—fuels, food, housing—into equilibrium can now be very great—great enough to put damaging strains on wage and price stability. The obvious remedy is to anticipate such shortages and, through public action, expand supply or reduce use. That such action has already been forced on modern governments in peacetime—and in the United States on an avowedly conservative administration—is a guide to expectation. (The character of the action is not changed by referring to planners as czars.) Since the problems of both supply and use are transnational, there will have to be cooperation between national planning authorities for these tasks. And supranational organization becomes a prospect. Again, notably in the cases of energy and food, circumstances are forcing the pace and, as ever, on those who are ideologically reluctant.

6. The problem of instability in international exchanges will recur; no more in the future than in the past will unpredictability seem a solution. International currency stabilization will, however, only be possible when national economies are stable—when the industrial countries have succeeded in combining reasonably high employment with tolerably stable prices. Until then all talk of international currency reform will be in a vacuum and can safely be ignored except by those whose employment depends on the discussion. It can be assumed that any future system will need lending capacity vastly in excess of the Bretton Woods system, even as it has been enlarged in recent times.[6] On the assumption that large blocs of mobile currencies will continue to accrue in the hands of banks, multinational corporations and (in lesser degree) free-lance speculators, eventual reform will have also to include some regulation of international currency movements.

There is another prospect—one for which we can profoundly pray. It is that policy in the future will be based not on forecasts but on the current reality. The reason for this we have sufficiently seen; not only is economic forecasting highly imperfect, something that is conceded even by the forecasters except when offering a new forecast, but official forecasting has an ineluctable tendency to error. On all but the rarest occasions it is biased by what policy-makers hope to have happen or need to have happen. Or, in the manner of the Vietnam war expenditures, it cannot contradict larger official promise. The solution is not better forecasts but prompt and unapologetic accommodation to what exists and prompt and unapologetic change when that no longer exists. In the late summer of 1974, Gerald Ford, newly arrived in the Presidency, proclaimed inflation the major threat to the American economy. Less than half a year later, with unemployment rising rapidly, production falling and prices leveling off, he proclaimed a recession to be the major threat. Such reversal of emphasis is not a confession of error. We should applaud prompt reaction to the current circumstance. The new President's error was not in changing his mind. It was in supposing that inflation could only be cured by recession—that the market power of corporations and unions could only be curbed by unemployment and declining output. No economic policy can be very satisfactory that provides only a choice between inflation and depression. But of this error there has been sufficient discussion.

There is one final prospect, also deeply rooted in this history. Nothing, it is worth repeating once more, lasts forever. That is true of inflation. It is true of recession. Each stirs the attitudes, engenders the action which seeks to bring itself to an end—and eventually does. But we have seen that the action required, including the action needed to avoid the increasingly probable combination of inflation with recession, is demanding and complex. And it becomes ever more so. The increasingly demanding character is the main message of this [article]. If anything is certain from this history, it is that those who see themselves as the strongest defenders of the system, those who proclaim themselves the most stalwart friends of free enterprise, even capitalism, will be the most fearful of measures designed to conserve the system. They will be the most antagonistic to the action that will improve its performance, enhance its reputation, increase its capacity to survive. Those who pray for the end of capitalism should never welcome the activist and affirmative spirit of the New Deal, World War II and after, or the New Frontier. This spirit, however on occasion the victim of its own enthusiasm, optimism or obligation to appease its opposition,

---

[6] Through provision of Special Drawing Rights and other steps, the Bretton Woods system has been much enlarged beyond the original design, although with no really significant departure from the original loan principle. The amounts available remain small in relation to potential international transfers of funds.

is open to the efforts that make the system work. When motivated by such spirit, the system has worked—in the United States to the satisfaction of, at a minimum, something exceeding a majority. Those who yearn for the end of capitalism should pray for government by men who believe that all positive action is inimical to what they call thoughtfully the fundamental principles of free enterprise.

Why Controls Failed

HERBERT STEIN

A past chairman of the Council of Economic Advisers, Herbert Stein is currently professor of economics at the University of Virginia. He is a specialist in stabilization theory and has written numerous books and articles on the subject. In this selection, excerpted from "Price-Fixing As Seen by a Price Fixer, Part II," he reflects on why the 1971–1974 controls failed.

The [1971–1974] controls obviously failed in the sense that there was an acceleration of the inflation rate before they ended and an even greater acceleration afterwards. They failed for a number of reasons, some of which are common to most price control experiments, and some of which may have been unusual although not unique.

1. The underlying rationale of the controls was faulty. If there is to be less inflation after a temporary price control system than before it, something must have changed during the controls period. The postcontrols situation must be less inflationary than the precontrols situation was. The argument for the 1971–1974 controls was that they would exorcise the expectation of inflation and lead people to make smaller price and wage increases than they would otherwise have made in similar conditions. This is the rationale that is now being used to explain a temporary incomes policy. But in fact the controls and the incomes policy do not have that effect. They only create the expectation that when the controls, or the incomes policy, end prices will rise more rapidly.

2. The controls were accompanied by a strongly expansionary fiscal and monetary policy, and in fact probably helped to make that policy more expansionary than it would otherwise have been. The economic officials of the time were aware of the fact that this had been the cause of the breakdown of controls and incomes policy systems in the past. Being aware of it, they thought they would avoid at least that error. But they did not. They were misled by the apparent success of the controls in their early months into thinking that there was more room for noninflationary expansion than there actually was.

Perhaps this is not an inherent defect of controls. But it has been encountered so often as to suggest that it is in fact an inescapable concomitant of controls, even if not a logical necessity. A government does not ordinarily get into controls in peacetime unless it feels a strong desire to pump up demand close to the inflationary danger point. And when prices are under control it becomes difficult to tell when the danger point is being neared.

3. Prices began to rise sharply in two important sectors where controls are hardest to maintain even for a short while—raw agricultural products and imports. When these prices began to rise sharply it became very difficult to keep the rest of the price structure steady. Any practicable price control system will

Herbert Stein, "Why Controls Failed" from "Price-Fixing As Seen by a Price Fixer, Part II," in William Fellner (ed.), *Contemporary Economic Problems 1978* (Washington, D.C.: American Enterprise Institute for Public Policy Research, 1978), pp. 133–135. Reprinted by permission of the publisher.

allow for the pass-through of cost increases, and wage controls will have to respond to the cost of living, so it is quite possible to have a cost-price spiral within the controls sytem if a few key prices go into motion exogenously. It may be said that the poor crops and the booming world markets were unfortunate accidents which need not have occurred, but they are the kinds of accidents that occur frequently.

4. The controls failed because they were basically in conflict with the way the American public, or at least powerful forces within it, want the political economic system to work. This is true despite the majority that is commonly revealed by public opinion polls to be in favor of price and wage controls. Once the first flush of enthusiasm has passed, and controls become a matter of continuing regulation that is increasingly detailed, labor and business become more and more resentful and resistant, and a larger and more irritating bureaucratic machine is required in an effort to achieve compliance. This was most obvious in the case of the labor organizations. Although there never was any union defiance of the system, the labor leadership clearly felt that the controls had displaced them from their role as the source of wage increases for their members, and their continued cooperation could be obtained even for a while only by a significant relaxation of the controls. Also businesses were becoming more determined and skillful in trying to find their way through ambiguities and gaps in the regulations. An attempt to make the controls work in those conditions would have required the exercise of government power over the economy on a scale which hardly anyone wanted.

The history of 1971–1974 is not recounted as conclusive evidence that price and wage controls can never work in a beneficial way. To prove that would require much more historical evidence and analysis than is presented here.

The conclusions I draw from this history are much narrower. The first is that incautious actions and talk did a great deal to lead the country to a policy which hardly anyone had wanted—namely, mandatory controls. The actions included irresponsible provision of legal authority for controls and mild steps in the direction of incomes policy, which were intended to stave off demands for controls, but only sharpened the appetite for them. The talk consisted in part of overly optimistic predictions of the speed and ease with which inflation would be controlled, leading to disappointment with conventional policies when the predictions turned out to be wrong. The talk also included a flood of argument for nonmandatory incomes policy, which turned out to convince the public of the need for controls of some kind—the degree of coercion involved being a secondary consideration.

The second conclusion is that the generally acknowledged failure of the controls in 1971–1974 cannot be convincingly attributed to the lack of enthusiasm of those who ran the control system or other easily remediable deficiencies in the management of the system.

These conclusions suggest two lessons for today. We should not evaluate the possible use of controls under the impression that the difficulties previously experienced will be escaped if the controls are managed by different people or in a different way. More important, all steps taken in this field or words uttered should be carefully considered in the light of the expectations they will arouse, the options they will close, and the momentum they will generate in directions that are unintended.

Controls Are Not the Answer

C. JACKSON GRAYSON, JR.

C. Jackson Grayson, Jr., is dean of the School of Business Administration, Southern Methodist University. After serving as chairman of the 1971 Price Commission, he wrote a book titled *Confessions of a Price Controller* as well as several articles about his experience. The selection presented here is one of those articles.

I will make one clear assertion at the outset: Wage-price controls are not the answer to inflation.

And yet I will also make the following prediction: We will turn again in the United States, in desperation, to some form of controls over wages and prices—just as people have done over the centuries. And the answer will still be the same—they may make some short-term gains, but at the expense of the long-run welfare.

The lessons of history seem pretty clear. Centralized efforts to fight inflation were started before Christ was born. Rome, for instance, fought inflation by various means for centuries. Finally, in A.D. 301, the emperor Diocletian imposed the first extensive price-wage control program. His edict (referred to as "commanded cheapness") set schedules for 76 different wage categories and for 890 different price categories (222 of which were for food!). The penalty for an offense was death. Thirteen years later, the program, in shambles, was abandoned. In the thirteenth century, the great Mongol, Kublai Khan, decreed maximum prices. And Medieval Europe had a "just price" code.

Not many people are aware of it, but the United States began some attempts at wage-price controls during its early years. The American Puritans imposed a code of wage and price limitations in 1636; those who violated the code were classed with "adulterers and whoremongers." The Continental Congress set price ceilings even before the Declaration of Independence. A few states enacted price control laws. Inflation became so severe that General George Washington complained in April 1779 that "a wagonload of money will scarcely purchase a wagonload of provisions." The attempts at control were sporadic, highly controversial, and not comprehensive. All efforts were largely abandoned by 1780.

Most modern nations have instituted wage-price controls during periods of war, but it was in Europe right after World War II that almost every nation tried some form of comprehensive peacetime controls (remembering the inflation that had torn apart European economics after World War I). Some European nations had succeeded with their "incomes policies" for a period of time. Some were started, stopped, and reinstated in another version. But none has lasted continuously.

Though specific "lessons" are difficult to transfer across international

C. Jackson Grayson, Jr., "Controls Are Not the Answer," *Challenge*, November/December 1974, pp. 9–12. Copyright © 1974 by M. E. Sharpe, Inc. Reprinted by permission of M. E. Sharpe, Inc.

boundaries, and even difficult to use in one nation from one time to another, it might be helpful to look at a summary that I have made of European experiences with controls (see table).

These experiences were summarized succinctly by Lloyd Ulman and Robert Flanagan in their book, *Wage Restraint—A Study of Incomes Policies in Western Europe:* "Incomes policy, to generalize from the experience of the countries in this account, has not been very successful." My conclusions about the accomplishments of the Price Commission do not vary from that. Perhaps we did obtain some short-range impact on price-wage levels, but they were gained under special conditions (slack in the economy, followed by productivity gains from a highly stimulated economy, and cooperation of business and labor) and at the cost of some long-term negative results.

As a result of my sixteen months as a price controller, I can list seven ways that controls interfere (negatively) with the market system and hasten its metamorphosis into a centralized economy.

First, wage-price controls lead to distortions in the economic system, which can be minimized only in the short run. The longer controls are in effect, the harder it is to discern real from artificial signals. No matter how cleverly any group designs a control system, distortions and inequities will appear. It happened in European control programs; it started to happen in Phase II.

For instance, lumber controls were beginning to lead to artificial middlemen, black markets, and sawmill shutdowns. Companies trapped with low base-period profit margins were beginning to consider selling out to those with

---

General Lessons from European Incomes Policies

1. If either labor or business does not cooperate, a wage-price controls programs will not work.
2. Incomes policies do not work for long. They erode with time.
3. Getting into controls is easier than getting out.
4. Rising profits drive wage demands up.
5. Neither business nor labor is very satisfied with any given distribution of their share of income at any given time. Both will seek to improve their share.
6. Voluntary incomes policies have been limited in success and in time. The tendency is toward mandatory policies.
7. Labor nearly always believes that the government figure for estimated productivity in setting wage guidelines is low. History shows that labor is generally right.
8. A wage "drift" occurs over time as business and labor cooperate to break many of the wage guidelines.
9. Efforts to restrain business and labor through education and exhortation have very limited success.
10. It is increasingly difficult to make incomes policies work as demand increases and unemployment decreases.
11. If prices are to be controlled, then so must wages be. The only exception is France, which has had a limited price control program but no wage control program.
12. Cost of living escalators accelerate inflation.
13. Less productive labor groups eventually demand comparability in wages with the more highly productive labor sectors, thereby eroding the wage guideline.
14. Expectations feed inflation.
15. Increasingly interdependent world trade can intrude upon and upset a nation's incomes policies.

higher base period margins, sending their capital overseas, or reducing their operations. Elsewhere, instances of false job upgrading—actually "raises" in disguise—were reported on a scattered but increasing basis. To keep away from profit-margin controls, some companies were considering dropping products where costs, and thus prices, had increased. And shortages of certain products (such as molasses and fertilizer) were appearing because artificially suppressed domestic prices had allowed higher world prices to pull domestic supplies abroad.

Exceptions and special regulations can handle some of these distortions, but the task grows more difficult as each correction breeds the need for another.

Second, during a period of controls, the public forgets that not all wage-price increases are inflationary. In a freely competitive economy, wage and price increases occur because of real consumer demand shifts and supply shortages. The resulting wage and price increases signal to businesses, "make more," or to labor, "move here," or to the public, "use less."

Controls interfere with this signaling mechanism. An artificially suppressed price can eventually cause shortages; natural gas is an example. Similar examples can be found in the labor market, where suppressed wages do not attract labor to areas in which there are shortages of skills or workers. But with wage-price controls in place, the public believes that all increases are inflationary—almost antisocial—and the clamor is for no increases, or at least very small ones.

"You can eliminate the middleman, but not his function"—this old business saying applies equally to our economic system. We live in a world of scarce resources, and, as much as some would like to repeal the laws of supply and demand, it cannot be done. Some system must allocate resources, we hope to the most efficient use for society. If wage-price controls, other government regulatory rules, or business-labor monopolies prohibit the price system from performing its natural function, then another rationing system (such as central planning and control) must be used. You can eliminate the price system, but not its function.

Third, during a control period, the public forgets what profits are all about. Even before the recent wage-price controls, the public believed profits were "too high," though they actually declined from 6.2 percent of GNP in 1966 to 3.6 percent in 1970, and increased only to 4.3 percent in the boom year of 1972. And with profit increases raised to the top of the news during the recovery of 1972 and early 1973, the negative public sentiment against profits increased. Why? The control system itself heightened the public's negative attitude toward profits at a time when capital regeneration, the fuel of the capitalist engine, was already alarmingly low.

Fourth, wage-price controls provide a convenient stone for those who have economic or political axes to grind, particularly those interested in promoting a centralized economic system. For example, in 1972 Ralph Nader argued that the control system should be used to prohibit automobile companies from raising their prices to reflect style changes. Others argued that price increases should not be given to companies that employ insufficient numbers of minorities or pollute the environment. Nor should wage increases go to uncooperative unions. And so on.

Fifth, wage-price controls can easily become a security blanket against the cold winds of free-market uncertainties. They tell people what the limits are; they help employers fight unions; and they provide union leaders with excuses to placate demands for "more" from their rank and file. The controlled become dependent on the controllers and want regulations continued in preference to the competition of a dynamic market. At the same time, the controllers themselves can become so enamored of their task that they don't want to let go.

The public begins to fear what will happen when controls are ended and seeks continuance. Witness the fears of moving from Phase II to Phase III, and the public (and congressional) pressure for the freeze to replace Phase III. Even Wall Street seemed terrified at the thought of returning to supply and demand in the market. It is much easier to get into controls than to get out.

Sixth, under controls, business and labor leaders begin to pay more attention to the regulatory body than to the dynamics of the marketplace. They inevitably come to the same conclusion, summed up by one executive: "We know that all of our sophisticated analysis and planning can be wiped out in the blink of a Washington controller's eye."

Seventh, and most dangerous, wage-price controls misguide the public. They draw attention away from the fundamental factors that affect inflation—fiscal and monetary policies, tax rates, import-export policies, productivity, competitive restrictions, and the like. The danger is that attention will become permanently focused on the symptom-treating control mechanism rather than on the underlying problems.

In summary, perhaps the most dramatic way I can underscore my views is to point out the recent example of Britain, where years of successive stop-go economic policies and various types of controls (including guideposts) have led that nation to where it is today, economically and politically in a crisis state with one of the lowest income growth rates of modern nations and raging inflation.

Controls are not the answer.

What Price Guideposts?[1]

MILTON FRIEDMAN

In the following selection, excerpted from an article by the same name, Milton Friedman argues against the use of guideposts.

The student of inflation is tempted to rejoin, "I've heard that one before," to exhortations now emanating from Washington. Since the time of Diocletian, and very probably long before, the sovereign has repeatedly responded to generally rising prices in precisely the same way: by berating the "profiteers," calling on private persons to show social responsibility by holding down the prices at which they sell their products or their services, and trying, through legal prohibitions or other devices, to prevent individual prices from rising.[2] The result of such measures has always been the same: complete failure. Inflation has been stopped when and only when the quantity of money has been kept from rising too fast, and that cure has been effective whether or not the other measures were taken. . . . Direct control of prices and wages does not eliminate inflationary pressure. It simply shifts the pressure elsewhere and suppresses some of its manifestations.

Inflation is always and everywhere a monetary phenomenon, resulting from and accompanied by a rise in the quantity of money relative to output. This generalization is not an arithmetical proposition or a truism, and it does not require a rigid relation between the rates of rise in prices and in the quantity of money. The precise rate at which prices rise for a given rate of rise in the quantity of money depends on such factors as past price behavior, current changes in the structure of labor and product markets, and fiscal policy. The monetary character of inflation . . . is an empirical generalization backed by a wide range of evidence which suggests that substantial changes in the demand for money seldom occur except as a reaction to a sequence of events set in train

---

[1] The author has drawn at various points in this paper on his book, *Inflation: Causes and Consequences* (New York: Asia Publishing House, 1963), which contains two lectures that he gave in Bombay, India, in 1963.

[2] In a market economy, prices of particular goods and services, including labor services, are always changing relatively to one another, some rising, others falling, some rising rapidly, others slowly, and so on. When rises predominate, in some sense which allows for the relative importance of the items whose prices are considered, there is inflation; when declines predominate, there is deflation. This definition is purposely vague because there is no unique way to measure the "average" behavior of prices; different indexes often give different answers not only about the size of any price change, but even about its direction. These differences are sometimes very large and are important for many purposes. In the context of this paper, however, they are not. We shall restrict attention to cases in which the general tendency for prices to rise is so clear and widespread that it would be reflected in just about every broadly based index number.

by changes in the quantity of money. It follows that the only effective way to stop inflation is to restrain the rate of growth of the quantity of money.[3]

Given inflationary pressure, rises in recorded or quoted prices and wages can be suppressed to some extent. The less severe the inflationary pressure, and the more vigorous and effective the enforcement of price controls, the greater the extent to which the manifestations of inflation can be suppressed. . . . Such suppressed inflation is far more harmful, both to efficiency and freedom, than open inflation, and the more effective the suppression, the greater the harm. It is highly desirable to avoid inflation but if, for whatever reason, that is not feasible, it is far better that inflation be open than that it be suppressed. . . .

WHAT HARM WILL BE DONE BY THE GUIDEPOSTS?

Even granted that legally imposed and vigorously enforced wage and price ceilings covering a wide range of the economy would do enormous harm, some may argue that the enunciation of guideposts, their approval by businessmen and labor leaders, and voluntary compliance with them, or even lip service to them, is a palliative that can do no harm and can temporarily help until more effective measures are taken. At the very least, it may be said, it will enable businessmen and labor leaders to display their sense of social responsibility.

This view seems to me mistaken. The guideposts do harm even when only lip service is paid to them, and the more extensive the compliance, the greater the harm.

In the first place, the guideposts confuse the issue and make correct policy less likely. If there is inflation or inflationary pressure, the governmental monetary (or, some would say, fiscal) authorities are responsible. It is they who must take corrective measures if the inflation is to be stopped. Naturally, the authorities want to shift the blame, so they castigate the rapacious businessman and the selfish labor leader. By approving guidelines, the businessman and the labor leader implicitly whitewash the government for its role and plead guilty to the charge. They thereby encourage the government to postpone taking the corrective measures that alone can succeed.

In the second place, whatever measure of actual compliance there is introduces just that much distortion into the allocation of resources and the distribution of output. To whatever extent the price system is displaced, some other system of organizing resources and rationing output must be adopted. As in the example of the controls on foreign loans by banks, one adverse effect is to foster private collusive arrangements, so that a measure undertaken to keep prices down leads to government support and encouragement of private monopolistic arrangements.

---

[3]As Robert Solow pointed out in his comments on this paper at [the Conference on Formal and Informal Controls at The University of Chicago, April 1966], the argument of the other sections of this paper (sections I, III, [not included here] and IV) is almost entirely independent of my generalization about the central role of the quantity of money in the inflationary process. The words inflationary pressure can be interpreted to mean an aggregate nominal demand in excess of the value of prior (or potential) output at prior prices. Whether this excess nominal demand reflects a change in the quantity of money, as I believe it generally does, or a change in velocity produced, for example, by changes in fiscal policy or investment demand, as others may believe, the analysis of the effects of price and wage guidelines or controls is precisely the same.

I am indebted to Mr. Solow for making this point explicit at the conference.

In the third place, "voluntary" controls invite the use of extralegal powers to produce compliance. And, in the modern world, such powers are ample. There is hardly a business concern that could not have great costs imposed on it by antitrust investigations, tax inquiries, government boycott, or rigid enforcement of any of a myriad of laws, or on the other side of the ledger, that can see no potential benefits from government orders, guarantees of loans, or similar measures. Which of us as an individual could not be, at the very least, seriously inconvenienced by investigation of his income tax returns, no matter how faithfully and carefully prepared, or by the enforcement to the letter of laws we may not even know about? This threat casts a shadow well beyond any particular instance. In a dissenting opinion in a recent court case involving a "stand-in" in a public library, Justice Black wrote, "It should be remembered that if one group can take over libraries for one cause, other groups will assert the right to do it for causes which, while wholly legal, may not be so appealing to this court." Precisely the same point applies here. If legal powers granted for other purposes can today be used for the "good" purpose of holding down prices, tomorrow they can be used for other purposes that will seem equally "good" to the men in power—such as simply keeping themselves in power. It is notable how sharp has been the decline in the number of businessmen willing to be quoted by name when they make adverse comments on government.

In the fourth place, compliance with voluntary controls imposes a severe conflict of responsibilities on businessmen and labor leaders. The corporate official is an agent of his stockholders; the labor leader, of the members of his union. He has a responsibility to promote their interests. He is now told that he must sacrifice their interests to some supposedly higher social responsibility. Even supposing that he can know what "social responsibility" demands—say by simply accepting on that question the gospel according to the Council of Economic Advisers—to what extent is it proper for him to do so? If he is to become a civil servant in fact, will he long remain an employee of the stockholders or an agent of the workers in name? Will they not discharge him? Or, alternatively, will not the government exert authority over him in name as in fact?

CONCLUSION

Inflation being always and everywhere a monetary phenomenon, the responsibility for controlling it is governmental. Legally enforced price and wage ceilings do not eliminate inflationary pressure. At most they suppress it. And suppressed inflation is vastly more harmful than open inflation.

Guideposts and pleas for voluntary compliance are a halfway house whose only merit is that they can more readily be abandoned than legally imposed controls. They are not an alternative to other effective measures to stem inflation, but at most a smokescreen to conceal the lack of action. Even if not complied with they do harm, and the more faithfully they are complied with, the more harm they do.

Nonetheless, we should not exaggerate either the problem or the harm that will be done by false cures. Prices will almost surely rise in coming months. We shall probably continue to experience inflationary pressure on the average over the coming years. The price rise, however, will be moderate. A major war aside,

I cannot conceive that the monetary authorities will permit the quantity of money to rise at a rate that would produce inflation of more than, say, 3-to-10 per cent a year. Such inflation will be unfortunate, but if permitted to occur reasonably openly and freely, not disastrous. And, despite all the talk, prices and wages will be permitted to rise in one way or another. The guideposts will be more talked about than they will be voluntarily complied with or enforced by extralegal pressure. Hypocrisy will enable effective evasion to be combined with self-congratulation. Debasing the coin of public and private morality is unfortunate, but in moderate doses not disastrous. The greatest harm will continue to be done by the measures taken to peg exchange rates. It is well to keep in mind Adam Smith's famous comment, "There is much ruin in a nation," but only to avoid overstating a good case, not to condone bad policy.

The Case Against the Case Against the Guideposts

ROBERT M. SOLOW

In this companion piece to the Friedman article, Robert M. Solow defends the use of guidelines and stresses their importance as a means of educating people about wage-price-productivity relationships.

I choose this defensive-sounding title because it points to an important truth. The wage-price guideposts, to the extent that they can be said to constitute a policy, are not the sort of policy you would invent if you were inventing policies from scratch. They are the type of policy you back into as you search for ways to protect an imperfect economy from the worst consequences of its imperfect behavior. . . .

WOULD THE GUIDEPOSTS FREEZE THE DISTRIBUTION OF INCOME AND INTERFERE WITH FREE MARKETS?

It is often remarked . . . that if wage rates on the average were to rise precisely as fast as productivity, while the price levels were to remain constant, then the proportions of the national income going to labor and to property would stay unchanged. To take some very round numbers, suppose production per man-year were $10,000 and the annual wage $7,500, so that $2,500 went to owners of capital. If productivity and the annual wage were both to rise by that famous 3.2 per cent, and prices were unchanged, then output per man-year would go to $10,320 and the wage $7,740. This would leave $2,580 in property income. Notice that the $320 of new output per man-year has been divided in the same 75–25 proportions as the original $10,000, so that the overall proportional distribution of the national income is undisturbed.

This algebraic fact has led to criticism of the guidepost concept. The argument is not at all about the equity or justice of the current distribution of income. The argument is that the distribution of income—before taxes and transfers—is part of the market process in our economy. Changes in incomes are supposed to guide efficiently the allocation of resources. To freeze the distribution of income in a pattern that may be suitable to current conditions can lead to distortions and inefficiencies if economic conditions change and call for a changed distribution of income.

It seems to me that this argument has no practical weight at all. It is rendered trivial by two facts. The first is that the division of the national income between labor and property incomes is among the slower-changing charac-

Robert M. Solow, "The Case Against the Case Against the Guideposts," in George P. Shultz and Robert Z. Aliber (eds.), *Guidelines, Informal Controls, and the Market Place* (Chicago: The University of Chicago Press, 1966), pp. 41, 48–54. Copyright © 1966 by the University of Chicago. Reprinted by permission of the publisher.

teristics of our economy, or of any Western economy. The second is that neither the guideposts nor any other such quantitative prescription can be satisfied *exactly*. Suppose that wage rates do follow the guideposts exactly. Then if the price level, instead of remaining constant, goes up by, say, 1 per cent in a year, the share of wages in national income will fall by 1 per cent—that is, by about ¾ of one percentage point. If, on the other hand, the price level should fall by 1 per cent, the share of wages in national income would rise by ¾ of 1 percentage point. That may not seem like much, but actually it is quite a lot, more than enough to provide all the flexibility that our economic system is likely to need.

In the twenty years since the end of the war, the proportion of "compensation of employees" to national income has moved about within a narrow range, say from 65 per cent to 71 per cent. There is no reason to suppose that market forces will always want to keep the figure within those bounds, but there is every reason to believe that market forces will never, or hardly ever, want to move the proportional distribution of income very rapidly. As the numerical example shows, if wages adhered to the guidelines, the distribution of income could get from one end of its postwar range to the other in about eight years, with an annual rate of inflation or deflation never exceeding 1 per cent.

There is no practical question, then, of freezing the distribution of income. The normal amount of play in any such policy gives all the room needed for the market to operate. It would be possible to provide formally for more flexibility if that were needed. If the wages guideposts were expressed in terms of a fairly narrow range, say from 3.0 to 3.5 per cent per year, this would serve two purposes. For one thing, it would more nearly express the uncertainty in any estimate of the trend increase in productivity. And secondly, it would permit the outcome to be nearer the bottom of the top of the range, depending on "market forces." Even a steady price level would then permit some drift in the distribution of income.

Even apart from this question of distribution, one hears it said that the guideposts are a dangerous interference in the free market, even a form of price control. At least this criticism is inconsistent with the other one that claims the guideposts to be ineffective. With some ingenuity, one could probably cook up a set of assumptions under which the guideposts had no effect on wage-price behavior, yet managed to do harm to the market economy. But this seems farfetched to me. If they are a real interference with the market, they must be partially effective.

I would contend that it is also farfetched to describe the wage-price guideposts as anything remotely like a system of wage and price controls. But in any case I am not concerned with the way the guideposts have been used by this President or that President, but with the way they were intended. They were intended, as I mentioned earlier, as a device for the education and mobilization of public opinion. The January 1962 Economic Report said:

> Individual wage and price decisions assume national importance when they involve large numbers of workers and large amounts of output directly, or when they are regarded by large segments of the economy as setting a pattern. Because such decisions affect the progress of the whole economy, there is legitimate reason for public interest in their content and consequences. An informed public, aware of the significance of major

wage bargains and price decisions, and equipped to judge for itself their compatibility with the national interest, can help to create an atmosphere in which the parties to such decisions will exercise their powers responsibly. . . . The guideposts suggested here as aids to public understanding are not concerned primarily with the relation of employers and employees to each other, but rather with their joint relation to the rest of the economy. (Pp. 185–86.)

It is no doubt inevitable that an activist President will want to help public opinion along. But that is still a far cry from wage and price control.

Moreover, by both intent and necessity, the guideposts can influence only those wage and price decisions in which the parties have a certain amount of discretion. Atomistic textbook competitors, having no discretion, will not be much influenced by either public opinion or the White House. But where there is enough market power, and hence enough discretion, for the guideposts to be a force, there is little or no reason to believe that the "free market" outcome will be in the public interest. The usual presumption against public interference in the market process does not hold. This conclusion does not depend on any very exact evaluation of the amount of competition to which the steel industry, or the aluminum industry, or the tobacco industry, or the United Automobile Workers, or the building trades unions are subject. It is enough that none of them is, and none of them thinks it is, selling against a nearly infinitely elastic demand curve.

Naturally, the fact that a concentrated industry and a strong union may make decisions not in the public interest does not automatically mean that what the guideposts suggest will be better. That question needs to be decided on its merits. Yet, the guideposts are intended to give a summary description of a well-functioning market economy; within limits they can be expected to represent the public interest fairly well. But it is much more important to realize that the public interest does need representation.

It is worth remembering, in this connection, that the guideposts are intended to have an effect on the general level of money wages and prices, not on relative wages and relative prices. Most of the things we expect free markets to accomplish are "real" things, more or less independent of the price level. Ideally, the guideposts should permit markets to allocate resources freely, insuring only that the price level not drift up in the process. The January 1962 Economic Report said: "It is desirable that labor and management should bargain explicitly about the distribution of the income of particular firms or industries. It is, however, undesirable that they should bargain implicitly about general price level." (P. 188.) In practice, one must admit, the guideposts will operate unevenly; relative prices and resource allocation may thus be affected. One can hope that these effects are second-order.

UNEVENNESS AND INEQUITY

This inevitable unevenness in operation strikes me as the main weakness in the guideposts. Public opinion is bound to have its greatest impact on markets that are centralized and conspicuous. That may not be all bad; centralization and discretionary power over prices and wages may be correlated. But there are obvious instances in which the correlation is broken, in which considerable market power in local markets goes along with decentralization and near-immunity to pressure from public opinion. The construction industry and the building trades unions are the standard illustration; parts of trade and transportation may provide other examples.

This weakness must simply be admitted. It is dangerous not only because it invites inefficient relative price effects, but because policy that tries to mobilize public opinion on behalf of the public interest will inevitably find its foundations sapped by obvious inequity.

There is probably no general solution to the problem. There may, however, be ad hoc solutions in special cases. If, as may well be the case, the Davis-Bacon Act is one of those legally enforced restrictions on competition whose main effect is to allow one segment of the labor market to exploit the others—and to hamper full-employment policy in the bargain—then repeal may well be in order.

Another possible solution to the problem of uneven impact might be to formalize the guideposts into some sort of advance-notice and/or public hearing procedure, perhaps through a committee of Congress. I am opposed to this sort of development. It would be a move away from the original conception of the guideposts as an educational device, in the direction of a system of semiformal price controls. It is unlikely that Congress would favor that much of a break with the past; if we are to espouse unlikely legislation, I would rather favor the promotion of competition and the reduction of tariff protection.

There is a different respect in which the involvement of Congress might be a good idea. Up to now, the burden of informing and mobilizing public opinion has fallen to the President and to the Chairman of the Council of Economic Advisers. This seems to be a mistake. The prestige of the President is probably too important a commodity to be spent in a way that invites occasional rebuff. And the prestige of the Council of Economic Advisers, taken by itself, is probably insufficient to carry the load. It might be helpful, therefore, if individual senators and congressmen would take part in the public debate, in their capacity as leaders and formers of public opinion. Even hearings are a possibility, provided they are hearings devoted to ordinary pieces of legislation—past or future—or to expect testimony and not to individual wage bargains or price decisions.

HOW SHOULD THE GUIDEPOST FIGURE BE SET?

In principle, the guidepost figure for wages is supposed to be the trend-increase in productivity for the economy as a whole. This is a difficult thing to measure; indeed, the concept is not entirely free of ambiguity. For example, one clearly wants a figure free of the effects of short-term changes in capacity utilization in industry, because otherwise the result would be to transfer the risks of enterprise from profits to wages, and that is not the intent. This suggests using a long-run trend figure. On the other hand, it seems faintly ridiculous that the permissible wage increase today should be made to depend on what was happening to productivity a few decades ago. Actually, this particular problem is primarily a matter of measurement, not of ambiguity in principle. A group of technicians could probably come to reasonable agreement. The difficulty is, however, that this number produced by technicians needs to be believed and used by the public and others.

Consider the unedifying spectacle of earlier this year [1966]. Should the administration continue to promulgate last year's guidepost figure of 3.2 per cent per year, or should it continue to use the method by which last year's figure was calculated, which would yield 3.6 per cent for this year? The decision to stay with 3.2 per cent was clearly the right one in substance; nobody with any sense believes that the steady-state rate of increase of output per man-hour in the private economy is now 3.6 per cent annually. The whole difficulty was created by the explicit adoption of a five-year moving average as the "official" method for calculating the trend-increase in productivity. This is clearly not a technician's method; a technician would make a more explicit statistical decomposition into cyclical and secular productivity change. The five-year moving average was clearly a compromise expedient—a method anyone could understand, which happened to give the same numerical answer as the technician's methods.

I am inclined to think that the technician's methods should prevail. I realize that there are grave difficulties with this view. In the first place, the parties to collective bargaining are likely to resent being presented with a figure they had no part in setting. That is understandable. The trouble is that the parties' mutual relationship is naturally a bargaining one; presented with an opportunity to set or influence the guidepost figure, they will naturally bargain over it. But that would destroy any claim that the guidepost figure might have to be an objectively determined number. In the second place, I gather that some members of Congress would like to take a hand in guidepost-setting. Again, one can understand why. But in principle the guidepost figure is not something one sets, it is something that one finds out. Congress can investigate, of course, but it is far from clear that its methods are ideal for investigating the subtler properties of economic time series. I can imagine that every so often Congress might like to hear expert testimony on how the exercise is being carried out; that would be salutary. But that would be different from an airing of predictable majority, minority, and interested-party views.

There is another sort of problem which is not open to technical solution and on which exchanges of opinion might be useful. It was easy to begin talking about wage-price guideposts in 1962 because the immediate history was one of approximate price stability. But suppose prices have been rising, and suppose that it is very unlikely that they can be made to level out in one year. Then it is difficult for labor to acquiesce in a figure for money wage increases which would give the right real-wage increase only if prices were constant.

That would be to acquiesce to a subnormal increase in real wages and a supernormal increase in profits. On the other hand, to add the current rate of price increase to the rate of productivity increase would be to throw the entire burden onto profits or, more likely, guarantee that prices will continue to rise. What is needed is some target pace for slowing down the price trend over a couple of years. One can imagine rational discussion of such a problem in a small country with centralized and enlightened trade union and employer association leadership. (Even then I'm not sure one can imagine anything actually being accomplished on so difficult a matter.) It is less easy to imagine such discussion in the United States.

CONCLUSION

. . . Wage-price guideposts are not an ideal or complete policy for the control of inflation. They may, however, under appropriate circumstances, offer a little help at even less cost. Alternatives sometimes proposed may be very costly or very unrealistic. Let me quote an English author, Henry Smith (*Lloyd's Bank Review*, January, 1966, p. 40):

> If the ideal answer is to allow the pricing system all the freedom that is possible, while creating an atmosphere which induces the maximum restraint on the use of strategic power capable of pushing up money wages and increasing prices, and this is probably the ideal solution, then out of the debate great good may come. If we go through the motions of working out what is called an incomes policy, although we cannot in reality put it into practice, then everybody on a position of strategic authority may think twice before using it. This may not seem to be a great deal. However, the agreed objectives of British economic policy—rising productivity, expanding exports, economy in the use of manpower, high employment—all depend for their success upon the containment of the inflationary forces which their pursuit may generate.

Fact Sheet on Inflation Plan

ASSOCIATED PRESS

Despite the acknowledged problems with guidelines, the United States has continually flirted with them. In October 1978 a new guideline policy was implemented. The following news summary is a brief report on this program.

The following is the fact sheet on President Carter's anti-inflation program, released by the White House.

FEDERAL ACTIONS

The Federal Government alone cannot solve the inflation problem, but it must take the lead. The Administration will do anything in its power to ensure that its actions are consistent with the objectives of the anti-inflation program.

Budgetary Policy: Substantial progress has been made in reducing the rate of unemployment. But further progress in reducing unemployment will depend on our success in reducing the rate of inflation. The budget that will be submitted in January will give top priority to moderating inflation. To achieve that goal the President will:

- Put a tight rein on the growth of Federal spending. He has pledged to cut the share of gross national product accounted for by Federal spending from 23 percent in fiscal year 1976 to about 21 percent in fiscal year 1980.

- Reduce the Federal deficit. In fiscal year 1976, the Federal deficit was $66 billion. In just three years, by 1979, the deficit will be cut to below $40 billion. In the 1980 budget, the deficit will be reduced still further—to less than one-half the 1976 deficit.

In order to contribute to these goals, the President has imposed severe limits on the hiring of Federal employees. Effective immediately, for an indefinite period, Federal agencies will be permitted to fill only one out of two vacancies as they occur.

Programs to protect the environment and the health and safety of workers and consumers are vital. But the achievement of these critical objectives should not place unnecessary burdens on the economy. Regulatory agencies are now required to analyze major new regulations to identify and compare benefits and costs. In addition, the President has:

- Directed the formation of a Regulatory Council. This Council will include all regulatory departments and agencies. The Council will have the important task of coordinating duplicative and overlapping regulations, in concert with the Office of Management and Budget's efforts to enforce the regulatory-process Executive Order 12044.

- Directed the new Regulatory Council to develop a unified calendar of major regulations. The calendar will provide, for the first time, a comprehensive list of major regulations to be proposed by the various agencies of the Federal Government. This calendar will facilitate a comprehensive and consistent approach to the evaulation of costs and benefits of proposed regulations. The council will help to ensure that regulatory objectives are achieved at the lowest possible cost.

- Pledged to use his authority to ensure that regulations are issued only when necessary and that they achieve their goals at the lowest possible cost.

- Directed each executive branch regulatory agency to include additional regulations that have a major economic impact in the "sunset" reviews that are required by Executive Order 12044.

PRIVATE ACTIONS

Success of this anti-inflation effort will depend upon the cooperation of the private sector. To this end, the President has set forth explicit numerical standards of behavior for pay and prices in the year ahead.

Pay Standard: Annual increases in wages and private fringe benefits should not exceed 7 percent.

- Workers earning less than $4 per hour will be exempt as well as wage contracts already signed.

- In new collective bargaining situations, a contract in which wage and fringe benefit increases average no more than 7 percent annually over the life of the contract will be consistent with the standard. In evaluating a contract for consistency with the standard, cost-of-living clauses will be evaluated using a 6 percent per year rate of price inflation over the life of the contract.

- No more than an 8 percent pay increase should be included in the first year of a multi-year contract.

- Increases above the standard will be acceptable to the extent that they reflect changes in work rules and practices that show demonstrable productivity improvements.

- The standard does not apply to individual workers. The standard applies to average pay increases for groups of workers. Companies will be expected to divide their work force into three categories:
  a. management employees,
  b. groups of employees covered by separate collectively bargained contracts, and
  c. all other employees.

Price Standard: Individual companies are expected to limit their price increases over the next year to one-half of 1 percentage point below their average annual rate of price increase during 1976–77.

- If the wage-rate increases for a company decelerate by more than one-half percentage point from the 1976–77 base period, greater deceleration in prices will be required in order to ensure that savings are reflected in prices.

- The standard does not apply to specific products, but to a company's overall average price.

- Companies unable to meet the one-half percent deceleration standard due to unavoidable cost increases must demonstrate, as an alternative, that their before-tax profit margins are no higher than in the best two of the last three years.

Program Objectives: The pay and price standards have been developed to be consistent with one another.

- The deceleration standard for prices can be related to the wage standard by adding 0.5 percentage point to the 7 percent wage standard to reflect scheduled increases in legislatively mandated payroll costs and deducting 1¾ percentage points for productivity growth.

The result is a 5¾ percent economywide rate of increase in unit labor costs. If companies reduced their average price increases by the price standard—that is, if they reduce their average price increase by one-half percentage point below the average rate of price increase in 1976–77—the result would be a 5¾ percent increase in prices of nonfood commodities and services. The pay and price standards are thus consistent with one another.

- Because of the allowances necessary to deal with a complex economy—such as the treatment of wage contracts already signed and the existence of some uncontrollable cost increases—widespread observance of the standards would lead to an overall rate of inflation of 6 to 6½ percent in the year ahead, well below the rate of inflation in 1978 to date.

Real Wage Insurance: The President will recommend to the Congress a program of "real wage insurance." Under this program, workers who are members of groups that meet the pay standard would receive a tax rebate if the rate of inflation in the year ahead exceeds 7 percent. The program will be developed for submission to the Congress in January. Although final decisions remain to be made, the broad outlines of the program are as follows:

- The amount of the rebate would be equal to the difference between the actual rate of inflation and 7 percent, multiplied by an individual worker's pay, up to some reasonable limit.

- Workers who are members of groups that meet the 7 percent pay limitation would be eligible for the real wage insurance.

- The rebate would be paid only if the rate of inflation in the year ahead actually exceeds 7 percent.

INCENTIVES

The Administration will interpret wage and price increases above the standards as indications of inflationary conditions, such as shortages, excessive market power or shelter from competition. Thus, increases in excess of the standards will trigger actions by the Government such as:

- Re-examining various restrictions on imports and, where possible and appropriate, relaxing them.
- Asking regulatory agencies to review rate levels and other rules in light of the standards for wages and prices.
- Seeking modification in those regulations that set minimum levels for prices or wages in specific situations.

Government Purchases: The Federal Government itself is a major purchaser of goods and services. By channeling its procurement to those firms whose price and wage decisions meet the standards, it can realize long-term savings in its procurement budget and simultaneously take the lead in fighting inflation.

- To the extent consistent with legal requirements and ensuring national security, the President will direct Government agencies to limit purchases to those companies observing the pay and price standards.
- After Jan. 1, the Government will require companies awarded contracts in excess of $5 million to certify that they are observing the standards.
- This program will be administered by the Office of Federal Procurement Policy of the OMB.
- Specific procedures to carry out this policy will be announced soon by Federal Procurement Office and by the Council on Wage and Price Stability.

Monitoring: The Council on Wage and Price Stability will be expanded by about 100 persons to monitor the adherence to the wage and price standards by companies and employee groups.

- The Council has the authority to obtain, where necessary, required information on prices, profits and wage rates. It will publicly identify areas of the economy and companies that are not complying with the standards.
- In addition, the Council will monitor on a regular basis wage and price developments of individual companies whose annual sales exceed $500 million. It will also monitor individually all major collective bargaining settlements.

IV/
ECONOMIC INCOMES POLICIES

Man has almost constant occasion for the help of his brethren, and it is in vain for him to expect it from their benevolence only. He will be more likely to prevail, if he can interest their self-love in his favour, and show them that it is for their own advantage to do for him what he requires of them. Whoever offers to another a bargain of any kind proposes to do this. Give me that which I want, and you shall have this which you want, is the meaning of every such offer; and it is in this manner that we obtain from one another the far greater part of those good offices which we stand in need of. It is not from the benevolence of the butcher, the brewer, or the baker, that we expect our dinner, but from their regard to their own interest. We address ourselves, not to their humanity but to their self-love, and never talk to them of our own necessities but of their advantages.

ADAM SMITH

To politicians, choosing between monetary restriction and wage and price controls is equivalent to choosing the type of rope that will be used to hang them. It is little wonder then that politicians flit from one policy to the other, attempting to loosen the noose whenever it begins to tighten, always searching for a better way.

This need to make a choice has spawned many new approaches to the inflation problem. As mainline theory flounders, the fringes flourish; the ideas of "cranks" metamorphize, becoming the ideas of some "respected" economists, which then become the ideas of mainline economics. After the fact, it is difficult to imagine that mainline economists ever thought any other way. This process happened with Keynes's theory; it happened with the monetarists' theory; and (according to its proponents) it is slowly happening with economic-based incomes policies.

The concept of an economic-based incomes policy seems, at first glance, to be a contradiction in terms. Are not controls the antithesis of the market and the pricing mechanism? Upon reflection, however, it is easily seen that they are not; the market and pricing mechanisms are merely subtler forms of control. The problem with wage and price controls is that they are too rigid and do not allow the necessary relative price and wage adjustments. Economic-based incomes policies avoid the rigidities of direct wage and price controls by using a pricing or taxing mechanism to exert control. Precisely as is done in other markets, they use the incentive system to control *indirectly* the individual's decision toward a socially desirable end. They establish new social rules that recognize the contribution made to inflation when individuals raise their wages or prices.

Under our present system, individuals do not bear the cost of that contribution, and, as with anything else, when they do not pay the cost, too much of it is demanded. In this case, "it" is too much inflation. Economic incomes policies incorporate this contribution into the individual's decision without directly controlling that decision.

TAX-BASED INCOMES POLICIES
The most developed of the economic incomes policies are called tax-based incomes policies (TIPs). Although tax (or subsidy) anti-inflation proposals have been around for a

while and have received attention in academic journals since as early as 1961 (and, I suspect, much earlier), they have only recently received serious policy consideration. Recent attention is largely attributable to four individuals: Sidney Weintraub, Henry Wallich, Arthur Okun, and Laurence S. Seidman. The first article, from *Business Week*, provides an initial overview of the TIP concept and its advantages and difficulties.

In the reading by Laurence Seidman we find a fuller description of the Wallich-Weintraub TIP proposal, together with Seidman's view of the underlying theory. He equates inflation to an externality and argues that the natural "economic" approach to inflation should be the same as it is to other externalities; in other words, it should be taxed.

In "TIP: A Tax-Based Incomes Policy to Stop Stagflation," Sidney Weintraub offers a slightly different approach to the underlying theory of TIP. Emphasizing the macro-economic approach, he suggests that all economies face the problem of income gearing, or of relating nominal to real income. Western market economies specifically, he argues, "have lacked a mechanism to accomplish the task, relying instead on the imperfect mechanics of monetary policy. . . ." By contrasting a market economy with the command and control economy, he suggests that we should be able to build upon the incentive aspects of the tax mechanism to design a workable incomes policy.

Arthur Okun's testimony before the Committee on Banking, Housing, and Urban Affairs, along with his other writings, were instrumental in "selling" TIP. In this piece, he nicely sums up the feelings of most TIP proponents: "I am a proponent of a tax-based incomes policy, not because that policy is beautiful, but because it is a lot less ugly than alternative policy strategies." He then outlines the policy options and sketches a "reward TIP" based on wages, but he leaves open the question of whether there should be a TIP on prices.

TIP has political appeal; it combines the free market virtues with the incomes policy virtues, allowing the politician to favor both. The selection by Mancur Olson was originally an internal memo, written in 1976 for Jimmy Carter's presidential campaign. It reveals some of the political forces pushing our economy toward economic-based incomes policies.

As we have seen above, the need for equity among all types of income consistently creates a stumbling block for incomes policies. In this respect, TIP is no exception. Everyone wants equity, but the administrative arguments (and costs) do not call for equity. Wages are easier to control than prices, and therefore wages are burdened with controls. In the next paper, I suggest that we can make an "end run" around the problem by not designing a TIP around wages but rather by designing it around value added per unit input. Although this sounds rather formidable, it is argued that the idea is simple. One can control prices either by controlling output prices or by controlling input prices. If we can combine wages and profits together by controlling total value added of a firm, the political problems are avoided at no added costs in administrative difficulties. The idea is still new and fluid; some believe negative productivity effects will make the plan undesirable while others believe either that those effects are minor or that adjustments can be made that meet the productivity objections.

In "Some Questions and Answers about TIP," Abba Lerner responds to questions raised by Senator William Proxmire about this topic and suggests that a fair and administratively feasible TIP can be designed.

In the next piece, Gardner Ackley states what is probably the "mainline economic" position on TIP: It's an interesting idea but let's wait and see. We then look at a more negative position in the selection by Norman Ture. After presenting a list of problems with the Okun and Wallich-Weintraub TIPs, Ture concludes with a belief that TIP is not the answer.

MARKET-BASED INCOMES POLICIES (MIP)

Besides instituting an economic incomes policy through the tax system, it could also be implemented through the market. To my knowledge, three such policies have been proposed. In 1974 Christian von Weitsäcker and I each developed separate market proposals, both of which circulated in draft form among economists. Significant interest in market-based incomes policies, however, did not develop until 1976, when Professor Abba Lerner developed his Wage Increase Permit Plan (WIPP), which was a combination of von Weitsäcker's permit plan on prices and the TIP proposals. Instead of using permits for price increases, as called for in von Weitsäcker's plan, Lerner proposed permits for wage increases, allowing a firm to give above-guideline wage increases if it bought the necessary permits from another firm that gave a below-guideline figure.

Because of Lerner's distinguished reputation and lucid writing style, his proposal attracted significant attention among economists. However, the political problems of the proposal seeming antilabor and unresolved administrative questions prevented its serious practical consideration. In 1978 Professor Lerner and I decided to combine our plans, and we jointly developed the Market Anti-Inflation Plan (MAP), one version of which is presented as the last selection in this volume. As you read it, note the similarities and differences in the reasoning between Hayek's "market solution" and MAP. Although each uses the market, they are quite different. Or are they?

As you read these articles consider carefully the advantages and disadvantages of a tax-based incomes policy and a market-based incomes policy. Should they even be called incomes policies? Is one plan more practical than the other? If the government controls the price of anti-inflation credits, does MAP become identical to TIP? For what price will these anti-inflation credits sell? Will the price quickly fall to zero?

CONCLUSION

It should be clear from the readings that economic-based incomes policies provide no easy answer. They do not avoid the "good for the soul" suffering of monetary policy that is the only real solution to inflation; they merely make it bearable by equally sharing the burden, channeling the power of monetary policy directly into prices, and yet avoiding the administrative problems of direct controls. Thus incomes policies offer a compromise between the other two types of solutions. They *are* controls, but they are flexible controls, giving guidance while leaving the actual decisions to the individual. (Thus they are no different from any other type of market control.) In the final analysis, the question is not whether to control or not to control prices; it is what method of control is best. Do we want the tyranny of the federal government, the tyranny of the market, or the tyranny of taxes?

The final verdict on tax- and market-based incomes policies is not in. Both plans are still developing, and much work remains to be done before we can decide whether they are indeed the "least worst" tyranny or whether they are merely the scribblings of wild-eyed academicians.

Another Weapon Against Inflation: Tax Policy

BUSINESS WEEK

Interest in economic policies have been generated by newspapers and magazines, which have carefully followed the development of TIP. This article from *Business Week* provides a good introduction to the TIP proposals.

With the nation undergoing a new bout of stagflation and with fiscal and monetary policy making little headway against the combination of high unemployment and high inflation, economists are again looking wistfully at the wide range of incomes-policy schemes tried or proposed in the past. The Carter Administration has strongly disavowed any intention to resort even to milder forms, such as voluntary wage and price guidelines, but the economics profession is looking with increasing excitement at a variation called TIP, for tax-based incomes policy.

Behind this approach is the acknowledgment, even by liberal economists, that the term "underlying inflation rate" so popular in Washington for the last two years is a euphemism for cost-push inflation, and that most of the push is in wage increases that far outstrip productivity gains. With labor compensation accounting for 75% of national income, the so-called underlying inflation rate of 6% cannot be cracked without slowing the rate of wage gains, which have been running close to or above 8% a year since 1973.

Although there are grave questions over whether labor or management will ever accept TIP, proponents argue that the scheme would largely circumvent the problems and inequities created by previous incomes-policy experiments. According to Federal Reserve Board Governor Henry C. Wallich, who designed TIP with Sidney Weintraub of the University of Pennsylvania, the new proposal differs from the failed wage and price controls of 1971–74 or the guideposts of the 1960s by "relying on market forces" rather than "versions that do violence to the market."

In its simplest form, TIP would hit companies with a surcharge on their corporate income tax if they grant their employees wage increases in excess of some government-set standard. Similarly, by holding their average wage increases below the standard, the companies would be eligible for a tax reduction. Wallich and Weintraub would grant corporations in general a tax-rate reduction big enough to restore to the private sector any funds drained off to the Treasury by the surtax.

"If the TIP pulls in more revenue than it puts out, it's not working," says Weintraub, "and both the TIP tax and the general reduction would have to be increased the next year. The idea is not to raise revenues, any more than a 55-mph speed limit should. The idea is to keep people from killing themselves in the attempt to go faster."

But even with the 55-mph limit—that is, a productivity-based standard that government would set for wage increases—labor and management would still sit in the driver's seat. Unions and business would be free to negotiate wage settlements above or below the guideline, or to negotiate differential settlements for different plants and types of workers within a company, according to the labor market demands of that concern.

As Wallich puts it: "No company would need an exception of the type used under controls. If the employer needs to attract labor and wants to exceed the wage standard, he obviously is generating good profits and can afford the extra tax." But the same employer would have an incentive to "backbone" labor on the size of the wage increase, since his competitors might enhance their market position by gaining the tax break and a better rate of return.

THE RISK

For the same reason, the company that followed the current practice of trying to pass through every wage increase in an automatic price markup would run into competitive pressures from some rival, who just might find that it pays to hold the price line. Wallich and Weintraub acknowledge that this backboning entails the risk of increasing strikes, but if labor at some point realizes that what matters are real wage gains instead of nominal inflation gains, the wage-price-wage spiral could be broken.

In short, TIP ideally would increase rather than diminish reliance on the market system, and would allow for flexibility in the negotiating process. In past incomes-policy schemes, government standards or regulations inevitably became price controls that prevented relative wage and price adjustments in response to the market signals of supply and demand.

The problem is whether labor and management will ever take the risk of breaking the present pattern. Union leaders win approval for getting bigger pay increases than other unionists, which is why the 1960s' ceilings wound up as floors for settlements. And management, operating in a climate where everyone now expects business to just keep raising prices, maximizes profits and minimizes risk of labor unrest by caving in to labor demands and simply passing the increases on to consumers. Furthermore, both sides may view TIP as only a subtle new form of coercion.

In a masterpiece of understatement, Wallich is certain that "neither business nor labor will like this idea if TIP is viewed only as a stick, a penalty, which hits both profits and wages. But if it does no more than stabilize income shares between labor and capital, it would be no worse than the guideposts of the 1960s. If it also lowered the overall rate of inflation, everyone would benefit."

MAKING SENSE NOW

TIP, to be sure, abounds in practical limitations—administrative complexity being only second to the gut opposition of labor and management, which may be why it has not received serious consideration before now. The idea, in fact, dates to a Wallich-Weintraub paper in the *Journal of Economic Issues* of June, 1971, when Wallich was a Yale professor, and to expositions of TIP by Weintraub for years before that. What is new, however, is that TIP and some variations on the scheme are starting to make sense to economists in the current economic context.

The Congressional Budget Office, for example, cited TIP in a study last July as one of several "innovative anti-inflation mechanisms" that merits "further research and perhaps some experimentation." Congress' Joint Economic Committee takes a similar position in mid-session review issued this week. And the venerable Abba P. Lerner of Queens College in New York City has dropped his past opposition to TIP and argues strongly for it.

Surprisingly, the liberal Lerner takes no exception to the focus of TIP on wages alone. For Wallich and Weintraub cite historical evidence that "the average markup of prices over unit labor costs has been remarkably constant," with price gains exceeding labor gains by one to two index points a year. Put another way, they say, "the share of wages and sales in the national income, or in gross business income, has been historically constant," so that wage restraint implies restraint on price increases and no separate controls are required.

INCENTIVE

Both Wallich and Weintraub, as well as Lerner, favor an idea that could be used with TIP to make it more acceptable to labor: a reduction in payroll taxes for workers who settle for less than the "standard" wage increase. As developed by Laurence Seidman, another University of Pennsylvania economist, this payroll tax scheme would reinforce the stick of TIP with the carrot of a direct employee incentive to internalize the costs and benefits of fighting inflation, just as tax penalties and rewards have been proposed to fight pollution. Seidman considers wage increases in excess of average productivity gains a "pollution-like activity."

Seidman acknowledges that TIP would complicate the tax code. However, he notes: "Other tax incentives in the code are far from esthetic delights, but they make social and economic sense. The investment tax credit may be complex, but it works. Why should TIP be any less practical?"

Even economists with rival incomes-policy schemes are starting to voice support for TIP. Arthur Okun, of the Brookings Institution, has long argued for a "social contract" approach that would tie tax cuts to a commitment to anti-inflationary wage behavior by labor. But Okun is now willing to put his chips on TIP. "We're not beating inflation by stifling the recovery and throwing away half a trillion dollars in GNP," says Okun. "Either we find a way to live with inflation, or we do something about it besides making silly half-point shifts in the monetary growth targets. We must look at new ways to break out of inflation, and TIP is one of the most promising."

While the ideological spread between Wallich and Okun shows how wide support for TIP is among economists, there are some critics—especially among the pragmatists who have dealt for years with wage and price questions on the firing line of negotiations. Harvard's John T. Dunlop, former chairman of the Cost of Living Council, for example, reacts to TIP with his well-known position that "single, uniform standards for wages, as for prices, are simply not effective." And, he adds: "On the wage side, the existence of inflation implies that there already are distortions in the appropriate differentials between unions. A uniform standard for increases cannot eliminate that problem."

Dunlop's approach to wage inflation has always been to work behind the scenes with labor and management in problem areas, industry by industry, and that presumably is what he is still doing as head of the informal labor-management committee.

Marvin Kosters of the American Enterprise Institute takes an even dimmer view of TIP. Kosters, who helped design the 1971–74 controls program, warns: "To the extent TIP would be effective, it would inevitably interfere with market mechanisms. It might change relative prices a bit, but only by allowing low-wage industries to expand and forcing high-wage industries to contract. Wages would continue to rise as usual in the regulated industries or in others where there are cartelizing influences, and the result in the inflation rate could well be a wash."

Weintraub is not disheartened by this reaction. He insists that "TIP is the only wheel in town, and Washington may give it some spin of its own, but they'll come around to it eventually."

A New Approach to the Control of Inflation

LAURENCE S. SEIDMAN

A professor of economics at the University of Pennsylvania, Laurence S. Seidman has been instrumental in popularizing tax-based incomes policies through his many technical and popular articles on the subject. In the following selection he concisely gives the arguments for and against TIP.

Many countries over the last two decades have witnessed the failure of monetary and fiscal policy to maintain both price stability and full employment. They have turned to incomes policy in an attempt to restrain directly the advance of wages and salaries.

Monetarists correctly argue that excessive monetary expansion will cause inflation; and that any inflation will *eventually* end if the growth rate of the money supply is kept equal to the growth rate of potential real output. Unfortunately, monetarists also concede that, given the institutional features of a modern economy, their money supply policy—unassisted by incomes policy—will subject the economy to several years of high unemployment and slow growth in the process of subduing inflation. Other economists believe that even the estimate of several years is optimistic. Thus, while the correct money supply growth rate must be one element in a policy to achieve both price stability and full employment, it cannot be the only element.

Proper monetary and fiscal policy must be accompanied by an effective permanent incomes policy. The logic behind incomes policy derives from the observation—supported by common experience and econometric analysis—that the average business firm sets its price as a mark-up on its unit labor cost, and that while this mark-up fluctuates over the business cycle, its average value changes only very slowly over time. Firms with market power will tend to have larger mark-ups than firms in highly competitive industries, so that the average degree of market power in the economy will influence the average size of the mark-up. But as long as the average degree of market power changes very slowly, the average mark-up will change only very slowly. This has in fact been the case.

Thus, prices on average will be reasonably stable (some rising, some falling) if unit labor cost on average is stable (rising in some firms, falling in others). In turn, the growth rate in unit labor cost must by definition equal the growth rate in compensation per hour minus the growth rate in output per hour (productivity). Thus, the price level will be relatively stable (though, of course, occasionally buffeted by shocks, like the initial OPEC price rise) if the growth rate of wages and salaries stays equal to the growth rate in average productivity throughout the economy. The inflation rate will tend on average to equal the excess of the first growth rate over the second. These assertions are generally supported in

Laurence S. Seidman, "A New Apporoach to the Control of Inflation," *Challenge*, July-August 1976, pp. 39–43. Copyright ©1976 by M. E. Sharpe, Inc. Reprinted by permission of M. E. Sharpe, Inc.

the accompanying table. If the growth rate in compensation per hour today were 3 percent, as it was in the early 1960s, the inflation rate today would be minimal, as it was during that period.

The crucial question becomes: How can a permanent incomes policy be effectively implemented? It is at this vital step that incomes policy has thus far stumbled. While its theoretical justification remains compelling, unsatisfactory practical implementation has created considerable disillusionment with incomes policy. In virtually all countries that have attempted the policy, the same two methods have been tried. The first is voluntary restraint, introduced in the United States during the Kennedy Administration (the wage-price "guideposts"). The second is direct controls, introduced here during the Nixon Administration. Even advocates of incomes policy usually concede that each of these methods has serious weaknesses as a permanent policy.

Yet there is an alternative way to implement incomes policy permanently—one which has yet to be tried, and which should succeed in overcoming the major shortcomings of past attempts.

A MICROECONOMIC PROBLEM

This new method should actually be the most natural one for economists. Indeed, only the traditional designation of inflation as a macroeconomic, rather than a microeconomic problem, can account for the neglect of this approach thus far. From a microeconomic perspective, prices rise when the average business firm grants a wage and salary increase that exceeds the average growth rate of productivity in the economy. If the problem were regarded as microeconomic—the consequence of undesirable behavior by the average firm— economists would naturally propose a tax on the undesired activity in order to discourage it.

A comparison with the environmental pollution problem is instructive. Pollution is regarded by economists as a microeconomic problem. It arises because polluting firms are not charged for their use of a scarce resource—clean air or water. Economists almost unanimously recommend the use of effluent taxes (charges) to "internalize the externality," that is, to make polluting firms pay for the use of this valuable resource just as they must pay for any other. These traditional market incentives are generally regarded as the best method of controlling pollution. On the one hand, almost no one expects voluntary guideposts to be effective. In the microeconomic sphere, economists accept as an axiom that economic agents will behave according to their own self-interest, largely unaffected by what is best for society. On the other hand, most economists reject direct controls on polluters (except in extreme cases) because, in contrast to tax incentives and the market mechanism, controls are cumbersome, costly to administer, inflexible, and inefficient.

The microeconomic perspective, when applied to the traditionally macroeconomic problem of inflation, immediately reveals a similar "externality." When business firms grant wage and salary increases in excess of the average growth rate of productivity in the economy, they impose a cost on society by producing the public good ("bad") called inflation. Yet they are not charged for doing so, and therefore do not take this social cost into account when they make their wage-salary decisions. The question naturally arises: Why not tax business firms when they grant excessive wage and salary increases in order to "internalize this externality," and discourage them from such behavior? This is precisely the proposal that has been offered by Sidney Weintraub and Henry Wallich (*Journal of Economic Issues*, June 1971). They call this most natural way to implement incomes policy "The Tax-Based Incomes Policy (TIP)."

THE TAX-BASED INCOMES POLICY (TIP)

This policy has two unfortunate attributes that must be identified at the outset. First, TIP *appears* both to point the finger of blame at employees, or at their unions, and to penalize them by restraining their money incomes. Second, TIP *appears* to inflict an actual tax penalty on the average business firm. It must be emphasized that neither of these apparent aspects of TIP is actually part of the policy.

First, employees (or their unions) who seek higher wages and salaries to catch up with inflation, to stay ahead of it, or to maximize their earnings, are simply acting in their self-interest in exactly the same way managements do when they seek profits. Since labor is responding to the same incentives that drive all economic agents in our economy, fault-finding is unjustified. The aim of TIP is not to place blame, but to restructure incentives so that the outcome is best for society. TIP will slow the advance of money incomes, but it is incorrect to conclude that this will penalize labor. It is the advance of *real* income (the growth rate of money income minus the inflation rate) that determines labor's well-being, and this must on average equal the growth rate of real productivity. As the table illustrates, high growth rates of compensation on average cause high inflation rates; low growth rates of compensation cause low inflation rates. Since TIP will enable us to achieve a full employment economy, with its higher growth rate of productivity, TIP will improve, not reduce, the real income of labor.

Second, when TIP is introduced, the base corporate tax rate (now 48 percent) should be cut to offset the average surcharge. It will be shown that while the average business firm will be faced with a potential tax penalty under TIP if it continues to grant an excessive wage increase, it will not suffer an actual tax penalty when it responds as expected.

TIP would levy a surcharge on the ordinary corporate income tax—each firm's surcharge to be determined by its own annual wage and salary increase (including executive salaries, and the fringe benefits of all employees). Suppose the TIP guidepost (norm) were set at 3 percent—roughly the secular growth rate of average productivity in the economy. Then if the firm granted an 8 percent wage incrase, its surcharge would equal some multiple of the 5 percent excess over the norm. For instance, if the multiple were 4, the surcharge would be 20 percent.

Suppose that without TIP, the average wage increase in the economy would have been 8 percent and in response to TIP (with a multiple of 4) it is expected to be 5 percent. Then under TIP, the excess over the norm would average 2 percent, and the average surcharge would be 8 percent. When TIP is introduced, the base corporate tax rate should therefore be cut from 48 percent to 40 percent to offset the average surcharge. The firm that responds to TIP as expected by lowering its salary advance from 8 percent to 5 percent will continue to pay a corporate tax rate of 48 percent (the base rate of 40 percent plus the 8 percent surcharge). On the other hand, the firm that ignores TIP and continues to grant an 8 percent increase will suffer a surcharge of 20 percent, and a rise in its corporate tax rate to 60 percent.

Thus, TIP threatens a significant tax penalty if the firm ignores it. But if the firm responds as expected, no actual tax penalty is inflicted. Finally, if the firm grants an increase that is lower than expected, it will enjoy a net tax rate cut. Under TIP and the offsetting base rate adjustment, the total tax burden on corporations is expected to remain constant.

Thus, the threat of a tax penalty may be expected to stiffen the resistance of management against an excessive wage increase, reduce the resulting increase, and thereby on average avoid an actual tax penalty.

WILL TIP WORK?

At first glance, skeptical reaction to TIP might be, "Corporations will just ignore TIP, and 'pass on' the surcharge, thereby avoiding any decline in after-tax profit." It must be grasped that, if the TIP multiple is set sufficiently high, such a response is impossible. Suppose that the TIP multiple in the example above were set at 12, and the base rate lowered to 24 percent. Then the firm that responded to TIP as expected and granted a 5 percent increase would still pay 48 percent (the base rate of 24 percent plus a 24 percent surcharge). But a firm that ignored TIP and granted a 9 percent increase would suffer a tax rate of 96 percent. Obviously, the firm would be unable to maintain its after-tax profit, no matter how it tried to "pass on" the tax. If the multiple were only 7 and the base rate 34 percent, this firm would incur a rate increase of 28 to 76 percent and would have to double its before-tax profit to earn the same after-tax profit.

Even a small surcharge should be difficult to pass on. Economists disagree over whether firms can quickly pass on a modest increase in the ordinary corporate tax rate. It would be much harder, however, for a firm to shift its TIP surcharge because all its competitors might not have incurred as large a surcharge. In sharp contrast to an ordinary corporate rate increase, the TIP surcharge would vary across firms.

Thus, TIP should succeed in strengthening the resistance of managements to pay increases. Since it is the interaction of labor's push with management's resistance that determines the outcome, the result should be a lower rate of wage and salary increase at any unemployment rate, and therefore, a lower rate of inflation at full employment.

But labor may fear that profits will increase at the expense of wages; and business may fear that after-tax profit will be squeezed relative to wages. Neither fear should prove justified. As long as the growth rate of prices continues, on average, to be roughly equal to the growth rate of unit labor cost, then the ratio of aggregate profit to aggregate labor income must on average be unaffected by TIP. The slower growth rate of money compensation will automatically be followed (perhaps with a short lag) by a slower growth rate in money profits, both before and after tax. Real compensation and real profit will continue to advance at the growth rate of real output. Nevertheless, if the ratio of after-tax profit to after-tax compensation should alter in a way that is regarded as undesirable, then personal, payroll, or corporate tax rates can always be adjusted to secure a more desirable balance.

THE AUTOMATIC FLEXIBILITY OF TIP

TIP's great advantage over direct controls is its automatic flexibility. Suppose that without TIP, a firm with a labor shortage granted a 10 percent increase, while a firm with abundant labor granted 7 percent. Then under TIP, the increases might be 6 percent and 3 percent. Since TIP merely adds one additional condition to those already confronting the firm, it does not eliminate

PRICE-UNIT LABOR COST RELATIONSHIP
(PERCENT CHANGE FROM THE PREVIOUS PERIOD)

Year	Output Per Hour	Compensation Per Hour	Unit Labor Costs	Implicit Price Deflator
1948	3.1	2.9	5.6	6.6
1949	3.6	3.1	−0.5	1.0
1950	6.1	5.5	−0.6	1.7
1951	2.4	8.8	6.3	6.8
1952	2.2	5.5	3.2	1.7
1953	2.1	5.7	3.6	2.2
1954	1.8	3.2	1.3	1.6
1955	3.4	3.5	0.1	2.1
1956	−0.3	5.9	6.2	3.2
1957	2.3	5.7	3.4	3.5
1958	3.1	3.7	0.6	1.0
1959	3.2	4.6	1.3	2.2
1960	0.7	3.9	3.2	1.6
1961	3.4	3.3	−0.1	0.8
1962	4.1	4.2	0.0	1.5
1963	3.1	3.6	0.5	1.3
1964	3.6	4.8	1.2	1.3
1965	2.6	3.6	1.0	1.7
1966	3.1	6.2	3.0	2.8
1967	1.7	5.7	3.9	3.1
1968	2.6	7.4	4.7	4.1
1969	−0.4	6.7	7.1	4.7
1970	0.6	6.8	6.1	4.9
1971	3.4	6.8	3.3	4.7
1972	3.4	6.2	2.7	3.1
1973	2.0	7.8	5.7	4.2
1974	−2.4	9.5	12.2	10.1
1975[1]	0.9[1]	8.9[1]	8.0[1]	9.9[1]

[1] Projected by Bureau of Labor Statistics.
Note: All data are for the private, nonfarm economy.
Source: Bureau of Labor Statistics, Department of Labor, Presented in Table B-31 (p. 207), *The Economic Report of the President*, January 1976.

other market forces, which will therefore continue to generate desired relative wage and price patterns, thereby guiding resources efficiently.

This flexibility is automatic. There would be no direct interference in wage-salary setting. No new bureaucracy would be required. While there will obviously be technical problems that must be dealt with, such as the computation of the wage increase, the treatment of fringe benefits, etc., they should prove manageable. With respect to the complexity of its provisions, and opportunity for evasion, TIP should compare favorably with several existing taxes. While direct controls have seldom lasted, the tax-based incomes policy could become a permanent complement to proper monetary and fiscal policy. Together, these policies may at last be able to maintain both reasonable price stability and full employment.

TIP: A Tax-Based Incomes Policy to Stop Stagflation

SIDNEY WEINTRAUB

Sidney Weintraub, professor of economics at the University of Pennsylvania, has one of the longest lists of publications of any economist. His writings concern all areas of economic theory, and his insights into difficult questions have often preceded those of the profession. Together with Henry Wallich, Weintraub wrote what has become the seminal article on tax-based incomes policies. Currently the co-editor of *The Journal of Post Keynesian Economics*, he has recently completed two books, *Capitalism's Inflation and Unemployment Crisis* (1978) and *Keynes, Keynesians, and Monetarists* (1978). In the following selection, excerpted from his Frank M. Engle Lecture of the American College at Bryn Mawr, Pennsylvania, Weintraub looks at the theory of TIP and then discusses various methods of implementing the concept.

INCOME GEARING IN A MARKET ECONOMY

Whatever the institutions around which an economy may be organized, whether capitalist principles or socialist precepts, if production is going to grow by 3 percent per annum (especially in the consumer sector), it will not be possible for money incomes (and their expenditure) to advance by more than the same figure without the excess spilling over into higher prices or, as in the collectivist economies, resulting in queuing, shortages, and black markets induced at arbitrary state-sanctioned prices. Fundamentally there is a need for income *gearing*, of money payments in rough balance to parallel productivity trends. Collectivist economies accomplish the matching—imperfectly to be sure—by ukase. Market economies have lacked a mechanism to accomplish the task, relying instead on the imperfect mechanics of monetary policy, which carries the capability for creating unemployment while it strives erratically to fulfill the income-gearing function. Recent years make it painfully obvious that a more direct, precise, and less destructive mechanism must be devised if the market economy is to be healed of its stagflation sores.

What must be sought is a method of tying the money income track to productivity trends in a manner compatible with a market economy. The objective is to permit the system to operate harmoniously by relieving it of the mismatch which erupts in a telltale stagflation debacle.

The Incentive-Deterrent System

A market economy is inherently an incentive-deterrent system: it uses the carrot and the stick, with the latter being a pecuniary penalty to induce rational decisions while averting physical coercion. Specifically, the economy works

Sidney Weintraub, "TIP: A Tax-Based Incomes Policy to Stop Stagflation," M. Engle Lecture of The American College, Bryn Mawr, Pennsylvania, 1978, pp. 23–32. Reprinted from "TIP: A Tax-Based Incomes Policy to Stop Stagflation" by permission of The American College, Bryn Mawr, Pennsylvania. Copyright © 1978, The American College. All rights reserved.

through the stimuli of price-cost ratios. Favorable price-cost signals encourage production. Unfavorable ratios act as production deterrents. As businessmen weigh profit prospects they are induced to produce more or to produce less. Labor and capital are attracted into outlets where profit opportunities beckon; they tend likewise to shun the less attractive outlets. In the process, factors of production are hired and efficient resources are adapted to the underlying demand and supply manifestations. The price-cost ratios constitute the tangible signals of the "invisible hand" detected by Adam Smith, whereby individuals promote the general interest by making wanted goods and services available while pursuing their own profitable self-interest.

Expositors can differ in propounding the details of the price-cost-profit mechanics, including short-term impurities and long-term balances. But there can be no serious disagreement on its underlying pecuniary incentive-deterrent nature. The alternative to relying on price and income incentives, and deterrents, is a recourse to the coercive system: to prison warden jailers or the dictates of collectivist economies under which individuals are ordered to complete arduous and unattractive chores, and personal choices are narrowed to "Do it" or suffer dire physical discomfort menacing life itself.

When we apprehend the incentive-deterrent aspect of the market economy, it also becomes apparent that taxes partake of the same pecuniary incentive-deterrent features. In modern business ventures the intricacies of tax impairment are incessantly explored; investment opportunities are embraced only if they promise favorable aftertax outcomes, while other resource uses are abandoned under adverse tax pressures. The tax mechanism, like the price-cost system, is familiar; tax legislation contains financial penalties as a deterrent to enterprise and may promise lucrative income prizes in forging an incentive haven.

TIP: A TAX-BASED INCOMES POLICY

We should be able to build on this incentive-deterrent aspect of the tax mechanism in designing a workable incomes policy, or income gearing, for a full employment market economy free of the inflation fevers.

To anticipate an obvious objection, although our focus is on tax-oriented policies, the purpose is *not* to amass tax revenue. The proposals are aimed at eradicating inflationary incomes conduct, not collecting taxes. Actually, tax rates can be reduced through ensuing continuous full employment, and government outlays required for the jobless in the unemployment model can be curtailed.

A Speed Limit Analogy

A speed limit analogy can make the salient points to render the concept more apparent. An urban speed limit is not aimed at collecting revenue: if we were obsessed with collections, we would put the limit down to, say, 3 mph. Everybody would be busy all day paying a fine! Instead, the objective is to deter suicidal road conduct, especially when the actions menace the life and limb of others. In emergencies, individuals can surpass the limit, recognizing that they will have to pay a penalty. This prospect constitutes a safety valve; and an escape feature for special circumstances makes good legislation.

TIP (an acronym for a tax-based incomes policy) builds on this speeding analogy. Others might proffer a carrot approach to speeders; it might be possible to "bribe" individuals by giving them (small?) sums to stick to speeds under the limit, while denying the bounty to those surpassing the norm.

We shall see the bearing of these points in our discussion of the Wallich-Weintraub and the Okun approaches below. A new proposal (CAIP) is also unveiled as a promising vehicle for hastening the enactment of a more complete set of TIP measures.

The Wallich-Weintraub Proposal

To break the stagflation syndrome of unmitigated economic disaster fostered by bad theory and ensuing futile policies, in 1971 (early on in the stagflation misadventures) Professor Henry Wallich (now Federal Reserve governor) and I collaborated in sketching the outlines of the TIP concept. It was based on the perspective that price level stability required money incomes geared closely to productivity changes.

Briefly, TIP proposed that roughly the thousand largest corporations (measured in terms of employees), which are responsible for the lion's share of the GNP, maintain the *average* of their annual pay hikes for all employees—executive, managerial, clerical, production all included—to a norm, say, of 5 percent per annum. This would put a lid on the per annum price creep of about 2 percent.

To ensure compliance, firms that punctured the norm would be subject to a higher penalty rate of corporate income tax. The scale could be progressive, with the corporate income tax increased from the approximate average rate of 46 percent to 48 percent for small violations, rising for severe transgressions. The firm would thus have an incentive to resist extravagant pay demands; there would be a costly tax deterrent to docile submissiveness and systematic escalating prices of the infamous wage-price spiral. Too, various supplements could be conceived; for one, low-interest loans could be tendered to firms that adhered to the norm and whose settlements were rejected by union intransigence; or NLRB accreditation might be withdrawn from unions which persisted in staking out exorbitant claims. More dire penalties might involve denial of unemployment and (e.g., food stamps) to those who rejected noninflationary settlements. At the same time, those firms which consciously wanted to pay more than the norm, for reasons that seemed compelling to them, could do so—at a price. An escape hatch or safety valve option would be present.

In instituting TIP, *the normal corporate income tax level could be cut*, say, from 46 percent to 42 percent. This reduction would offset, by and large, any TIP collections. Business objections that TIP would erode corporate venture capital could not be legitimately sustained. Actually, as inflation is blocked and easier money ushers in full employment, steeper corporate tax reduction could be contemplated. Protests that TIP would block venturesome investment capital projects would thus misconstrue its nature entirely. (If the TIP norm is universally violated, the plan—like an ineffective speed limit—would be inoperative, and it could quickly be withdrawn.)

Administratively, TIP would add about six extra lines to the corporate income tax form. A firm would take its total wage and salary bill, and divide this by the number of full-time equivalent employees (this information is already reported on corporate income tax, Social Security, and personal income tax withholding forms). The firm would then calculate the *average* pay per employee for, say, 1977. It would do the same for 1978. If for 1977 the average pay was, say, $10,000, and for 1978 the figure was $10,500 (or less), this simple computation would end the matter. If the pay hike brought the average to $11,000—a 10 percent annual boost—the firm would be subject to an extra corporate income tax penalty.

To check the extra six to eight lines on the corporate tax form for the contemplated one thousand firms whose pay scales set the key income patterns would require about twenty more IRS auditors. Cost: approximately $500,000 to $1 million. Potential GNP gains: perhaps $100 billion or more. The difference appears as a most felicitous trade-off bargain.

Obviated is the cumbersome, denunciatory, politicized, harassing, and expensive bureaucratic legion of 100,000 to 500,000 employees (costing perhaps $5 billion to $10 billion) under traditional—and porous—wage and price controls. Officiousness would be absent, exasperating delays and arbitrary rulings would be precluded, and the costly field day enriching mainly lawyers while clogging court calendars, with a parade of petty snoopers and control enforcers creating a new breed of criminals out of consenting individuals engaged in market transactions, would be suppressed. The image of Captain Queeg counting strawberries is best erased from our economic life; it becomes only too visible under mandatory wage and price controls.

On all counts, TIP has unparalleled virtues compared to the defects of historic price and wage control practices.

TIP-CAP

Unions likewise would exercise their usual functions under TIP, albeit with more realistic ceilings to preclude the exaggerated pay hikes of the past. They might be able to eke out more than a 5 percent annual pay boost, through bargaining, as long as executive, managerial, and other nonunionized employees acquired less. Bargaining would focus on *relative* gains, which is where the conflict and controversy belong, rather than being concentrated on the absolute increments, as in the past. For if one union grabs off 12 percent and another 8 percent, with the average being 10 percent, while the price swing is 7 percent, what is accomplished is practically equivalent to a 6 percent gain for the one, 4 percent for the other, an average of 5 percent and a price move of, say, 2 percent—with fuller employment. The modestly revised income shuffle under practically noninflated prices would possess stronger attributes of equity and justice.

It is also conceivable to permit an addendum to the flat (hypothetical) 5 percent pay norm in recognition of more spectacular productivity achievements, with employees of the particular firms sharing, say, about half the exceptional gains. (I have described this as TIP-CAP, where CAP = corrected average product.) However, productivity gains in any single firm markedly above the economy's 3 percent average should ordinarily be translated into lower prices for the industry's product relative to other goods; under a stable price level it would mean lower absolute prices in sectors where productivity rises significantly.

Covering the thousand largest firms would extend the TIP income controls to employees responsible for 55 to 60 percent of business output. By emulation the influences would extend farther, to smaller enterprises. For government employees, across-the-board pay increases could be limited to 5 percent per annum and corrected where necessary every two or three years.

To an overwhelming degree, the market demands for professional services are regulated by incomes earned in the business sector of the economy. With most wage and salary incomes limited to 5 percent average increments per annum, we can suspect that professional fees and earnings will not skyrocket at the inordinate past pace. Farm prices, too, would be contained, inasmuch as they would reflect the industrial income stability.

The Okun TIP Variant

Dr. Arthur Okun, of the Brookings Institution, offered (in late 1977) a "carrot variant" of TIP. Noting that 1977 pay gains bordered on 8 percent, Okun would reward union employees who acceded to a 6 percent hike with a tax refund of about $225 per annum. After taxes, they would thus be (slightly) better off than with the higher 8 percent pay award. Inflation would be cut by about 2 percent, and the GNP could grow. Firms likewise would have their corporate taxes trimmed by 2.5 percent. As promulgated, the plan would be voluntary, not mandated.

There is the issue of whether the carrot is sweet enough or big enough: the proposal is akin to paying individuals for observing the speed limit or for behaving socially as they should behave. Apparently there is nothing to prevent unions from deciding to go for far more than 8 percent and then regaling their membership with tales of victories far larger than tax rebates. Too, the voluntary feature under limited tax benefits raises queries on how widespread its adoption would be. There is the added complication of equity protests from nonunion employees whose incomes have not risen by more than 6 percent, who would feel entitled to and would warrant a matching tax refund.

Nonetheless, in offering an incentive proposal and contributing vitally to the debate, the Okun proposal has achieved a prominence and intensity that has enabled the conflicting ideas to attract a public hearing, with their respective merits ventilated and more finely appraised.

CAIP

In view of the tax dimension to TIP, Congress is unlikely to move with dispatch. Judging by the delay in enacting an energy bill, we are still a long way—despite the urgency of a long-range national policy on incomes as well as energy—from dispelling our stagflation predicament. Modest improvement on the inflation front or in jobs might even kindle the political, and public, fiction that the trouble will vanish. Politicians are not unlike Mr. Micawber; they, too, wish something miraculous and soothing will turn up, magically, to relieve them of a painful prospect of antagonizing a constituency even when the injury is more illusory than real or even when, in the absence of enlightened dialogue, a benefit is misconstrued as an injury.

Faster progress might be made along another route. Despite protestations that incomes policy, or income gearing, is wholly a new departure, the federal government already has a partial one in operation in the form of the Walsh-

Healey and the Davis-Bacon acts. To be sure, these set income floors rather than ceilings.

Under Walsh-Healey, firms fulfilling government contracts are bound to pay prevailing minimum wages. Davis-Bacon requires workers on federal or federally assisted construction projects to be paid "prevailing wage scales," ordinarily interpreted liberally to mean about the maximum rates within a fifty-mile radius.

Why not also a ceiling in terms of *annual rates of pay change*? Entailed would be the insertion of a clause in government contracts to the effect that successful bidders must adhere to an annual limit of 5 percent on the *average wage and salary increase* over the life of the contract. Penalties for violators could be as follows: (1) future bids could be rejected, say, for a period of three years; (2) cost excesses from puncturing the norm could be precluded as cost deductions for income tax in computing company profits; (3) cost overruns attributable to magnanimous pay grants could be disapproved in compensatory negotiations.

Considering that the defense contractors comprise a veritable Who's Who among America's thousand largest firms, the proviso would thus blanket the same firms selected for TIP coverage. Subcontractors would probably also have to abide by equivalent rules to block evasive spin-off loopholes.

A contract-award incomes policy (CAIP) of this nature could thwart the pay escalation and mitigate the inflationary pressure emanating from the construction sector, which has been a notorious front-runner in the pay scramble. Money costs would thus be linked more closely to productivity progress in this important economic area. Depending on how the law was written, GNP activity of $100 billion to $500 billion might be effectively brought under income restraint. A huge and vital sector would thus be subject to noninflationary behavior.

License to inflate money income by raiding the federal Treasury under cost-plus negotiations would be withdrawn; firms making too good a personal thing, and aggrandizing executive compensation out of the necessary military business, would be deterred by effective "speed limits." Within a few months of the contract awards, unions—which often form a vocal lobby for defense contracts because "they spell jobs"—strike for higher pay; this would be stopped. After lobbying for the jobs and weapons systems, they would be subject to life-of-the-contract restricted pay enhancement. As matters now stand, once the government outlay is committed, the subsequent inflationary pay demands victimize all taxpayers through the federal budget process, and other union employees are injured after the Fed presses its tight money clutch to combat the price level disorders.

CAIP thus would have congenial moral, as well as economic, attributes. Too, as a natural short extension of Davis-Bacon, CAIP should be capable of earlier implementation than TIP. The latter, however, casts the wider net and constitutes the essence of a long-term rational solution.

LINCOLN AND "THE SLOWS"

Logic thus commends the need for new policies to cope with the new events that have impaired the functioning of our economy. Experience confirms that the dour outcome of the market economy on the price and job front hardly swells popular support for the system. A better chance for its sustenance and survival would ensue from even a modest institutional innovation. TIP is of this nature, compatible with the ultimate pecuniary incentive-deterrent principles of the market economy.

During the lamentable Nixon presidency there was, in his demeaning colloquial football analogies, much talk of an economic "game plan" involving "gradual" money supply deflation. It was thought that if the pace of the annual money supply increment slowly abated, then the economic perplexities would disappear; the object was to sort of sneak up on the instability. Unfortunately, the result of gradualism was the onset and perpetuation of stagflation until, in desperation and anxiety about a forthcoming reelection campaign, the impeachable president disavowed his oft-pronounced principle of "never" concerning wage and price controls, and implemented his assorted series of noxious control phases.

During Ford's incumbency, his economic advisers first gave us WIN buttons to stop inflation and reiterated the virtues of patience and inaction; they even advocated a tax hike in 1974, despite the obvious recession phenomena. Then at the close of the year there was the 180 degree field reversal and a show of pique at Congress's slight delay in enacting a tax cut! Through 1975 and 1976 the Ford advisers beguiled us with communiques, like a midwife reporting a bedside vigil, about the economy "bottoming out." (It was the largest postwar bottom, to be sure.)

The Carter presidency is now sixteen months old. On inflation it has made no real progress at all. Instead, it has dredged up a PR promotional image of "encouraging" business and labor "discussions." Presumably, talks always take place at contract time and before—more talk is hardly a policy. On jobs there has been some improvement from the 1976 rates of unemployment of 9 percent. Nonetheless, there remains a shortfall between skills and jobs; teenage unemployment and street-corner living are still with us in epidemic proportions.

After ten years of stagflation, therefore, we still lack a sense of urgency to eradicate the monumental ills that plague our society. Inflation touches all our difficulties, from farmers' problems, to Social Security pensions, to unemployment, to the international value of the dollar, to energy finance, to the stock market, to government budgets, to personal frustration, to a string of irrationalities in decision making—and this list of charges is not exhaustive.

Over a century ago, under the stress of a civil war, Abraham Lincoln moaned, more in sorrow than in anger, over what he termed a case of "the slows" on the part of his generals. Until he found Grant, he observed, he gave his commanders superior numbers and immense supplies, and acceded to their military plans. Yet they refused to budge from the drill camp and do battle: they had a case of "the slows."

On inflation, our political leaders, and professional economists too, have been exhibiting a profound case of "the slows." New policies to subdue this economic excrescence, so that we get on to resolve the other novel and grave problems of our age, are overdue. The older scourge of inflation should be eradicated, as has been the case with smallpox and malaria. TIP in one form or another, or some other imaginative use of incomes policy that ingenuity might yet devise, could be the serum for inoculating the economy against the virus of income and productivity imbalance.

REVISING THE DECLARATION OF INDEPENDENCE

When John Adams recommended Thomas Jefferson for the onerous chore of writing the draft of the Declaration of Independence, forgoing the task himself despite the entreaties of others on his own behalf, among the reasons he gave for his choice was Jefferson's gift of "a peculiar felicity of expression." For his part, Jefferson claimed only modest originality as he tried to incorporate in the document what he sensed as the prevailing democratic mood of the time.

If he were writing today, some of us might petition Mr. Jefferson to insert into the statement (with apologies to Locke) a remark on "labor's unalienable right to a job," an affirmation that work opportunities must abound to provide income choices. However, along with this "unalienable right" there goes an unalienable obligation—namely, a denial of any right of labor to inflate the price level. No group can have a mandate to do injury to others—as Jefferson well understood—by inviting system responses that end in unemployment.

An incomes policy such as TIP is *not* antilabor. It is *not* antibusiness. It is anit-inflation and pro-full employment. It can permit jobs for all, with money and real income advances tethered to productivity to permit the pursuit of "life, liberty, and happiness" in a smoothly functioning market economy under democratic institutions guaranteeing freedom and preserving liberty.

A Reward TIP[1]

ARTHUR M. OKUN

Arthur M. Okun is respected as one of the most knowledgeable economists in the United States. A former chairman of the Council of Economic Advisers, he is currently a Senior Fellow at Brookings Institution, where he serves as co-editor of the *Brookings Papers on Economic Activity*. One of the few economists who has an "economic law" named after him, Okun has been influential in publicizing TIP and in designing a practical and politically feasible proposal. In his testimony to the Senate Committee on Banking, Housing, and Urban Affairs, which is reproduced here, Okun outlines a proposal upon which President Carter modeled the guaranteed real wage insurance portion of his 1978 anti-inflation program.

I am a proponent of a tax-based incomes policy, not because that policy is beautiful, but because it is a lot less ugly than alternative policy strategies. Under present policies, inflation is proceeding at a pace that is unacceptable to the American people; it is not unwinding but rather tending to step up; it is not susceptible to any efficient cure from either fiscal-monetary restraint or price-wage controls.

THE PREAMBLE TO TIP

Despite persistent excess supplies for more than three years, our economy is suffering from an entrenched price-wage spiral with a 6-percent rate of price increase and an 8-percent rate of pay increase. And although the rate of price increase has been reasonably steady and well-predicted, inflation remains public enemy #1 in the eyes of the overwhelming majority of the American public. Currently inflation seems to be moving a bit above the 6-percent plateau, reflecting an inevitable catch-up of nonunion wages and the consequences of several cost-raising measures taken by the government.

Inflation could be slowed down once more by recession, as it was during 1974–75. But fighting inflation by curbing demand at a time when it is not being caused by excess demand is absurdly inefficient. It is like burning down the house to roast the pig. A wide variety of statistical estimates that I know agree that, under current conditions, a reduction of 1 percent in nominal GNP for 1979 would cost between 0.85 and 0.95 of a percentage point of production and save only between .05 and .15 of a percentage point in inflation. In their discussions on fiscal policy, the Administration and Congress show that they are not willing to pay that price; while in its decisions on monetary policy, the Federal Reserve apparently considers it essential to pay that price. Hence, the nation is facing

---

[1] The views expressed are my own and are not necessarily those of the officers, trustees, or other staff members of The Brookings Institution.

Arthur M. Okun, "A Reward TIP," statement before the Committee on Banking, Housing, and Urban Affairs, U.S. Senate, May 22, 1978.

the serious risk that fiscal policy and monetary policy may be on a collision course. In light of all these unfavorable circumstances, I simply cannot see a realistic happy ending to the present scenario of policy.

The momentum of inflation must be stopped—without another bloodletting of jobs and investment like that of 1974–75 and without a return to the brittle and distorting controls of 1971–72. The same opinion surveys that record the American people's antipathy toward inflation also reveal their basic support for a mutual deescalation of wages and prices. But because this is a decentralized economy, no single group of private decisionmakers can stop the spiral on its own. On the contrary, firms and unions must run ever faster to protect themselves from higher costs being imposed on them. The spiral can be broken only with the help of a collective, social decision.

Tax-based incomes policy (TIP) is a way of pursuing mutual deescalation. It is not tried and true; but the present scenario has been tried and found sadly wanting. It is not a substitute for lower rates of monetary growth and lower federal deficits as a remedy for inflation, but it is a way to make possible the necessary slowdown of money growth and turnaround of fiscal stimulus without the enormous economic and social costs of recession.

AN OUTLINE OF A REWARD TIP ON WAGES

I speak as the inventor of the reward TIP; the original, basic-model TIP produced by Henry Wallich and Sidney Weintraub relies on a stick, and I sought to convert it to a carrot. I see some distinct advantages and disadvantages in each of the two approaches. But, most of all, I believe that either of them could work effectively, and that both belong among the options from which the Congress might ultimately select an efficient cure for stagflation.

My thinking about how a reward TIP might best be implemented has evolved during the past six months in light of constructive criticisms and probing inquiries that I have received; and I expect it to change some more. But let me outline my current thoughts on the main features of that program. To begin with, I would like the legislation implementing a reward-TIP for wages to be enacted for a three-year period, with the understanding that the ceiling on the wage increase that qualifies for the reward and the size of the tax credit would be determined annually by the Congress. I would hope to be able to declare victory and let TIP expire after the three-year period, but I would like to hold open the possibility of renewal.

As I envision it, forms would be sent to all employers in the nation on October 1 in the year prior to the initiation of TIP, asking them to enlist in the program. To participate at that time, the firm would have to pledge to limit the *average* pay increase for its workers in the next year to no more than 6 percent. Pay would be defined as wages plus private fringe benefits, and the definition of fringes would be spelled out in detail. The pledge would leave the firm free to grant promotions and merit raises of any size to individual workers so long as its overall average increase in pay was within the limit.

By participating, the firm would qualify all its employees for a tax reduction during the year ahead equal to 1½ percent of their wage and salary income up to some level, say $20,000. For most workers, that tax credit would be the equivalent of a raise a little bigger than 2 percent (before-tax). In other words, the worker would be better off with a 6-percent raise and the tax credit in combination, than with an 8-percent raise and no tax cut. The credit would then be subtracted in calculating the worker's withholding tax, in effect offsetting a portion of the present payroll tax.

The firm would also be asked to state in the initial form how it intended to measure its units of employment for the two consecutive years—for example, as total person-hours or as full-time equivalent employees. It would also be asked to specify how it planned to calculate its average wage increase—for example, simply by using the totality of all pay and all workers, or by weighting increases for distinct occupational groups, plants, subsidiaries, or the like. Once the firm made these decisions, it would be required to stick with them for the next tax year.

I believe that workers would strongly prefer getting the bonus right from the beginning of the year in their take-home paychecks, and that is why I emphasize advance commitments by firms to participate. But some firms may be unable to predict their wage increases in advance or might become unable to keep wages on target under some contingencies they might encounter during the calendar year.

Hence, I think that firms should be given an option to fill out the form, displaying an interest in the program without making a commitment; they would hold open the possibility of qualifying their workers for refunds after the year ends, if they meet the wage limit. In contrast to those firms that delay their decision, any firm that makes an advance commitment must take the responsibility of fulfilling its pledge and must assume the full liability for any subsequent determination that the reduction in withholding taxes from workers was unjustified. For carrying those responsibilities, the firms that sign up in advance (*not* those that only qualify ex post) should receive some reward for themselves—perhaps one-fourth of the amount that is rebated to their workers through withholding.

Thus, the key features of the plan can be summarized as follows:

1. A qualified worker receives an anti-inflationary tax credit equal to 1½ percent of his wage or salary income up to $20,000—equivalent to an extra raise of 2+ percent (before-tax).
2. A worker becomes qualified when his employer either:
   A. Pledges in advance that the overall average pay increase for the year will not exceed 6 percent (and then the worker gets the credit in take-home pay through reduced withholding); or
   B. Reports on its tax return, ex post, that its average pay increase for the year in fact did not exceed 6 percent (and then the worker gets a tax refund).
3. A firm that enlists in advance (as in 2A above) receives for itself a tax credit equal to one-fourth the total reduction in withholding taxes granted to its workers.

Under present circumstances, I would expect the overwhelming majority of nonunion employers to enlist in the program, with virtually all governmental units and nonprofit institutions leading the parade. Employees would be informed that they would receive tax credits, and, I would expect, most would be assured by the firms that, if their relative wage position should fall behind during the course of the program, it would be subsequently restored. I would expect a significant fraction—though probably only a minority—of unionized firms to participate during the initial year of the program. In fact, the size of the pay increases scheduled for the second year and third year of many existing three-year contracts would make participation worthwhile to the workers. Indeed, a substantial fraction of union contracts average less than 8 percent over the life of the contract, even though the average is apparently above 9 percent. As a rough guess, I would expect that about two-thirds of all workers would be enrolled in the program. If the Congress could afford to make the rebate 2 or 2½ percent rather than 1½, that figure might be raised to 80 or 90 percent.

Firms will want to participate in a reward TIP because—and only because—the tax credit to their workers would help them to slow down wages; and that is the basic guarantee that the program would be effectively anti-inflationary. I would expect—and, indeed, I would want—the average wage slowdown to be somewhat smaller than the tax credit so that labor is initially made better off, as well as gaining additional benefits from the subsequent slowdown of prices. I would also expect generally favorable effects from the recognition and the expectation of the deceleration of inflation.

Surely, the slowdown of wages in general will affect union contracts; the influence of relative wages works both ways—from nonunion to union sectors as well as the reverse. Moreover, the deceleration in consumer prices stemming from the slowdown in wages would automatically have further favorable anti-inflationary effects through cost-of-living escalator clauses.

During the second and third years of the program, I would expect an increasing fraction of union workers to be enrolled in it. All participation requires an implicit understanding with employers that, at the end of the program, any group that has fallen behind in relative wages would require some compensatory catch-up. But with broad participation, such adjustments would largely serve to restrain those who did not join up, rather than to compensate those who did.

At the end of each year, employers who qualified their workers for the credit (either by advance pledge or by ex post action) would fill out a supplemental form on their income taxes, totalling wages and all other deducted expenses that are classified as pay, and then dividing that total pay by the number of employment units (say, full-time equivalent workers or total manhours). The calculation would be made for the latest year and for the base year, to show that the 6-percent standard had been met.

There would be no monitoring, investigating, or approval or notification of any wage change during the course of the year. The auditing of tax returns would be the sole technique of enforcement, just as it is now for all provisions of the income tax. In these respects, all types of TIP contrast sharply with controls: no private behavior is prohibited, and no advance approval from the government is required.

If a firm has an acute labor shortage and really needs to raise wages by 12 percent to get the added workers it can profitably use, clearly it should and would stay out of the program. That firm and its workers should then recognize that, in all fairness, they are not entitled to an anti-inflationary tax credit.

Analogously, in the case of the investment tax credit, a firm that does not need more equipment is not obliged to invest; but neither does it have any justified complaint about not receiving a tax reward.

SOME FEATURES OF ALTERNATIVE PROPOSALS

The advantages and disadvantages of various approaches form an interesting balance sheet:

Revenue Costs The most obvious disadvantage of the reward-TIP relative to the penalty TIP is that the reward costs federal revenue, and that is a significant matter.

Scope. Secondly, the reward approach must be *universal*; the tax reductions must be available to employees of the corner grocer and the county sheriff's office as well as to those of major corporations. The penalty approach, on the other hand, can be confined to large firms which may be viewed as the pacesetters in the determination of wages. At a Brookings conference last month that covered this range of subjects, many participants viewed the opportunity for selectivity as a major advantage of the penalty approach, particularly because it avoided the problems of record-keeping, informing, and auditing for very small firms.

In my personal judgment, however, that is not a decisive matter. Small firms are now offered the opportunity of qualifying for the investment tax credit, the employment tax credit, capital gains advantages, deductible travel and entertainment expenses, and all of the other complex tax-minimizing provisions of the income tax. And all of these provisions are enforced solely through the low probability of subsequent audit of returns. But if the Congress should feel that an onerous burden would be placed on tiny firms, then enterprises with, say, less than twenty employees (as well as brand new firms operating in their initial year) could be given a special exemption, enabling them to qualify their workers for the tax credit simply by signing a pledge to adhere to the anti-inflationary spirit of the program. Any sensible employer would convert that into some slowdown of wages.

Special Situations Like any tax incentive program, any newly enacted TIP will run into some special situations that can reasonably be regarded as "inequities." For example, some firm may have granted no pay increases at all in the preceding year, and its workers might well feel that they deserve the elbow room to catch up. Alternatively, another firm might have raised pay by 10 percent on September 1 of the preceding year; that alone would push up the calendar-year average incrase of the next year above the 6 percent hurdle, even if no further pay increases were awarded during that calendar year. No manageable set of provisions can "fix up" such special problems. If these are inequities, they are surely far less serious than the inequities imposed by stagflation. The Congress would have to accept some imperfections to ensure an administratively feasible and economically effective program. I suspect that such a course would be more acceptable if the victims of "special situations" are merely deprived of rewards rather than subjected to penalties. In the history of tax legislation, "grandfather clauses" have been typical for newly stiffened rules, but not for new benefits, like the investment or employment tax credits. So this difference is another advantage of the reward approach.

In a somewhat related manner, the reward approach builds in a better incentive for compliance by making employers liable for any unwarranted rebates of taxation to their workers. Firms are much less likely to risk IRS punishment for unjustified claims that benefit workers directly than for minimization or avoidance to shave their own liability for penalties.

Pass-through In the penalty approach, firms that pay higher taxes because of large wage increases may conceivably pass on the tax penalty to their customers in the form of even higher prices. I do not view the pass-through as an overwhelming problem, but it is avoided by the reward approach.

Fairness to Workers Both the reward and the penalty TIP apply leverage directly to wages rather than to prices. That aspect of TIP needs to be clearly understood. Every TIP proponent knows that labor has *not* been the villain in the present inflation and that wages are *not* out of line on the high side. The reason for focusing on wages is quite different. According to a vast body of statistical evidence, a slowdown in wages is fully and reliably translated, after a reasonably short lag, into a slowdown of prices. The evidence on the conversion of price slowdowns into wage slowdowns is much less clear. Some studies suggest that a 1 percentage point slowdown in prices will slow wages by only 0.2 percentage point, while others give answers as high as 0.9. Mainly, the problem is that economists just don't know. If we were sure that a price slowdown would generate a prompt and substantial wage slowdown, we could break the spiral by a direct attack on consumer prices—for example, a federal program to "buy out" state sales taxes (or to slash federal payroll taxes on employers). I think those steps are well worth taking, but I do not have the faith in their effectiveness to rely entirely on them.

At least in part, wage inflation must be the direct target of any effective TIP. With a reward TIP, I do not see a substantive equity problem: the average take-home pay of workers would probably be increased a little initially, even before they benefit from a slowdown of price inflation.

With the penalty approach, there is a problem of ensuring fairness to workers. They would be better off before long, and would be far better off than they would be if inflation speeds up or if it is curbed by recession. But they are not immediately indemnified for the initial slowdown of wages that is being induced by the tax penalty. As some see a penalty TIP, it requires workers (and only workers) to ante up for the deal, so to speak. Henry Wallich and Sidney Weintraub have been sensitive to such criticisms and have suggested added provisions to achieve equity—like a contingent tax on any shift of income to profits.

Problems of this sort are most relevant in the first year of a penalty TIP, since the statistical evidence warns that it takes a little while for a wage slowdown to be translated fully into a price slowdown. It could help to combine the stick on excessive wage increases with a general carrot for all wage earners in that year—e.g. by enacting an income-tax cut for low and middle income families or, even better, a cut in federal payroll taxes on workers, or, best of all, a federal grant program to induce cuts in state sales taxes.

A PRICE RESTRAINT CREDIT?

In the search for still greater evenhandedness, I suggested last fall [1977] that a tax reward (perhaps a discount on income taxes) might be offered to those businesses that limited to 4 percent their price increases on a value-added basis (that is, above and beyond increased costs of purchased materials, energy, and supplies). On this proposal, the criticisms that I have received from my professional colleagues have generally been more adverse and, to me, more persuasive than those on the wage reward TIP. I was searching for symmetry, but the economy has a basic asymmetry: it is much harder to measure increases in product prices than increases in wages. New products, quality changes, and widely varied types of output complicate the calculation. I now believe that a price reward can be incorporated into the program *if* the Congress insists that the burden of proof rests on any claimant for such a tax credit—that the firm is responsible to develop the kind of systematic price indexes that would justify its deduction. But my critics would emphasize that such an accounting task would be inherently less difficult for large manufacturing firms, airlines, communications companies, and utilities than for small enterprises.

Frankly, I never expected much additional benefit in slowing inflation from the price reward, but felt that the forging of a social compact would be enhanced by treating wages and prices symmetrically. Now, however, I am concerned that a provision that was intended to reassure workers might turn out to bestow tax cuts arbitrarily on big business. At this point, I would not advocate a tax credit for price restraint.

In summary, TIP requires much more discussion and a major educational effort; and this committee deserves our gratitude for promoting that discussion. Clearly, the basic current controversy is not among alternative forms of TIP. Rather, it is between slowing the wage-price spiral by some form of TIP or other innovative cost-reducing strategy, on the one hand, and the hideous alternatives of letting inflation rip, fighting it by recession, or suppressing it by wage-price controls, on the other. The need to lick stagflation cooperatively and sensibly is the biggest economic challenge facing our nation, and also one of the biggest challenges to our democratic political process.

On Getting Really Full Employment Without Inflation

MANCUR OLSON

A highly respected public finance specialist, Mancur Olson has written on diverse areas of economic analysis. He has taught at Princeton University and is currently professor of economics at the University of Maryland. This memo was written during the time he served as an adviser to Jimmy Carter in the 1976 election campaign.

One problem that is likely to be decisively important after the election, and which can be relevant even in the last days of the campaign, is of course how to get the unemployment rate down to an appealing level without generating inflation. This memo proposes a tool that can help solve that problem after the election, and which might possibly be mentioned in the last days of the campaign to document the claim that a Carter-Mondale administration would provide both full employment and price stability.

As is well known, the American economy like most others has experienced significant inflation whenever the unemployment has fallen to generally acceptable levels and sometimes even when unemployment is very high and increasing. Many voters think a Carter-Mondale administration would lower the rate of unemployment, but perhaps only at the expense of a higher rate of inflation than the Republicans would generate. Thus any measure that could promise both lower unemployment and lower inflation would have considerable electoral appeal as well as economic usefulness.

Those economists who might best be called "hard line monetarists" rule out the possibility that inflation during periods when the economy has an unusual amount of excess capacity could owe anything at all to the freedom of action of labor unions or firms with a lot of market power. Their best argument seems to be that there has been no sign of an *increase* in union membership or monopoly power during any recent inflation; since decisionmakers would have an incentive to set prices or wages that reflected their market power as soon as they obtained that power, there is no reason why they should increase wages or prices in the absence of a monetary or fiscal expansion. The very conservative emotions of most of the economists who make this argument should not obscure the fact that it contains a great deal of truth where firms as opposed to unions are at issue.

For unions, on the other hand, this hard line monetarist position is much too simple, and the reasons why it is inadequate point the way to a scheme that can bring full employment without any serious inflation. Unlike the firm, the labor union does not have one overriding objective like profits; it wants higher

Mancur Olson, "On Getting Really Full Employment Without Inflation: An Idea for the Last Days of the Campaign and the Next Four Years," internal memo during Jimmy Carter's presidential campaign, 1976. Reprinted by permission of the author.

wages for its members, but when wages rise firms will normally have an incentive to hire less labor, so the union must (consciously or subconsciously) trade-off the higher wages against reduced employment, which means a risk of unemployment or shorter work weeks for its members. It is entirely possible that unions can decide to give a higher relative weight to higher wages in some circumstances than others, thereby bringing about either an increase in unemployment or (if monetary and fiscal expansion maintains full employment) inflation. They may do this because coalitions of relatively senior workers who would not be laid off succeed in getting the union to demand higher wages; because union members often do not have much basis for judging their leaders' performance except by comparing their wage increases with comparable workers in other unions and may demand wage increases that match whichever reference union happens to have obtained the largest increase; because workers in less fortunate industries, occupations, or regions may out of a sense of fairness demand wage increases equal to those of their better placed brethren; and because astute union leaders may find their leadership roles easier if they demand regular periodic increases in wages rather than adjust the wage demand to the vagaries of the labor market.

If what has been said is correct, it follows that good monetary and fiscal policy may not be enough to obtain both full employment and price stability and that the initial impetus for any wage-price spiral on the supply side comes from wages rather than prices. It does not follow, however, that the proper policy for dealing with this problem is to attack or discriminate against unions; this would not be an optimal policy, in view of the many contributions unions make, nor even a viable policy, particularly in a Democratic administration.

The usual way of dealing with this problem has of course been through "guidelines" or "income policies" which prohibit or discourage wage and price increases above specified levels. Labor union support for these policies is sometimes sought with "social contract" proposals that endeavor to trade some government policies favorable to blue collar workers for promises of support for the guidelines by organized labor. Well intentioned and sensible as such policies can be, their record of success has not been very encouraging, either in this country or in others. They have also regularly proved to be political liabilities for the administration in power. If the program is altogether rigid, as in a mandatory price-wage freeze, the price system cannot perform the function of allocating resoures and inefficiences, queues, and black markets develop if the controls are kept on very long. If, on the other hand, there is some flexibility or an element of voluntary compliance in the program, some exceptional wage or price increases are granted, and these exceptions generate pressure for further exceptions, so that in the end the policy is no longer effective. There is also the danger that firms and unions will choose larger price and wage increases than they would otherwise have chosen in anticipation of the imposition or reimposition of controls. These disadvantages of the conventional guidelines or controls do not show that they are of no help, but they do suggest that it is desirable to look for an alternative policy that would be more effective and less costly.

The key to a better policy is found in the paradoxical fact that workers gain fully as much from the control of inflation as other major sectors of the population, yet support aggressive union action that rules out either price stability or full employment. Why, if excessive wage increases lead to price rises which eat up most or all of the increases in money wages, and in addition block policy changes favorable to wage earners, do the inflationary wage increases take place? The reason, surely, is that it isn't rational for an individual labor union that represents only a tiny percentage of the work force to consider the effects of its policies on the wage-earning class as a whole. If a union represents even as many as half a million workers, its own members will still bear less than one percent of the burden of any inflation caused by any wage increase it wins. If the union foregoes an effort to obtain the wage increase it would otherwise want in the interest of preventing inflation, its own members will get less than one percent of whatever reduction in inflation results, but they will lose *all* of the money their inhibition made them forego. This illustration, and the general consideration that an inflationary act by an individual union is an "external diseconomy" which the rational and self-interested union will ignore, suggest that guidelines on income policies are going to be very fragile indeed, because it is not in the interest of individual unions to adhere to them. Union leaders are no doubt as public spirited as other groups in the population, but they cannot be expected to sell out the interests of their members, or give up much of their own social function, both of which they must do under normal guidelines or income policies.

If what has been said so far is correct, an appropriate policy must:

1. Limit the wage increases that are the initial source of the problem;

2. Avoid anti-union actions which ignore the importance of unions to a democratic and pluralistic society or which deprive union leaders of one of their basic social functions;

3. Provide incentives for *individual* unions, rather than unions or workers as a whole, to practice wage-restraint;

4. Allow flexibility, so that labor can be attracted with appropriate wage increases into rapidly growing firms and industries;

5. Avoid the "exceptions" that will destroy the policy and the credibility of those who enforce it.

It might seem that no single policy could meet all of these criteria at once, but that is not true. All of these criteria can be satisfied by a policy which limits wage increases indirectly, by changing the incentives *individual* firms have to grant wage increases, thereby leaving each union leader free to obtain the best bargain he or she can obtain in the existing situation, and by using subsidies or taxes rather than prohibitions or controls to influence behavior. Suppose that the corporate income tax were increased, but at the same time each firm whose wage bill divided by its number of employees rose no more than (say) the guidelines allowed, would get a substantial subsidy. This subsidy would decrease more rapidly as wages rose above the guideline level and could be supplemented with a surtax if wage increases became higher still. Such a policy would give individual firms an incentive to drive a harder bargain with the individual unions with which they dealt, but no union leader would be kept from driving the best bargain he could for his members, and those firms that had a reason to take on additional labor would find it advantageous to grant larger wage increases than those that did not. Every unusually large wage increase would be matched by an unusually large loss of subsidy or increase in taxation, so there would be no reason why any such unusual wage increase should create a demand for others, and if they did the tax/subsidy cost of inflationary wage settlements could be increased until the average level of wage increases fell to an acceptable level.

The general type of policy that is being suggested has been proposed before by a number of economists of diverse persuasions, for example by Weintraub and Wallich, Meade, and Portes, though usually on the assumption that only taxes, rather than subsidies and taxes, would be used. Given the opposition that a proposed new tax, even on large firms in the corporate sector, can provoke, it may make more political sense to speak of the use of subsidies and taxes than just of taxes. But the economic difference is negligible: a firm will find that the cost to it of granting a wage increase higher than the target level is the same, whether it must pay (say) a 50% tax on all wage payments beyond the target level or whether it loses subsidy payments equal to 50% of its wage payments above that level: in both cases the loss of revenue is of course the same. There doesn't even have to be any difference in the effect on income distribution: a tax on wage payments/number of employees that was more than X% above last year's level which brought in, say, 5 billion dollars would have the same direct effect on the post-tax income of the corporate sector as an across-the-board increase in the corporate tax combined with a subsidy which returned the same amount to those firms whose wage payments were no more than the target level, but took 5 billion more on balance from those firms whose wages went up more than this.

Presumably the incentive structure facing firms should be made progressive, in the sense that firms whose wage increases exceeded the guidelines by a large percentage would pay a disproportionately higher tax. No doubt it would not be desirable to have subsidies so large that cutting them in response to an exceptional wage increase would make the cost to the firm, say, triple the supra-guideline increase actually received by the workers. For these most progressive and rarely used parts of the structure there should be reliance on taxes. This would mean that firms which were exceptionally craven in bargaining with unions would find that their tax payments under the sort of scheme proposed here would far exceed any subsidy they received. But the total tax collections from corporations in the aggregate under the scheme still need not exceed the total of subsidies to corporations in the aggregate. To repeat, this point has no economic importance, but it does show that it is possible with absolute truthfulness to say that a scheme of the sort proposed here could be introduced with no net increase in taxation.

Since wage push is surely a phenomenon that has significance only in substantial firms, the plan could be applied only in firms with a fair number of employees. This could keep the administrative costs to a very low level. The fact that Hungary has used a somewhat similar plan successfully doesn't tell us much about the effects the plan would have here, given the difference between Hungary's "guided market" system and our own, but it does suggest that any administrative problems would be tractable. If the plan were in effect permanently with the provision that it applied only to larger firms, it could cause noticeable inefficiency by discriminating against these large firms, but inflation is really serious only episodically, and the use of the plan should destroy inflationary expectations, so there should be no need to use the scheme on more than a temporary basis.

It must be conceded that the plan as proposed would discourage firms from switching from unskilled to skilled workers, because this would raise pay per worker even if there were no increase in wage rates at a given skill level. Though this could produce minor inefficiency in some cases, in the United States today, where unemployment is highest at low skill levels and there are several policies (e.g., minimum wage laws) which discriminate against the use of unskilled labor, it could be an advantage. If, however, there was no desire to counteract the forces that militate against the employment of unskilled labor, then the plan should be changed. Instead of simply dividing the wage bill by the number of employees for each year to calculate the increase on which any tax would be assessed, the firm could be required to list the number of workers and the wage rate in each category, and the index of its average wage rate could be compared from year to year.

In short, the scheme proposes using monetary incentives rather than bureaucratic regulation to control wage increases that would result either in inflation or unemployment. It involves nothing more than the application of the classic microeconomic principle that actions which have social costs or benefits beyond those experienced by the actor should be taxed or subsidized. If a wage bargain has inflationary implications for the economy as a whole, it ought to be taxed in the same way as any other external diseconomy.

A Value Added Tax-Based Incomes Policy[1]

DAVID C. COLANDER

David C. Colander is a public finance specialist and the editor of this volume. In this selection he presents one of many possible variations of the TIP concept.

Tax-based incomes policies (TIP) have come to the front line in the battle against inflation. As the subject of both House and Senate hearings, a Brookings Conference, and many economists' papers, it is more than the scribblings of some wild academicians. Bucking what is often harsh criticism, TIP is nevertheless slowly taking shape.

The concept is intriguing: By increasing the cost to firms of raising the absolute wage level, wage inflation is slowed while relative wage movements are allowed. Since administrative decisions about relative wage changes are avoided, these TIPs make an incomes policy administratively more acceptable. Unfortunately the concentration of all TIP proposals on *wage increases* have made them politically unacceptable. Labor understandably reasons: *Why should wages and not all income be controlled?* The AFL-CIO states simply that every source of income—profits, dividends, rents, interest rates, and executive compensation—must be controlled.

The equity arguments in favor of treating all income alike are indisputable; the administrative arguments are not. It is generally believed that income other than wage income is administratively difficult, if not impossible, to control. And even if it were administratively feasible for the government to control all forms of income separately, doing so would mean that the government and not the market would have to determine the relative distribution among different types of incomes. This is an administrative burden which the government is *unable* and *unwilling* to undertake. The government also rules out the alternative to income control—explicit price control—which involves equally difficult administrative complexities.

Thus, as a practical policy, incomes policies have always been interpreted as wage-incomes policies, and they have been imposed with the hope that since wages are the most important income factor, comprising 80 percent of total incomes, wage control will be sufficient. Labor finds these administrative arguments—arguments that can be reduced to "he who is most easily caught is most controlled"—unacceptable. And without labor's support, a meaningful tax-based incomes policy cannot be instituted.

[1] I would like to thank Arthur Okun, Richard Slitor, George Perry, and Abba Lerner, who have given helpful comments on early drafts of this paper. All remaining mistakes are mine alone.

David C. Colander, "A Value Added Tax-Based Incomes Policy," mimeo, 1978.

A NEW APPROACH

I suggest that there is an equitable method for a tax-based incomes policy to control all factor incomes. That method bases the TIP guideline not on increases in the *wage rate*, but on increases in the *value added rate*.[2]

Although value added may sound complicated to noneconomists, it is a well-known concept in economics. It is fundamental to an understanding of the gross national product accounting and it forms the basis of the value added tax in many European countries. Value added is defined as the increase in value of a product at each stage of production where "value" includes all wages, profits, rents, and interest that the firm pays out in income. The sum of all firms' value added equals the total domestic income. Because it includes all income, it can be taxed neutrally.

The *value added rate* is a new concept, but it is central to the analysis of inflation; it is the average rate of pay dispersed to all inputs. It is a combined measure of a firm's increase in profit rates, interest rates, rental rates, and wage rates. The important adjective is *combined*. No one type of income is singled out for control—only the total. Since value added is total income, the increase in the value added rate equals the rate of inflation; thus by controlling the average value added rate in the economy, inflation is, by definition, controlled.[3]

CALCULATION OF A VALUE ADDED RATE

As long as the firm does not change its inputs, calculation of increases in the value added rate is simple; one need only look at the increase in the value added. Unfortunately, inputs are constantly changing through labor turnover, capital changes, and training. Thus calculations are slightly more difficult to make. Numerous methods could be followed in calculating the *value added rate* when inputs change. One possibility would be as follows: Start with the increase in value added of the firm. Then adjust the firm's specific allowable increase in value added (its guideline figure) for all investment by adding or subtracting from the allowable guideline an amount equal to the investment multiplied by the risk-adjusted prime interest rate and for all employment by adjusting for its labor input.

The following example will give you an idea of how the proposal would work. Say a firm's guideline figure is $1,400,000, but it actually has a value added of $1,500,000, an excess of 7.2 percent. However, it made new invetments

[2] I first used the concept of a value added rate as the basis for my market-based incomes policy (MIP) proposal, which I called the "Free Market Solution to Inflation." Professor Abba Lerner and I have since decided to collaborate and have developed a Market Anti-Inflation Plan (MAP) that is designed around the value added concept. [EDITOR'S NOTE: The MAP proposal is discussed on pages 210–220.]

[3] The value added approach resulted from the study of numerous attempts to devise an acceptable incomes policy. In those attempts, a pattern, which can be expressed in the following law, quickly became apparent: The administrative and political difficulties of an incomes policy vary directly with the potential permutations of the number of relative share decisions made. Thus, if a pay board tried to control three aggregates, the political and administrative decisions would be seven times more difficult than if one aggregate were controlled. The reason for this law is obvious. Some groups or combinations of groups inevitably feel slighted relative to some other group or combination of groups. The more groups, the more likely that some group will feel slighted. Controlling value added makes all groups feel equally slighted, which is as close to fairness as one can hope to come.

of $400,000 in that year and had increased its employment by 5000 hours valued at $6 per hour. Its guideline is, therefore, increased by 10 percent of $400,000, or $40,000, for this year and for future years to take account of investment, and by $30,000 to take account of increased employment. Thus, its new value added guideline is $1,470,000 rather than $1,400,000, and the value added rate has only been exceeded by 2.2 percent. If the firm or factors decrease their investment, or if the firm decreases its employment, the guideline is likewise reduced.

Having calculated the value added rate, we are in a position to say whether a firm's overall pricing policy is, or is not, inflationary. Any increases above the guideline contribute to inflation and must be discouraged if we are to slow inflation; increases below the guideline slow inflation and must be encouraged. The essence of the value added TIP is to create an incentive structure so that all relative price changes are centered around the guideline, rather than around an inflated numeraire. To accomplish this, a tax is instituted that depends on how much a firm's value added rate exceeds the guideline rate.

Firms are allowed to increase their value added rate by more than the guideline but they must *offset* their contribution to inflation by paying a tax on the inflationary part of their increase. The tax revenue is used to induce an offsetting price change by some other firm below the guideline. This avoids the normal inflationary price and wage changes where *all* prices rise by, say, 6 percent merely to keep even, and ensures that all price changes are relative price changes, not price level changes.

This TIP tax is not meant to penalize firms. *It is not a penalty: It is merely a market incentive to bring about a desirable result.* "Penalty" implies that the firm or individual has done something wrong; there is, however, nothing necessarily wrong with high relative wages or high relative profits. The point is to make any changes in the wage and price level reflect actual changes in relative prices, not merely changes in the average price level. By placing a cost on firms that raise absolute prices and wages, and by using the money to subsidize firms that lower their prices and wages, the necessary relative price changes are allowed without the inflationary consequences. This is the essence of TIPs.

The firm can easily avoid the TIP tax by merely lowering its price. Thus TIP will be a success even if no firm pays the TIP tax, because if they do not, it means they are following the guidelines.

PRODUCTIVITY EFFECTS OF A VALUE ADDED TIP

The relationship between the value added TIP and productivity is easily confused. Since TIP is a tax on increases in value added, some critics have suggested that it is a tax on productivity. It is not; it is merely a tax on increases in productivity gains that are not passed on to the consumer through lower prices. This point is lost by many TIP critics who confuse the effects of unexpected changes in sales on output per unit with productivity changes. In fact, many of the measured variations in productivity are not changes in productivity at all; they are merely reflections of whether or not the firm had higher or lower sales than expected. When a firm has higher than expected sales, output per unit input (or measured productivity) *temporarily* rises; if it has lower sales than expected, measured productivity temporarily falls. These changes in measured productivity are not true changes in productivity but are merely temporary fluctuations. Over a number of years, the good years and the bad years even out.[4] True increases in productivity are generally the result of investment. Since the guideline figure increases with increases in investment, true productivity is not discouraged.

It is true that the value added TIP increases the tax on firms that have good years and decreases the tax on firms that experience bad years. However, it does not affect the average "expected" profits of firms; it only reduces the variance. According to standard corporate finance theory, a reduction in variance reduces risk, and, therefore, this risk reduction is desirable and should have a positive rather than a negative effect on economic efficiency.

The fact that the value added TIP reduces the variance in the profit is important for two reasons: (1) It makes the plan fairer than the wage board TIPs, and (2) it removes one of the significant causes of inflation.

Consider the following example: A firm grants a 6 percent average wage increase, which is precisely the guideline figure. However, it increases its average profit rate by 10 percent, which results in a profit increase for the firm of millions of dollars and a value added rate increase of 7 percent. Under a wage TIP the firm would pay no surcharge.

Under the value added TIP the firm would be subject to a surcharge on the 1 percent increase above the guidelines, which is precisely as it is in the case where it grants wage increases above the guidelines. (Alternatively, a firm that decreases its profit margin could actually offset, in the calculation of value added, part of its wage increases.) Neither wages nor profits are discriminated against. This even-handed treatment of all income has a second advantage: It mitigates an important source of inflation. In the collective bargaining that determines wage rates, one of the important considerations is the profitability of the firm. Workers in a firm with high profits see the high profits and feel they deserve a share of the wealth. In their negotiations they "catch up," generally winning significant wage increases. Since institutional rigidities hold prices and wages up once they are raised, other prices and wages must adjust upward to match the lead industry's raises, bringing relative wages and prices in the economy into equilibrium through an upward rise in the price level. In almost all econometric studies of the determination of wages, increases in profits have been highly correlated with increases in money wages. Since the value added TIP channels the good years into *lower prices rather than higher profits*, workers will not feel the need to catch up. Thus the value added TIP reduces one of the inflationary biases in the system.

CONCLUSION

There are many other design variables that must be considered in deciding on a tax-based incomes policy. Some include its expected duration, the extent of the coverage, the net accompanying macroeconomic effect, the progressivity in the

---

[4]Another adjustment that improves the equity of the incomes policy and reduces the variance in the value added measure is to use a multi-year moving average of the rates. Thus if the rates of increase in value added were 6 percent, 14 percent, 6 percent, and 16 percent, the value added three-year moving average increase would be 8 percent and 12 percent in the last two years rather than 6 percent and 16 percent. This moving average better reflects the underlying inflationary tendencies by smoothing out extreme years. Other, more sophisticated, chain indices could also be used.

rates, and the statutory payee. In this paper I have discussed none of these issues, nor have I discussed the technical issues involved in the calculation of the value added rate. Therefore, this paper must be seen as merely an introduction to a new approach that can make TIPs equitable and therefore politically feasible.

Two final points should be reiterated: (1) TIP is not a substitute for the appropriate monetary and fiscal policy, and (2) nobody desires the imposition of TIP. Any form of controls—and structuring tax incentives is merely an alternative form of control—is not pleasant. All controls are administratively costly; they detract from individual freedom; and they impose efficiency losses. Undesirable as they are, the question is, What are the alternatives? Restrictive monetary policy used alone causes unacceptable unemployment, while wage and price controls do not allow sufficient flexibility in relative prices and involve far more administrative complexities than does TIP. Hard choices must be made, and deciding to implement TIP is a hard choice. But considering the alternatives, either it—or some other form of incentive-based incomes policy—is probably the best of the bad.

Some Questions and Answers about TIP

ABBA LERNER

Currently a professor of economics at Florida State University, Abba Lerner is one of the most original and highly respected economists of our time. A student of Keynes, Lerner played a major role in "spreading the Keynesian revolution" to the United States and has since been instrumental in determining the direction that revolution has taken. His *Economics of Control* (1943) is a classic in the discipline, and his writings in all fields of economics are always insightful and beautifully written.

This selection, taken from an exchange of letters with Senator William Proxmire of Wisconsin, focuses on some practical political questions related to implementation of TIP.

Q Are special types of programs such as "TIP" needed to combat inflation in general, and the type of inflation currently afflicting our economy in particular?

A A special program which, like TIP, mobilizes direct incentives to induce restraint by those who determine wage rate increases (and thereby cost increases and price increases) is absolutely necessary if we are to slow down or stop the inflation in a reasonable time. To depend on appeals for voluntary restraint on wage and price increases when others are getting them, is no more rational than to depend on appeals to the public to refrain from taking goods from stores if we abolish the requirement that they must be paid for.

Q What benefits would be gained through "TIP" that cannot be derived through other types of anti-inflation programs? What are the costs to the economy that would accrue through "TIP"?

A The only other effective anti-inflation program consists of reducing total demand by monetary and fiscal policy. This works only by reducing sales and output and employment, and relying on the induced unemployment to hold down wages, and thus costs, and thus prices. At less than 10% unemployment the rate of increase of wages shows hardly any response to increases in unemployment. To achieve the response it would be necessary either to starve the workers by cutting off unemployment pay, welfare payments, food stamp plans, etc., or so to tighten the monetary-fiscal restraints as to induce 20 or 30% unemployment. No government will of course do either of these so the answer to the first part of question 2 is: No, the benefits that would be gained through TIP (curing inflation and permitting unemployment to be reduced from about 7% to about 5%) *cannot* be gained through other types of anti-inflation programs.

There are costs of administering TIP, and many forms of TIP . . . would give rise to maldistribution of resources, to extensive litigation and possibly to strikes of workers against the strengthened resistance to inflationary wage

Abba Lerner, "Some Questions and Answers about TIP," letter to Senator William Proxmire, May 10, 1978. Reprinted by permission.

demands. But all these could never come to more than one or two percent of the $50–100 billion of potential annual output we are losing because of the excess unemployment from the current government efforts to check the inflation by holding down total spending in the economy.

Q What type of "TIP" program would be best, . . . a penalty or rewards approach, [and should it be] instituted for a limited period or permanently?

A Stabilizing either prices or efficiency wages (money wages adjusted for increases in productivity—i.e., in output per man) would break the spiral of our expectational inflation; but of the two, wages are by far the preferable target. This is because:

1. prices are much more complicated, and quality variation makes evasion much easier,
2. wages are already largely governed by collective bargaining and similar large scale decisions,
3. average prices adjust automatically to average wages in a fairly steadily declining ratio because of a stable average degree of competition (or monopoly) and a steady decline in costs relative to wages because of increasing average productivity. Wage increases adjust to decelerating price increases only by the pressure of severe additional unemployment.

Stabilizing *both* prices and wages is most inadvisable. It would mean arbitrarily establishing a ratio of average wages to average prices and having this ratio [increase] with productivity. If these established ratios happen to coincide with the somewhat fluctuating average degree of competition and average degree of productivity increase, the price stabilization would be innocuous and meaningless. But if there was any discrepancy, it would conflict with and disrupt the free competition on which our economy depends.

The distinction between "penalty" and "reward" is thoroughly misleading. *Only a "penalty"* for wage increases can be an incentive for resisting them. "Reward" means penalizing agreement to wage increases by reducing the reward; "penalty" means rewarding resistance to wage increases by reducing the penalty. A reward program can only be a combination of a *grant* (or tax cut) that is independent of the wage paid (what economists call "lump sum"), together with a *charge* or tax that is greater for greater wage increases. "Reward" has been called a "carrot" as opposed to a "stick," but it is really a carrot plus a stick, or rather a carrot given to obtain consent to the use of the stick.

Any of the TIP programs, whatever its particular inadequacies, if kept in operation for, say, a year, would reach its chosen "norm" of reduced wage level rate of increase (and the correspondingly reduced price level rate of increase), providing the charges on wage increases are applied at the appropriate rates. The appropriate rate would be continually diminishing. As a lowered rate of inflation reduced the inflationary pressure for inflationary wage increases, there would be less and less pressure for the charge to offset. The appropriate charge, and the adjustments in it, would have to be reached by trial and error. . . .

TIP would thus be self liquidated when it had reached the designed wage increase norm (and the corresponding inflation rate). The excessive pressure for wage increases, and the appropriate charge, would then fall to zero. . . .

Q Can an effective set of tax based incomes policies be devised that would treat everyone fairly?

A The charges would be nondiscriminatory, and thus fair, if (as in Seidman's form of TIP) they are proportional to the amount of wage bill increases due to wage rate increases. The grants, which have to be equal to the total of the amount collected in the charges (so as to offset the effect of total demand), can never be given in a form that would seem fair to all without being made just equal to the charges and thus negating the whole business. Furthermore, the offsetting would inevitably be considered as "compensation" for "hardships," which they are not, and there will be other demands made on them. Perhaps the fairest way would be to spread them equally over the whole population (as a negative income tax), but there will be pressures to have them concentrated on the more needy by reason of poverty, illness, national disaster or whatnot.

Furthermore, the reductions in the TIP charges required by the reduced inflationary pressure as the TIP norm is approached could be endangered by Congress' reluctance to see tax revenues disappear. The same is true for the correspondingly increasing "reward" that would be called for as the norm is approached. (The diminution in the reduction of the reward is the reduced incentive appropriate for resisting the same reduced inflationary pressure.) This increasing "reward" would not only be resisted by an expense-conscious Congress—it would be defended by its recipients as (an inadequate) recognition of the part they will have played (in response to the "inducement") in the reduction of the inflation. . . .

Q What problems should the Congress be mindful of as it considers proposals for "TIP"? What safeguards would, therefore, need to be built into a workable version of "TIP"?

A Workers might fear that the holding down of wages would not result [in] a corresponding holding down of prices, and [that] real wages would fall. As a safeguard, the government could guarantee to recompense all employees after a year of the plan, not only against a fall [in] average real wages but also against a failure of average wages to *increase* as real purchasing power by, say, 1 percent.[1] The money needed for this would become available to the government in such a case from the additional taxes collected from the exorbitant profits which would have been earned if prices did rise enough, relative to wages, to keep real wages from rising by as much as 1 percent.

There would also have to be measures for dealing with the inequities that would arise from any sudden end to inflation. Those whose wages were about to be raised would suffer [at] the expense of those whose wages were raised just before the plan was imposed. One proposed solution is a *gradual* disinflation, reducing the wage increase rate from 9 percent to 3 percent (and thus the price increase from 6 percent to zero) by, say, 1 percent a year over 6 years, by having the wage increase norm 8 percent the first year, 7 percent the second year and down to 3 percent by the sixth year.

This would involve continuing the Stagflation, although at a diminishing

---

[1] [In] the Harris Survey of 3/20/78, 54% as against 32% said they preferred an assured "pay raise *less* than rise in cost of living" to a "pay raise more than the cost of living but not assured" (by a controlled cost of living).

rate, with a loss of output through the six years of between $150 and $300 billion—averaging half the rate at which we are losing output at the present time. It would cost the economy much less to give the most generous benefits to those [who] feel that they had lost by having been caught by TIP while waiting in line for their wage increase. One possibility is to adjust everybody's wage immediately, up to or down to, say, his average wage over the past year plus a half of one year's average increase of all wages over that year, and have that be the base for further bargaining subject to TIP . . . provisions for controlling the inflations pressures.

This seems a fair compromise, but even a much more generous settlement for those who will have lost some of the benefit they would have got from having "jumped the gun" would be very small compared with the loss of output and the other disturbances, inconveniences and inequities from the continuing though gradually diminishing inflation. These would be more disturbing than the fairly constant rate of inflation we have been experiencing in the more recent years, because much harder to anticipate and adjust for.

There is a more serious objection to such a "gradualist" approach. The basic goal of all the TIP's . . . is to break the vicious *expectational* cycle. All the plans assume that the expectations are based on and can be changed only by experience, and not by jawboning, by hell-fire threats of economic doom or by appeals to patriotism or ideology. TIP . . . aim[s] at providing the *experience* of stabilized prices by the use of material incentives which bring them about, and the demonstration has to be convincing.

There are bound to be all sorts of disturbances such as happen all the time—bad harvests, unexpected foreign competition, sudden increases in costs of raw materials—even though another quadrupling of oil prices is unlikely. These can give rise to temporary ups and downs in the price level. A slow reduction of the inflation rate can easily be more than offset, although temporarily, by these random and unforseeable incidents. And they could easily be enough to make it appear that the cure is not working and to force its abandonment before the incident is over. Gradualism is too dangerous.

Q Would "TIP" best be implemented by applying it to large firms only, to all corporations, or still more broadly?

A Applying TIP to only a part of the economy, whether as a trial or to simplify the administration, would provide a temptation for firms that have to pay wage increases above the norm to try to escape from the problem (say by splitting to below the critical size); and conversely for those who can pay less than the norm wage increase. . . .

Q Can and should the tax system be used to implement anti-inflation guideposts? What special problems would this cause for the tax system, and are solutions possible and at what cost?

A The tax system is of course involved in the charges and in the offsets of all forms of TIP. . . . The only special problems that occur to me are those concerned with the efficiency of the charges, and the fairness of the offsets discussed above when seen as "subsidies."

Fiscal and monetary policy remains responsible for keeping total spending in the economy large enough to provide full employment (with only genuinely *structural* unemployment) but not so large as to create excess demand—demand for more than the economy can produce with full employment. This is Functional Finance. With a successful stabilization of the average rate of wage increase and the corresponding price level movement, the pressure for Functional Finance is greatly strengthened. Any excess spending all goes into profits and none into raising wages, and any deficiency falls entirely on profits and employment. The pressure for a national level of spending adequate for full employment without inflation will be overwhelming. Without Functional Finance . . . TIP . . . [cannot] succeed or even survive. Functional Finance is necessary but not sufficient for curing Stagflation. TIP [is] . . . only [an attempt] to complement it. the combination is necessary *and* sufficient.

Q What would be the cost to the Treasury of implementation of "TIP"?

A There need be no direct cost or benefit to the Treasury. The tax revenues from TIP would have to be offset by the grants to avoid inflationary or deflationary fiscal pressures. (The Treasury would, of course, benefit from the increased tax revenues from increased economic activity as the victory over inflation led the government to give up its "anti-inflationary" restriction of economic activity.)

Any other expenditure by the Treasury, such as administering the charges and the grants and monitoring the observance of the regulations (which would be watched keenly by both employers and workers), would constitute increases in income that offset the taxes and would warrant an equal reduction in the grants. . . .

Q Do you view "TIP" as being related to mandatory wage and price controls, or to a social contract among government, labor, and business?

A TIP . . . share[s] with wage and/or price controls only the *objective* of trying to cure inflation. They involve no mandatory controls over wages or prices. They can be considered as part of a social contract but not between government, labor, and business as entities.

Like all civil governments, they are part of a general contract between citizens to limit some individual freedoms (like the freedom to grab another's property) for the greater freedom and well-being of all.

Okun's New Tax-Based Incomes-Policy Proposal

GARDNER ACKLEY

Currently a professor of economics at the University of Michigan, Gardner Ackley, a former chairman of the Council of Economic Advisers, has long been active in designing macroeconomic policy. His textbook, *Macroeconomic Theory*, is considered a standard text in the field, and his other writings are always highly regarded. In this selection, he voices a few cautionary words about Arthur Okun's reward TIP.

It is clear that recent and prospective levels of economic activity pose no significant threat of new inflationary pressures. Our roughly 6-percent chronic rate of price increase is clearly a residual infection, remaining from earlier bouts of demand-pull inflation in the late 1960s and of imported cost-push inflation in the early 1970s. Prices now continue to rise because domestic wage costs rise more rapidly than worker productivity; and wage costs continue to rise because workers pay rising prices. It is a classic case of the self-maintaining spiral; and it is a debilitating condition. Until it is cured, our economy will never be really healthy, able to deal fully and resolutely with such problems as excessive unemployment, inadequate investment, scarce and insecure energy, and the weakened dollar.

Almost no expert now prescribes the drastic therapy of prolonged fasting or bloodletting—raising the unemployment rate to 8 or 10 percent, and holding it there until the fever departs. It is not clear that it would work; in any case, the cure would be worse than the disease. And almost no one wants to try mandatory controls again, or even "voluntary" guideposts enforced by "jaw-boning." Yet the malaise is too serious to ignore.

THE NEW PROPOSAL

The most attractive new idea proposed to deal with this residual inflationary infection comes from Arthur Okun. Others (Sidney Weintraub, Henry Wallich) had long ago proposed taxing firms that granted wage increases above some standard increase consistent with stable average unit labor costs; but no one liked the idea. More recently, A.P. Lerner proposed requiring permits for wage increases, issued in an aggregate dollar amount that would allow only that average rise of wage costs which could be absorbed by productivity gains; these permits would be freely marketable among firms. The concept is theoretically superb, but clearly too "far out" for serious consideration.[1]

[1] See A.M. Okun, "The Great Stagflation Swamp," *Challenge*, 20, November/December 1977: H.C. Wallich and S. Weintraub, "A Tax-Based Incomes Policy," *Journal of Economic Issues*, 5, June 1971; A.P. Lerner, "Stagflation—Its Cause and Cure." *Challenge*, 20, September/October 1977.

Okun, however, now turns the Weintraub-Wallich tax penalty into a tax incentive: employers who give wage-rate increases not in excess of a clearly defined non-inflationary standard would qualify their *employees* for generous tax rebates; by avoiding any widening of gross margins over their unit labor costs the *firms*, too, would earn tax reductions.

No one would be forced to do anything; but by choosing to restrain their wage- and price-setting, workers and firms would earn tax rewards that made it easy to advance the public interest. If most chose to take advantage, they would earn a further reward: even though nominal wages and prices would advance more slowly, the resulting slower infaltion would maintain the *real value* of the reduced nominal gains.

I admire Okun's ingenuity. But I am not ready to jump on the bandwagon that is rapidly forming behind his invention until I see the fine print. The basic concept is splendid—but the details worry me. If some are going to be awarded tax rebates and others denied them, the standards and procedures must be precisely definable in the tax law, and able to withstand court review of their fairness.

POTENTIAL PROBLEMS

From my experience in designing and administering price controls during World War II, and again, in a policy role, during the Korean War, I retain keen, and sometimes bitter, memories of great ideas about ways to restrain wage and price increases for which the fine print could never be written—or, if it could be written, filled endless volumes of the *Federal Register* with constant revisions, exceptions, and adjustments necessary to cover special situations that could never have been dreamed of in advance by the most imaginative economists, accountants, and lawyers. Okun's proposal raises some of these old problems.

For example, Okun's firms must be told how to define each wage rate, and thus how to measure its increase—presumably to include all benefits, including pension rights, dental-care plans, executive stock options, and changed eligibility for overtime pay. Whose estimates of these costs would be accepted? How would cost-of-living escalators in contracts be evaluated? Instructions must then be given as to how to compute an *average* wage rate increase—the old "index-number" problem. Must this average increase be calculated for the entire firm or can it be calculated by divisions, plants, or categories or workers? Would account be taken of changes in the mix of higher-wage and lower-wage workers, or of effects on the average wage arising from new product lines, acquisitions, spin-offs, or shut-downs?

How does one visualize a union bargaining with an industry composed of many firms differently affected by a given wage increase? How could an employer assure a union that a proposed agreement would or would not qualify its workers for the tax rebate, until much bookkeeping (and IRS review) had been completed? Indeed, could it give any assurances before its tax year was finished? Can a union live with an industry-wide contract which permits the employees of some firms to qualify for tax benefits that others don't get? What about the firm bargaining with many unions, on different calendars, the wage increase for no *one* of which would cause the employer's *average* wage to increase enough to prevent its workers from qualifying for the tax rebate?

Would qualification be based on a life-of-the-contract calculation, or for each year at a time? How about contracts that cover periods not corresponding to tax years?

Are exceptions to be made for that portion of wage increases that merely lets workers "catch up" with wage increases already granted to other workers, or that remove long-standing "inequities"? Is it possible to deny all exceptions to the wage standard (such as there were to the "guideposts" of the 1960s); can the exceptions be defined without writing the equivalent of a wage-control regulation—to which further exceptions must be allowed?[2]

In computing the firms' margins over materials plus labor costs, how are inventories to be valued? What operating unit is to be used (if less than the entire firm, how are the joint costs to be allocated)? If overhead costs should be excluded, what are overhead costs? How will new firms become eligible? Won't there have to be provisions for adjusting abnormally low base-period margins, due to special sales, close-outs of unprofitable lines, and many other unusual circumstances?

I shall never forget the "Manufacturer's Price Regulation" (CPR 22) issued by the Office of Price Stabilization during the Korean War, to cover most sectors of the economy other than services, agriculture, mining, and distribution. I was in charge of the team that wrote it. It required each firm to calculate a simple historical gross margin for the appropriate manufacturing unit. The basic idea could be summarized in a few paragraphs and was generally accepted as fair and reasonable. But by the time the regulation was finally drafted it covered tens of finely printed pages in the *Federal Register*. And that was only the beginning. It took a growing army of economists, commodity experts, statisticians, and lawyers to deal with the questions and problems that arose: not about the general principle, but about how to define, apply, and measure it in all the infinite variety of its applications. Hardly an issue of the *Federal Register* thereafter was without its quota of amendments, special orders, individual adjustments, and official interpretations of CPR 22. Many industries had to be taken completely out from under the regulation and given special treatment. Each elaboration or exception dealt with a meritorious claim (always with strong political support). We found that a difference of a few words in a definition could mean millions of dollars to a large company; thus, its lawyers and lobbyists could easily earn their pay by getting the definition changed or an exception made. The corresponding Okun tax provisions might also mean millions of dollars in taxes to many firms—and their workers.

Might Congress need to write something comparable to CPR 22 into the tax code, and amend it frequently to deal with questions that were not anticipated or pressures that could not be avoided? And would it not need also to write into the tax code the equivalent of a complete wage control system in order to define the wage increases which would qualify workers for their tax rebates?

There are millions of small firms: retail stores, doctor's offices, farm enterprises, most not incorporated and having extremely rudimentary accounting. Could they be denied the opportunity to qualify for tax advantages for themselves and their workers? But could rules be written which they could understand and apply?

[2]All of the above problems apply equally to the Wallich-Weintraub and Lerner schemes.

THE NEED TO BEGIN PROMPTLY

I don't know the answers to these questions, and I doubt that anyone does. Thus, if the idea is to be taken seriously, some imaginative group of economists, tax lawyers, accountants, and labor experts should immediately start thinking through the problems, preparing a draft of the legislation and operating instructions, and trying them out on a variety of the firms and unions which would be affected. This consultation needs to involve not merely executives, who will debate the general principles, but the working experts down the line, who would have to administer them, and who would envisage at least some of the problems which would arise.

Until that happens, I have to reserve judgment on the Okun plan—much as I admire its ingenuity, and much as I hope that some workable plan can be found.

Tax-Based Incomes Policy: Pain or Pleasure in Pursuit of Price-Level Stability

NORMAN B. TURE

Norman Ture is currently president of an economic consulting firm. A highly respected economist, he has written numerous books and articles on federal tax and fiscal policy, has worked on the staffs of the Joint Economic Committee and the Treasury Department, and has served as a member of both President John Kennedy's and President Richard Nixon's Task Force on Taxation. In the following article, Ture questions the usefulness of both the Okun and the Wallich TIP proposals.

When two major personalities in the field of public economic policy advance a "new" proposal for restraining inflation, policy makers are likely to give it their attention. A current case in point is the so-called tax-based incomes policy (TIP). Calling his proposal the "stick" approach, Henry Wallich of the Federal Reserve Board urges that the 1,000 or 2,000 largest corporations be subject to punishment if they give their employees wage increases in excess of some given rate; the punishment would take the form of an increase in the corporate income tax rate at some multiple—4 or 5—of the rate of wage increase deemed to be excessive.[1] The "guideline"—Wallich's nostalgic nomenclature—for nonexcessive wage increases would be the sum of the nationwide average productivity gain plus some fraction, perhaps one-half, of the going rate of inflation. If inflation is 7 percent and the long-term, nationwide productivity gain were 2 percent, the stick would beat on employers allowing wage increases in excess of 5.5 percent.

Arthur Okun of the Brookings Institution argues for a "carrot" approach to TIP; he would reward employees who keep wage hikes at or below some designated percentage by giving them income tax credits and would provide some tax reduction to employers who make and carry through a commitment to hold wage increases below that percentage. Employers would be asked to make advance pledges to restrict wage increases to rates not more than 6 percent. Employees of firms taking this pledge would get an income tax credit of 1.5 percent of wage or salary income up to $20,000; the credit would be reflected in

---

[1]Alternatively, the offending company would be denied deductibility of wages in excess of the designated amount. Wallich also considers a third tax increase for miscreant employers—an increase in their payroll tax liabilities—but he's currently far less enthusiastic about this form of knuckle rapping. Politically, a payroll tax increase is a no-no, at least until the dust settles over the current OASI tax increases. As a matter of economic strategy, Wallich wants the punishment for "excessive" wage hikes to rest on the employer, not the employee, and he must surely be aware of the fact that most, if not all, of the employer's share of the payroll tax in fact is borne by the employee. Hence, this third alternative may be dismissed from consideration.

Norman B. Ture, "Tax-Based Incomes Policy: Pain or Pleasure in Pursuit of Price-Level Stability," *Tax Review*, Vol. XXXIX, No. 6, June 1978, pp. 23–30. Reprinted with permission of the Tax Foundation, Inc.

current withheld taxes. Where a firm did not make this pledge but did in fact hold wage increases within the specified percentage, the tax credit would go to its employees in the form of a tax refund. Firms that sign up in advance would be rewarded by having their tax liabilities reduced in an amount equal to one-fourth of the amount of the credit allowed their employees. If an employer were not to carry through on his pledge, on the other hand, he would be liable for payment of the under-withheld taxes, and, of course, he'd not get the cut in his own tax liability.

Both Okun and Wallich regard their respective alternatives as variations on a single theme—the use of taxes, instead of direct controls, to restrain wage increases. Both claim as a major advantage of either TIP that it would not interfere with market-based decisions—would not distort the wage structure. Both Wallich and Okun believe that moderating wage increases will also moderate price increases. Okun explicity asserts that the recent and ongoing inflation is "cost-push" in character rather than the result of excess demand; Wallich doesn't go this far, but in asserting that restraint of wages means restraint on prices, he arrives at very nearly the same position. Both Wallich and Okun avow that TIP is not an alternative to monetary and fiscal restraint as a means of curbing inflation. Okun views TIP as "a way to make possible the necessary slowdown of money growth and turnaround of fiscal stimulus without the enormous economic and social costs of recession"; Wallich believes that fiscal and monetary constraints, though still necessary, take effect slowly and argues for consideration of TIP as a means of hastening the "winding down" of inflation.

Two sets of questions should be posed in evaluating the TIP proposals. The first is whether there is any substantial evidence that basic fiscal and monetary constraints are ineffectual, too slow, or too costly means for curbing inflation. The second is whether either the carrot or stick approach would *per se* contribute significantly to moderating inflation and what costs each would impose.

HAVE FISCAL AND MONETARY CONSTRAINTS FAILED?

Before concluding that either fiscal or monetary constraints are ineffectual, too slow, or too costly, one should first determine whether in fact they have been imposed. The inflation problem with which the nation is today concerned is not a brand new development; neither is it a long-standing phenomenon. In essence, 1978's inflation is a continuation of a development which became noticeable and a matter of widespread concern in the mid 1960's. For the period 1949 through 1965, the GNP implicit price deflator, the broadest measure of over-all price change, increased at an average annual rate of 2.2 percent. Since 1965, however, the average rate of increase in this index has been 5.5 percent a year—2.5 times the inflation rate of the earlier period.

Did this marked acceleration of inflation occur in the face of a tight fiscal policy, demonstrating that fiscal policy is inadequate to the task of holding back increases in the price level? The answer clearly is no.

If fiscal constraints were imposed during the past 12 years, the evidence will have to be found elsewhere than in the financial records of the Federal government. From 1965 through 1977, Federal expenditures (as measured in the national income accounts) increased at an average annual rate of 10.8 percent.

While taxes also advanced briskly over these years—at an average annual rate of 9.6 percent—Federal deficits have been enormous by the standard of any peacetime experience: for the 12 years since 1965, these deficits aggregate almost $255 billion, close to $174 billion of which were realized in the last three calendar years. Surely this fiscal performance must be characterized as extraordinarily expansionary and inflationary—anything but restrictive. Recent experience affords no basis for the assertion that fiscal constraints are ineffectual, too slow, or too costly a means for holding back inflationary pressures since no fiscal restraints were imposed.[2]

It's equally difficult to find evidence of the use of monetary restraint to curb inflation. Over the period 1949–1965, the average annual rate of growth of the M_1 measure of the money stock (currency plus demand deposits) was 2.7 percent. From 1965 through 1977, in contrast, this measure of the money stock increased more than twice as rapidly—on the average by 5.8 percent a year. In 1977, the growth rate increased to 7.4 percent, surely not indicative of an anti-inflationary monetary policy stance. The same conclusion emerges from using broader measures of money, including time deposits at commercial banks—M_2—and deposits at thrift institutions—M_3. The latter measure, for example, grew on the average by 7.6 percent a year from 1959 through 1965 and by 9.3 percent a year from 1965 through 1977. The growth rate was markedly higher in the last three years—11.3 percent in 1975, 13.2 percent in 1976, and 11.1 percent in 1977.

It may be that Wallich and Okun are right in their views that fiscal and/or monetary policy alone cannot or should not be relied upon to provide a more moderate rate of increase in the price level. If they are, however, it is not because either has been tried and proved lacking during the last dozen years, and certainly not because the Federal government and the Federal Reserve have exerted fiscal and monetary constraints during the past three years. One is tempted to conclude that before messing around with TIP's it would be useful to see what cutting the rate of increase in Federal spending, reducing the Federal deficit, and retarding monetary expansion might do to slow inflation.

WHAT MIGHT ONE EXPECT OF TIPs?

The same evidence which shows that fiscal and monetary constraints haven't been applied in an effort to fight inflation also shows great reluctance on the part of fiscal and monetary policy makers to use the tools at hand. If one is convinced that there is little hope for cutting Federal spending, reducing the deficit, and slowing the growth in money stock, one may believe it necessary to look for other options. The disaster of wage and price controls, it is to be hoped, is still fresh enough in memory to eliminate any chance of their revival. Do tax devices of the sort Okun and Wallich propose promise some success in cutting back the inflation rate without the gross distortions of direct controls?

[2]Okun cites the 1974–1975 recession as an example of the excessive costs of curbing inflation by policies to restrict the growth of aggregate demand. But no fiscal policy impediments to the expansion of aggregate demand were imposed. Federal spending increased by 12.7 percent in 1974 over 1973 and by 19.3 percent in 1975 over 1974. The Federal deficit was $10.7 billion in 1974 and $70.2 billion in 1975. The GNP deflator increased by 5.6 percent in 1974 and by 9.6 percent in 1975. If the Federal government was pursuing an anti-inflationary policy in 1974–75 by attempting to repress aggregate demand and by promoting recession it certainly wasn't relying on fiscal policy to this end.

The answer is, emphatically, no. Neither plan would be likely to have any material effect on curbing wage rate increases. To the extent they did succeed in slowing these increases it would be at the cost of warping the structure of relative wage rates, penalizing employees and employers in firms and industries with relatively high rates of gain in productivity and efficiency and rewarding those in low productivity-gain industries. The Wallich plan would impose an additional distortion by increasing the cost of capital in those firms with brisk advances in productivity or with little ability to resist wage increases. It would also adversely affect total employment and real output. Both the Okun and Wallich variants would be burdensome to administer; the former would be a nightmare for employers and the government, while the latter would require a large increase in IRS audit personnel with knowledge of labor law and regulations as well as tax audit competence. Finally, neither variant would itself do much to restrain inflation nor to facilitate the use of broad fiscal and monetary constraints.

Implicit in both the Okun and Wallich TIPs is an unrealistic view of employers' ability to control wage increases. Wallich would confine his TIP to the largest 1,000 or 2,000 firms, both to limit administrative burdens and on the explicit assumption that ". . . these firms . . . are the pattern setters for wages so long as the economy is not overheating."[3] These 1,000 or 2,000 firms might well be eager to conform the wage increases for their employees to the guideline which would be prescribed in order to avoid significant increases in their corporate income tax liabilities, even at the risk of significantly increasing their problems in recruiting and retaining their labor force. It doesn't follow that the union representatives sitting across the bargaining tables would be equally eager to accommodate these companies. Suppose, for example, the inflation rate is 6.5 percent and that productivity is increasing at 2 percent. If the guideline were set at, say, 6 percent, unions would be asked to have their members accept a .5 percent *reduction* in real wages rather than realizing a 2 percent *increase*, equal to their productivity gains. Indeed, any wage increase less than 8.5 percent would be perceived by the employees, quite correctly, as a transfer of some part of their productivity gains to their employers.

The obstacles to workers' acceptance of wage increases less than the sum of the rate of productivity increase plus the rate of inflation are probably smaller the more personal the wage negotiation and the less skilled and specialized the employees. This suggests that the Wallich scheme would work better the smaller, not the larger, the firm and the less unionized its labor force. The Wallich stick would beat the wrong horses.

The Okun variant, on the other hand, would be universal; all employers, large and small, incorporated and unincorporated, public as well as private, would be solicited to participate. Of course, only the profit-making private firm could obtain the reward of a reduction in its, not merely its employees', tax liability, but Okun assumes that all employers would want to participate ". . . because—and only because—the tax credit to their workers would help them to slow down wages." Okun's assertion is undoubtedly correct if the tax credit

---

[3] A more accurate representation of the situation is that the outcome of wage negotiations between these firms and the unions to which their employees belong has some effect in setting patterns *within their respective industries;* even a casual glance at the data establishes that there is no uniformity *among industries* in the rates of wage increases.

were to be available to all employees without regard to the rate at which their wages advanced; the lower the marginal rate of tax imposed on labor income, the lower will be the pretax wage at which any given amount of labor services will be supplied. But confining the reward to those employees who seek or accept wage increases below some guideline, e.g., 6 percent, would surely limit the effectiveness of the proposed reward.

For example, consider the case of a $15,000 a year worker, married with two children, who's trying to get an 8 percent raise, to $16,200. If he gets it, his aftertax income (ignoring his FICA payroll tax, to keep things simple) would go up from $13,615 to $14,565. If he were to accept a 6 percent raise instead in order to get the 1.5 percent income tax credit, his aftertax income would go to $14,569. With the Okun TIP, the employee would be all of $4 a year better off, scarcely a handsome reward for his foregoing the 8 percent raise. His employer might be eager to sign up but this employee's wage demands are not likely to be effectively moderated by the TIP carrot. As a trade-off for smaller wage increases, the Okun TIP credit would have to be substantially larger than the proposed 1.5 percent to fire the imagination and engage the enthusiasm of any significant number of workers.

EFFECTS ON THE ALLOCATION OF RESOURCES

The likelihood of limited participation in either the Wallich or Okun TIP is probably the best thing that may be said of either. Insofar as either variant were to limit wage increases to amounts less than those that would be determined in the market, TIP would result in misallocation of labor services. For example, suppose that labor's productivity is advancing at the rate of 1 percent in industry X and at 4 percent in industry Y. With an inflation rate of, say, 6.5 percent, the unobstructed market-determined wage increase would be 7.5 percent in X and 10.5 percent in Y. This differential wage increase is essential to allow the market to work efficiently, i.e, to attract additional employees from X to Y. To the extent this wage differential were to be suppressed, it would no longer efficiently serve its function of directing the allocation of labor services to their most productive uses.

The Wallich TIP clearly would act as an artificial wage ceiling in any firm or industry in which the sum of the rate of increase in productivity and the inflation rate exceeded the TIP guideline. Like any price ceiling set below the market-clearing level, the principal result would be failure of the market to clear. At the artificially low wage rate, the quantity of labor services demanded in such firms and industries would exceed the quantity supplied. For these companies attempting to comply with the Wallich TIP guideline, the result would be labor-market disequilibrium.

The curtailment of the quantity of labor services employed in firms and industries with higher-than-average rates of advance in labor productivity obviously would also entail a curtailment of their output. This effect would also be reached, although by a different route, if potentially affected companies disregarded the guideline and incurred the substantial increases in their corporate tax liabilities. In this case, the resulting increase in the cost of capital to these companies would result in a lower rate of expansion—if not a reduction—in the amount of their real capital and, hence, in their use of capital services. This would, in turn, reduce the output of these companies. It would also reduce the rate of increase in the productivity of the labor services they employ.

It is difficult to perceive the social justification for any of these results. Fighting inflation is a hard enough chore without creating additional and unnecessary problems in the process. Efficiency in the use of production inputs is impaired by nonmarket constraints which prevent the substitution of one kind of input for other kinds when their relative prices change. If the cost of labor services is rising, raising the cost of capital services by increasing the tax on the returns for their use negates the impetus to use the former inputs more sparingly and the latter more extensively. In turn, it diminishes the advance in labor productivity, thereby increasing unit labor costs still further, and reduces employment of labor.

An anti-inflation strategy which depends on reducing the efficiency with which the economy's production inputs are used and/or which reduces the amount of inputs which will be supplied is counterproductive. Like explicit wage and price controls, it might temporarily disguise the inflation, but not for long and not without the costs of less efficiency and reduced real output.

The Okun TIP is somewhat less costly. There is, to be sure, a considerable number of workers whose productivity gains are low enough to leave them indifferent between accepting a trade-off of the Okun tax credit plus no more than a 6 percent wage hike for the larger wage increase they would otherwise obtain. Their doing so, however, would artificially widen the spread between the wage rates confronting firms and industries in which the rate of advance in labor's productivity was relatively fast compared with those in which it was slow. In effect, the Federal Treasury would be subsidizing employment in firms and industries at the low end of the productivity-advance scale. The result, as under the Wallich TIP, would be a loss of efficiency in the allocation of labor services.

Unlike the Wallich TIP, however, the Okun variant would not have a depressing effect on the aggregate supply of labor and capital inputs. In fact, since its initial effect would be to reduce (modestly, to be sure) the effective marginal tax rate for some workers and for some suppliers of capital without increasing it for any other taxpayers, the Okun TIP would result in some increase in employment, capital formation, and total output. But what an ungainly form of marginal tax rate reduction the Okun TIP would provide! Since increases in the supplies of production inputs, with the consequent expansion of output, would result from cuts in marginal tax rates generally, why should the rate cuts be designed to distort and impair the functioning of the market?

ADMINISTRATIVE AND COMPLIANCE BURDENS

Were there no other objections to the TIP proposals, the increase in administrative and compliance burdens they would impose would boggle the mind. To be sure, attributing complexity to a tax proposal one opposes is a tried and true way to duck the more pertinent issues to which the proposal is addressed. In this case, however, considerations of administration and compliance do not represent offsets to advantages but the compounding of disadvantages.

The Wallich stick would present less administration and compliance problems than the Okun carrot. Even so, it would be a trial. For one thing, under the

Wallich plan all elements of an employee's compensation would be taken into account. Whatever may be the degree of the corporation's control over the rate of gross cash wages and salaries, it must far exceed its control over the cost of providing, say, any given package of medical benefits stipulated in existing plans. Much the same is true regarding retirement benefits. Increases in the costs of these two items alone could exhaust the guideline increase in compensation. And insofar as these increases cannot be quickly curbed by the company, it might well face the necessity of attempting to renegotiate the pay package under its existing labor contracts to prevent total compensation increases from bumping well over the guideline.

The arithmetic required by the Wallich plan would be another stumper. Costing the diverse elements of a pay package is an imprecise business at best. How, for example, does one estimate the percentage gain in compensation from improvement in working conditions, one of the compensation elements Wallich specifies? Which would determine whether the company had met the guide-line—the overall average rate of compensation gain per hour or the percent increase in the average employee's total compensation over the year? How would the weighted average increase in compensation be determined—by establishment? by company? by all companies filing a single, consolidated return? by employment category? by all types of employment taken together? How would different employment categories be weighted—by number of employees? by initial compensation rate? How would changes in the composition of employment resulting from changes in the composition of output be taken into account? If the company cut back employment of high-gain employees and expanded employment of low-gain employees, while increasing compensation for each category more than the guideline, it might well come up with an overall increase at less than the guideline rate. Would—should—this company bear the Wallich penalty?

Questions of this sort scarcely ripple the surface of the sea of problems in which the company attempting to avoid the Wallich stick would founder. Personnel and labor management in these companies would be overwhelmed by fresh torrents of instructions about how to comply. And for each such problem identifiable by affected employers, there would be at least one additional problem for the Internal Revenue Service.

The Okun plan would pose all of the problems of administration and compliance in the Wallich plan, multiplied a thousand times over since all employers, except possibly tiny firms with less than, say, 20 employees, and brand new firms, would be asked to participate. Even if only a very small fraction of employers were to take the Okun pledge, the problem of checking results against promises would involve a huge number of firms. How would employers and the IRS handle the job of tracking down employees who were entitled to the refund but who were no longer with the same employer? How would IRS determine whether refunds claimed on individual tax returns were allowable? The audit problem would be enormous, far beyond the capacity of the IRS, even were it greatly enlarged. In fact, audits would have to be conducted on the basis of a miniscule sample; it wouldn't be long before participating companies would realize their chances of being audited were somewhat less than being struck by lightening. The plan would be an invitation to misrepresent intentions with little prospect of being found out and incurring a penalty. . . .

CONCLUSIONS: DON'T TIP THE ECONOMY

Neither the carrot nor the stick versions of the TIP offer the answer to the question of how to slow inflation. Even if one believes that wage increases are the cause, rather than the result, of inflation, neither version would materially reduce the rate of gain in nominal wages. Insofar as they did, however, this restraint on wage increases would be at the cost of misallocation of labor services and a consequent loss of economic efficiency. The Wallich plan would compound this loss with reductions in employment, real wage rates, and GNP. Neither TIP would either require or encourage the monetary authorities to slow the expansion of the stock of money. Nor would either variant lead to a less expansionary fiscal policy; indeed, each would result in a slightly larger Federal deficit than projected under present law. Both would impose huge additional burdens of compliance and administration.

The most damaging consequence of a TIP, whether carrot or stick, is that it would divert concern and energy from the real and extremely difficult problems of dealing effectively with inflation. Tax gimmicking in the form of a TIP is no more a solution to the inflation problem than any other "incomes" policy, whether it be as mild as jawboning or as severe as wage and price freezes. It's about time to try something which has not yet been attempted: slowing the expansion of the money stock, sharply reducing the increase in government spending, and reducing materially Federal deficits. At the same time, major revisions in the Federal tax system to moderate its existing bias against productive effort and private saving and investment would contribute importantly to slowing the increase in the price level. If the nation is serious about fighting inflation, these are the appropriate focuses for public policy. We certainly should not TIP our anti-inflation efforts off balance.

MAP: A Cure for Inflation

ABBA LERNER AND DAVID C. COLANDER

In the following selection Abba Lerner and David C. Colander provide a brief outline of the workings of a market anti-inflation plan (MAP).

A PARADOX?

To cure inflation and stagflation, we must first understand them. For the orthodox economic theory, stagflation presents a logical paradox. In that theory, inflation is always due to too much total spending. Since unemployment is due to too little (total) spending, stagflation seems to tell us, paradoxically, that we have too much spending and too little spending at the same time!

A paradox appears only when a failure of the facts to fit the theory is interpreted as a contradiction or an impossibility. But "the actual *is* possible," and when reality and theory conflict, it is the theory that must give way. The paradox disappears as soon as we escape from the dogma that inflation must be due to too much spending.

Stagflation is caused not by too much spending, but by self-fulfilling expectations. Prices rise to keep up with the cost of production. Wages rise to keep up with the increasing cost of living and with increasing output. Government, to avoid catastrophic depression, expands total spending in the economy to keep up with wages and prices. But to be able to counter charges that it is "ultimately"[1] responsible for the inflation, it puts an "anti-inflationary" *restraint* on the expansion as soon as the unemployment is not too catastrophic. This *restraint* is what turns inflation into stagflation.

A FLAW!

In this vicious circle of prices, wages, and spending chasing one another, each of the three actors continues the dance because he has to keep up with the others. The result is a continuing *expectational inflation-unemployment equilibrium*. The stagflation is a result of a *flaw* in the market mechanism that prevents it from working properly.

The flaw is a mutation of the older flaw that was responsible for the Great Depression of the 1930s. That flaw was diagnosed, and its cure prescribed, by Keynes in 1936. It consisted of the failure of prices and wages to fall far enough and fast enough to cure the unemployment (given the level of spending in the economy). The cure, since the prices would not adjust to the spending, was—a la Mohammed and the mountain—to adjust the spending to the prices. The

---

[1]"Ultimately," on the ground that "basically" the inflation must be due to too much spending. "Ultimately" and "basically" here mean "shut up and stop questioning the orthodox dogma."

Abba Lerner and David C. Colander, "MAP: A Cure for Inflation," mimeo, September 1978. Reprinted by permission.

mutation of the flaw is that prices and wages do not merely refuse to fall (as is necessary to cure a depression if spending does not rise); they keep rising, caught in the vicious circle of the spending, the prices and the wages all chasing one another. The simple Keynesian cure for the original flaw—providing adequate but not excessive total spending—cannot deal with the mutation.

PREVIOUS PLANS

It might seem that if any one of the three participants in the dance stopped running, the inflation would have to stop. But this turns out not to be so. *Spending* is the item that has most consistently been chosen as the one to be stopped. The weapon used for this is "sound finance," which relies on restrictionary monetary and fiscal policy to stop the inflationary increase in spending. But this works quickly enough only through catastrophic depression and unemployment. If the unemployment is severe but less than catastrophic, it works too slowly and is still too painful.

A few plans have been devised to work on *price increases*. However, these plans do not overcome the administrative problems stemming from the ease with which quality changes can be used to obscure, or to be disguised as, price changes.

It is also possible to work on *wage increases*. Limiting the average increase in wages to the average increase in output per person would stabilize average cost and average price. A number of plans on these lines are currently receiving wide attention. (They mostly propose only to *reduce* wage increases slightly so as to moderate the inflation slightly.) But all such plans give the impression of discriminating against labor by holding down wage increases while leaving profits unchecked. This is bound to make them unacceptable to labor and thus impossible to implement in a democratic society.

What we learn from this is that it is not enough to stop only one of the three inflationary elements in the tripartite expectational inflation. It turns out to be necessary to deal with wages and profits together. Once this is done the government will no longer have to keep expanding total spending to keep up with any rising prises. Since it will not have to prove it is not responsible for an ongoing inflation, the government will also feel free to give up the "anti-inflationary" restraint on the expansion that is responsible for the *stag* in the stagflation.

FAULTY SOCIAL ACCOUNTING

The mutated flaw which makes the wages and prices keep rising in the futile inflationary race to keep up with one another is a *social* flaw in the *private* accounting of firms. The inflationary impacts of wage and price decisions are not taken into account, just as environmental impacts, health impacts, and other socially important consequences are often not taken fully into account in the decisions of individuals or firms.

Individuals and firms can be made, and are being made, to take these environmental impacts into account through the imposition of incentives (usually taxes or subsidies) to correct the accounting, so as to have the private decisions made responsibly from a social point of view. The inflation cure must similarly apply such an incentive to stop the excessive (i.e., inflationary) wage and price increases.

Total spending in the economy must still be kept increasing enough to be able to buy the output of full employment, though not more than enough (which would bring excess demand inflation). Functional finance is still essential. But the cure for inflation is now faced with an additional *two-fold task*.

1. It must stabilize the *average* price (the price level), and at the same time

2. It must leave *actual* prices and wages free to be adjusted individually, by the market and by free bargaining, to the continuing changes in tastes, techniques, and availabilities. It must also be *fair* in its effects on the relations between wages and profits, and it must *not take too long* to achieve these objectives.

WHY PREVIOUS PLANS FAILED

Attempts to cure the inflation have failed so far because they have not satisfied all the necessary conditions. The same also seems to be true of the anti-inflation proposals now being considered.

Wage and price controls, when applied in the crudest possible way (sometimes as a preparatory step only) as a freeze of all wages and prices, immediately achieve objective (1), but they do nothing at all for objective (2). As the controls develop, they attempt to adjust the wages and prices to the changing tastes, techniques, and availabilities, but they do this not by using market and bargaining methods but by centralized administration. The task is too much for this method and the attempt regularly breaks down in an "administrative nightmare." Wage and price guidelines and guideposts have been greatly discredited, but they are proposed again from time to time only because nothing better has come up.

Similarly desperate (which means without hope) are attempts to stop the inflation by "jawboning"—attempts to persuade the public, even while they are experiencing the inflation going on, that the inflation is ending—so that they will stop raising wages and prices. This attacks the problem precisely the wrong way 'round. We must first stop the inflation. Only when the public sees that the inflation has stopped will it stop expecting the inflation to continue.

The necessity of dealing with both wages and prices was recognized in the wage and price guidelines and guideposts, but these failed because they attempted to handle administratively a task that requires the flexibility and the resistance to political pressure of a decentralized market mechanism.

MAP—THE MARKET ANTI-INFLATION PLAN

The market mechanism is needed to transmit the appropriate incentive against inflationary wage and price increases. Such incentives could be imposed by the government, as in most of the wage-oriented proposals. But the market mechanism is also required for *setting the appropriate level* of the incentive and for continually *adjusting the level* to changing conditions. This is what we believe is provided by the Market Mechanism Anti-Inflation Accounting Credit Plan. We have abbreviated this to Market Anti-Inflation Plan, or MAP, to indicate that it shows the way we have to go to cure our inflation and its stagflation offspring.

The basic idea of MAP is to correct the accounting flaw by translating the *social harm* from the inflationary element in price and wage increases into a *private cost* that the firm will try to avoid, and to do this through the market mechanism so as to avoid all administrative control or regulation of wages or prices. MAP leaves these free for determination by the market or by bargaining, as they are now, directing the market influences only on the (dollar) *Net Sales* or factor payments of the firm (gross sales minus purchases from other firms). Since Net Sales consists of the *combined* profits and wages, this clears MAP of any suspicion of bias between the two.

Prices in general rise, which is what we mean by inflation, when total national Dollar Net Sales is increasing faster than the total national (net) real output. This also means that national Net Sales per unit of input is increasing faster than national average output per unit of input—"productivity." A device that prevented every firm from increasing its Net Sales per unit of input by more than the national (average) increase in productivity would stop the inflation. But this would achieve only objective (1). It would *freeze* the economy, preventing the adjustments of *relative* Net Sales (the relative wages and profits) that are essential for the efficient working of a free and unregimented economy.

FUNCTIONAL RELATIVE AND NON-FUNCTIONAL INFLATIONARY INCREASES

To achieve objective (2) MAP must eliminate the non-functional inflationary part of the increases, which is *proportional*, without interfering with the functional *relative* changes.

The excess of a firm's increase in *Net Sales* per unit of input over the national average increase in *output* per unit of input may be called its "*inflationary impact*." It constitutes the firm's contribution to the inflation—in the sense that if this excess is added up for all the firms, it comes to the excess of the increase in national Net Sales over the increase in national net output, which is the inflation.

One might therefore be tempted to say that the greater a firm's "inflationary impact," the more it is to blame for the inflation (as seems to be assumed in some of the anti-inflation plans), and that a firm with a "deflationary impact" (Net Sales *decreasing* relative to national output per man) is to be praised.

This is not the case at all. The *differences* in various firms' "inflationary impact" reflect the functional *relative* changes and not the inflationary *proportional* changes. A firm's greater-than-average increase in Net Sales may be the completely warranted necessary changes in relative price, reflecting a greater-than-average scarcity of its product. Nevertheless we will find the "inflationary impact," cleared of all connection with blame or praise, of great use in achieving objective (2). If general inflation is to be prevented, every *greater-than-average* scarcity of a product must still be balanced by a *less-than-average* scarcity elsewhere, with a *less-than-average* increase (or an absolute decrease) in price and in Net Sales. Neither blame nor praise is deserved in either case, but the accounting flaw must be corrected in all cases.

A COUNTER-INFLATIONARY INCENTIVE

To correct the accounting flaw, which is the failure of firms to take into account the inflationary part of the increases in their Net Sales for which the inflationary pressure is responsible, a counterinflationary incentive must be imposed that is just equal to the inflationary pressure that it has to offset. Since an inflation affects *all* Net Sales, the counterinflationary incentive must also be applied to all Net Sales. It will then not interfere with the relative changes in Net Sales.

The appropriate counterinflationary incentive is that which is just sufficient to make *total* national Net Sales increase at the same rate as total national output. Average Net Sales per unit of input will then also be increasing at the same rate. This means that the rate of inflation will be zero, so that the total of the "inflationary impacts" of all the firms will add up to zero. The sum of positive "inflationary impacts" will be just equal to the sum of *negative* "inflationary impacts" (the "deflationary impacts"). This gives MAP the weapon needed to achieve objective (2).

ANTI-INFLATION ACCOUNTING CREDIT

Only the market can tell us what is the appropriate size of the counterinflationary incentive, but MAP can harness the market mechanism for this task. MAP creates *a new commodity* to be traded on the market—"Anti-Inflation Accounting Credit." It requires each firm to *buy* Anti-Inflation Accounting Credit in an amount equal to its "inflationary impacts," or enables it to *sell* such "credit" in an amount equal to its "deflationary impact," and it lets the market set the equilibrium price.

The free market price of the "credit," in discouraging demand and encouraging supply (which is what all prices always do) until they are equal in the market equilibrium, *ipso facto* discourages "inflationary impacts" and encourages "deflationary impacts" until *these* are equal. The inflationary and deflationary impacts then just cancel each other, and there is no inflation. The free market price of Anti-Inflation Accounting Credit *is* the incentive we need, is of just the strength we need, and is continuously adjusted by the market as conditions change.

All firms remain free to set their individual Net Sales as high or as low as they wish, after taking into account what they will have to pay or receive for the "credit" they buy or sell. This is how the social flaw in the private accounting is corrected. The firms are induced by the price of the "credit" freely to set their Net Sales, and thereby also the wages and prices, at the levels required for an inflation-free economy.

(In an *expectational deflation*, such as we had in the 1930s, all this would be reversed. The equilibrium price of "credit" would be negative and the price of "deficit" positive. Firms with deflationary impacts would be *required* to sell their "surplus credit" at the negative price. A generalized MAP would symmetrically require firms with deflationary impact to buy ADD (Anti-Deflationary Debits) to cancel their deflationary surplus "credit.")

A SELF-DEFLATING INFLATION DEFLATOR

Extra "credit" permits a firm to enjoy greater Net Sales. The higher the inflationary expectations, the more will firms be willing to pay for additional "credit" (or insist on getting paid for their spare "credit"), the higher will be the price of "credit," and the stronger will be the counterinflationary incentive— the price of "credit." MAP thus turns the inflationary pressure against itself, jujitsu fashion.

An important result is that as the inflationary pressure is weakened by the counterinflationary pressure, the price of "credit" falls and the counterinflationary pressure also weakens. As MAP deflates the inflation it is also itself deflated. When both the inflation and the expectation of inflation stop, the price of "credit" falls to zero or to whatever counterinflationary pressure may stil be required to offset any remaining upward pressures on prices and wages other than inflationary expectations.

There are many ways in which these principles can be applied. What follows is a very concrete picture of one way in which MAP could work. This might be called "model A."

MAP'S RULES

1. The responsibility for curing the inflation is given by Congress to the Federal Reserve. Its current responsibility for maintaining a sound money supply is interpreted as one *compatible* with prosperity and price stability (functional finance). Under MAP, the Federal Reserve had its responsibility extended by Congress to include responsibility for the *maintenance of price stability* through MAP.

MAP alone cannot prevent too much spending from causing excess demand or too little spending from causing depression and unemployment, while a functional finance spending policy alone cannot prevent expectational inflation. For prosperity, total spending must be enough to buy the output of full employment at the current prices. But that could leave us with inflation. For price stability, Net Sales (i.e., wages-plus-profit) must rise at the same rate as national output. But that could leave us with severe unemployment or with scarcities and black markets. With both functional finance *and* MAP we can have both prosperity and price stability.

MAP also provides better signals to indicate when total spending is too much or too little. An excess of total spending above that required for full employment, not being able to raise the average price or to increase employment and output, immediately shows itself in a rise in the price of Anti-Inflation Credit (AIC) and in shortages and black markets. Any deficiency of demand, having no way of reducing average price, immediately shows itself in swollen inventories or reduced employment and output (and in a negative price of "credit" and a positive price of "debit").

2. The Federal Reserve sets up an Anti-Inflation Credit (AIC) Office which monitors the Anti-Inflation Accounting position of each firm. At the initiation of MAP the AIC Office credits each firm with free AIC equal to 102 percent of its annual, pre-MAP (dollar) Net Sales (2 percent being the estimated national annual increase in productivity).

A firm is any employer who is subject to income tax. Net Sales consists of gross sales (including "internal sales," i.e., inventory increases at cost) *minus* purchases from other firms, and it is therefore equal to the firm's Profit *plus* its Wage Bill. Profit includes interest payments, rents, fees and other purchases from, and sales by, those firms. The Wage Bill includes all the costs of employment—wages, salaries, and the cost of all fringe benefits.

3. A firm's AIC (its Anti-Inflation Credit with the AIC Office) is the measure of its noninflationary Net Sales. Net Sales in excess of the firm's AIC constitutes an "inflationary impact" because it raises the average price level (unless offset by firms with Net Sales below their AIC). It can therefore be said to incur an Anti-Inflation Accounting *Deficit* and must cancel the deficit by buying additional AIC equal to this "deficit." Net Sales below a firm's AIC constitutes a "deflationary impact" because it lowers the average price level (unless offset by firms with Net Sales above their AIC) and can be said to earn Anti-Inflationary Accounting Credit "surplus," which is available for the "deficit" firms to buy.

The AIC Office maintains a market in AIC, buying and selling AIC freely to all comers, adjusting the price as may be necessary to bring supply and demand into equality. No AIC is created or destroyed in this trading, so that total AIC and total Net Sales are unchanged.

(In an *expectational deflation*, the price of "credit" would be *negative*. "Deflationary impact" firms would be required to buy ADD (Anti-Deflation Debits) to cancel the "surpluses" from their Net Sales growth falling below national average productivity.)

The money paid for additional AIC comes out of the Net Sales (i.e., the income or wages plus profit) of the buying firms and adds the same amount to the income of the selling firms. MAP can thus be said to consist of exactly equal amounts of "stick" and "carrot" incentives. MAP is also completely neutral in the sharing of such increases or decreases between profit and wages as it is in the sharing of income in general.

4. A newly hired employee (including all the employees of a new firm) entitles the firm to additional free AIC equal to his Wage (including fringe benefits) in his previous employment. Conversely, on the separation of an employee from a firm (which includes all the employees of a firm that closes down) the firm's AIC is reduced by the corresponding amount, calculated the same way.

Additional capital investment—whether financed by stocks, bonds, or reinvested (declared) profits (including all the investment of a new firm)—entitles the firm to AIC equal to interest on the additional investment at the prime rate of interest. Conversely, on the retirement of capital invested (which includes all the capital of a firm that closes down), the firm has its AIC reduced correspondingly.

5. The AIC Office keeps a continuous record of each firm's AIC as adjusted by hirings and separations of employees, by increases and reductions in capital invested, and by its purchases and sales of AIC. With this updated record of each firm's AIC, it is able to check whether the Net Sales corresponds to its total AIC.

6. Soon after the beginning of MAP the AIC Office starts off the trade in AIC by setting a price of AIC at which it expects to generate demand and supply in about equal quantities, guaranteeing to buy and sell AIC at this price up to an amount estimated as needed for a month's use. Beyond that limited guarantee it leaves the price entirely to the free market. Firms will then have two further months in which to adjust their total AIC to their Net Sales, or their Net Sales to their AIC. Check audits will be made at the end of a year when each firm's AIC is automatically increased by 2 percent to allow for increasing productivity. The national total AIC and Net Sales thus keeps up with both components of total national output: the output per unit of input and the volume of inputs. Net Sales stays proportional to output, so that the price level cannot change.

7. Government agencies and other institutions financed by government and private nonprofit corporations are subject to MAP just like private firms, but instead of "Net Sales" they would use "Net Income Generated—the cost of the labor and capital services or, namely, what is left of Net Sales if profit is eliminated. This may be considered the "price" paid for the service rendered, and it is most convenient to treat it as "Net Sales." Labor and capital, business and government, are thus all treated the same way.

HOW LONG WOULD MAP TAKE?

If MAP is imposed when an expectational inflation is going on, with prices rising at 6 percent, labor and capital inputs increasing at 2 percent, and productivity increasing at 2 percent per annum, total Net Sales will have been increasing at 10 percent. Suddenly Net Sales is reduced to 4 percent (the 102 percent basic AIC credited, increased a further 2 percent by the increase in labor and capital inputs). This is just enough to buy the increased output *at last year's prices*. Since prices have been rising, and are expected to continue to rise, there will be a demand for additional AIC to legitimize the increase in Net Sales from the *expected* increase in prices. The price of "credit" will be correspondingly high. But as it becomes apparent that the *actual* average increase is only 4 percent, the 10 percent expectation will diminish and with it also the demand for extra AIC. The price of "credit" will consequently fall.

Any continuing expectation of *any* inflation at all (which depends on Net Sales increasing at something *more* than 4 percent) is bound to be disappointed and revised downward. When the inflationary expectations have been completely eliminated by the disappointments, the expectational inflation will be completely cured. There would then be no "expectational inflation" demand for "credit," and its price would fall to zero or to what is required to offset any upward pressures on prices and wages due to causes other than expectations of continuing inflation.

As with all anti-inflation plans, there is a temptation to beat the gun by establishing higher base prices and wages for incorporation into the plan before it is jelled, and if the design of the plan permits this, it could result in a pre-plan spurt in the inflation. But such a possible development ends as soon as the base Net Sales are fixed. Once MAP is installed, the (initial) goal would be reached as soon as the rules are understood and obeyed. If, as seems pretty certain, there is a lively prior discussion, the cure could take very little time, or no time at all, or even *less than no time!*

Unless there is a general expectation of the inflation stopping or being significantly reduced soon after the imposition of MAP, there is no danger of MAP being imposed. Such an expectation would lead, after the base Net Sales of firms had been set, to anticipation of smaller future price increases and a greater willingness of sellers to accept lower price increases now rather than wait, as well as a greater readiness of buyers to wait rather than buy now. *This would result in at least a slowdown even if not a pre-emptive complete cessation of the inflation before MAP comes into effect.* But as soon as MAP *is* imposed, any remaining expectation of any average price increase will meet quick disappointment and reconsideration.

MAP IS A NEW USE OF AN OLD TRICK

MAP will indeed seem to many people a wild-eyed revoluntionary dream too good to be true. But it is, on the contrary, a well-established device that is operating under our eyes all the time. So familiar is it that it has become invisible—like Sherlock Holmes' invisible postman. This device regularly achieves the same two-fold task of keeping the *average* of a large number of quantities of some item fixed, while each *actual* quantity remains unregulated, for free determination by one of a large number of people. *MAP is no new invention.* MAP is just a plagiarism—a copy of this ancient device. What makes MAP seem strange is only that the item to which MAP is applied has not been treated in this normal way in the past.

One example of the only too familiar miracle will suffice. The price of oranges is adjusted by the market to make the demand equal to the supply. It achieves our objective (1) by making the *average* number demanded per consumer equal to the average number available per consumer, even while achieving our objective (2) by permitting the *actual* number of oranges demanded by each consumer to be chosen freely by the consumer when taking the price into consideration.

For this miracle to work, society at one time had to decide to make the ownership of oranges a legal property right of individuals. This undoubtedly was a shocking, impious, revolutionary, and "antisocial" idea when first suggested to the head of an unindividualized tribe. We expect some of the same resistance to MAP even if it is not accompanied by the claim that it could cure the inflation so quickly.

This bare-bone description of the operation of model A MAP, of course, leaves much to be filled in. We have heard hundreds of objections, nearly all of which have turned out to be either misunderstandings or problems for which we have been able to find satisfactory solutions. Some of the solutions, we hope, will be improved on, and other problems for which there are no satisfactory solutions could come to light. So far we have not met any fatal objections, and we feel that MAP *does* indicate the way we will have to go if we are to cure our inflation-stagflation.

This is not to say that we think we have a finished blueprint. The sketch of model A does, we hope, give a good idea of the general way in which MAP works. But many, if not most, of the actual numbers or time periods we have baldly pronounced may well be changed and improved.

COMPLICATIONS AND VARIATIONS

One possible variation of MAP is the extension of "the previous year" (for the determination of the grants of free AIC) to an average of several years, so as to diminish distortions from specially favorable or unfavorable years. Another is the restriction of MAP to firms above a certain size. This would be very important if some bureaucratic administration of wages or prices were involved, but it does not seem a very serious matter since MAP calls for only the *monitoring* of the truthfulness of the reports. This task is not different in kind from the monitoring and auditing of income tax and social security tax. There will, of course, be some cheating, but the incentives for cheating will be very much less than with income tax. The actual accounting task is comparable to what is being done by organizations like Master Charge.

There are many secondary problems, such as the determination of the amount of free AIC for new entrants to the labor force with no previous Wage. There might be some minimum wage before an employee is included in MAP. There is the possible hiring of retirees only for the sake of large, free AIC based on their last Wage. Some adjustment will have to be made to prevent shrinkage of a firm's Wage Bill, and its free AIC, from the retirement of high-Wage senior employees and from the recruitment of low-Wage beginners. This adjustment could provide for the up-grading of the Wage with seniority.

EFFECT ON THE DOLLAR

One effect of the end of inflation in the United States, until such time as the other countries stop their inflations too, will be a *rising* value of the dollar in terms of the other country's currency, equal (with lags and anticipation) to that country's inflation rate. The United States would gain about as much from the cheapening, in dollars, of its imports as it would lose from the cheapening, in dollars, of its exports. But the stabilization of the dollar in purchasing power would make it a much more desirable store of value and reserve currency for the rest of the world than it has ever been. If the Federal Reserve supplies all such foreign demand for U.S. dollars without permitting a tightening of liquidity and depression at home, this would develop an unprecedented scope for exchanging U.S. dollars for real imports or for philanthropic or political expenditures abroad.

A SLOW OR QUICK MAP?

Among the variations in the application of MAP is the issue of *slowing* the disinflation. Many people would be hurt by a sudden end to the inflation. Assets, such as houses, bought at superinflated prices based on the anticipation of further inflation will fall in value if the further inflation does not come about. There will also be other serious inequities. Workers with contracts for wage increases for several years at the high rates appropriate in continuing inflation will benefit from being able to spend their inflation-powered future wages on goods with stable prices, while those with contracts due for renewal soon after the imposition of MAP will have to get *less* than the 2 percent average rate of increase to balance the others' gains. Conversely, a quick MAP would be very hard on those with contractual monetary obligations undertaken in the expectation that they would be paid in more easily earned depreciating dollars. To soften such inequities a *gradual* disinflation has been suggested.

This could be done very simply by setting a higher initial Net Sales Increase Norm (beyond which additional AIC is required). This could be set not at 4 percent but at, say, 9 percent for one year (instead of the pre-MAP 10 percent), 8 percent for the next year, and so on, taking, say, six years to reach 4 percent and complete price stability.

It can be argued that such a slowing of MAP only spreads out the inequities of the disinflation over a longer period, during which it partially continues the inequities of the inflation. Another way of avoiding these inequities is a legal adjustment, at the beginning of MAP, which would deflate the monetary obligations so as to keep their value constant in *real* terms. This is a kind of indexation in reverse and would apply only to *pre-MAP* contracts, as contrasted with suggested *permanent* indexation to correct the inequities from continuing inflation. But such interfering with "the sacredness of contracts" is a matter for very serious consideration.

A quick MAP, or a fully anticipated slow MAP, if it could quickly reduce the price of AIC to zero, would have the great advantage that it would not give time for the development of a host of troubles that arise if we have positively priced AIC for a considerable time. But unless there is a successful legal deflation of inflation-powered contracts, the pressure for "catching up" by those left out by such contracts will necessitate high AIC prices for a considerable time.

In a slow MAP the gradual disinflation could be obscured by random changes in domestic or world conditions, so that for some time it may not be obvious that MAP is really stopping the inflation. To break the inflationary expectations a really dramatic demonstration may be desirable.

It is also possible that eliminating inflation quickly does not require a significantly higher price of AIC than does reducing the inflation gradually. If this is so, the case for a quick MAP is stronger.

A further difficulty for a quick MAP is the possibility that there is an inherent upward pressure on wages and prices even at less than full employment, and even in the absence of any expectations of inflation. Further study may be able to discover whether this is so. If it is, a quick MAP is an illusion and price stability will require a permanent positive price of AIC.

However, even if a careful weighting of the pros and cons should come out definitely in favor of a quick MAP, a gradual disinflation may be dictated by the political need to reduce resistance to MAP from those who would lose, or who think they might lose, as well as from those to whom all quick measures seem dangerous.

We believe we have explained the nature of our inflation-stagflation and derived from this a logical treatment. It is time we stopped repeating the doleful dirge, "Nobody knows what to do about the Great Paradox," and set about undertaking a look at the political and legislative procedures, at the border of which our MAP ends. *There is a cure* for Inflation-Stagflation. We should not limit our plans and our hopes to moderating their escalation, nor should we allow debate about possible improvements in a plan to postpone action indefinitely.